Transform
Chairwo

Transformational Chairwork

Using Psychotherapeutic Dialogues in Clinical Practice

Scott Kellogg

ROWMAN & LITTLEFIELD
Lanham • Boulder • New York • London

Published by Rowman & Littlefield
An imprint of The Rowman & Littlefield Publishing Group, Inc.
4501 Forbes Boulevard, Suite 200, Lanham, Maryland 20706
www.rowman.com

Unit A, Whitacre Mews, 26–34 Stannary Street, London SE11 4AB

British Library Cataloguing in Publication Information Available

Library of Congress Cataloging-in-Publication Data

Kellogg, Scott, 1954–, author.
Transformational chairwork : using psychotherapeutic dialogues in clinical practice / Scott Kellogg.
    p. ; cm.
Includes bibliographical references and index.
ISBN 978-1-4422-2953-2 (cloth : alk. paper))—ISBN 978-1-4422-4800-7 (pbk. : alk. paper)—ISBN 978-1-4422-2954-9 (electronic)
I. Title.
[DNLM: 1. Gestalt Therapy—methods. 2. Interview, Psychological—methods. WM 420.5.G3]
RC489.G4
616.89'143—dc23

2014039924

For Nadine,
With All My Love

Contents

Acknowledgments

Chairwork completely transformed my life as a psychotherapist. It altered my understanding of the nature of suffering and psychopathology, and it provided me with a method for treating patients that was exponentially more effective than anything I had done before. In 2001, when I began this journey, Chairwork was something of a lost art. Over time, a search for personal knowledge turned into a mission to reintroduce Chairwork to the world of psychotherapy with the hope that it would, once again, become a mainstream therapeutic intervention. This book is an outgrowth of that project.

Many people have assisted me in this endeavor and I would like to express my appreciation for their help and support. First and foremost, I would like to thank Dr. Fritz Perls for the extraordinary work he did in the 1960s and for developing Chairwork into a psychotherapeutic art form. Thank you, Fritz; you changed my life. I would also like to thank Dr. Jacob Moreno for the creation of Chairwork. The contributions of these two men, while under-acknowledged, continue to empower and inspire therapists around the world.

On a more personal level, I would like to thank Dr. Jeffrey Young, the creator of Schema Therapy. I am grateful for the years that I worked at the Schema Therapy Institute in New York City and I am grateful for the gift of Schema Therapy—which led me to Chairwork in the first place. Through your work, you are transforming, healing, and saving lives. Schema Therapy is the therapy for the present and the therapy for the future.

Dr. Vera Paster, of the Doctoral Program in Clinical Psychology at the City University of New York, was my dissertation mentor. You believed in me when many others did not; I strive to be worthy of that faith.

In 2004, I took the Gestalt-Experiential Therapy Seminar with the late John Mastro, LCSW—a faculty member at Gestalt Associates for Psychotherapy.

Your work challenged and stretched all of us who attended and I was never the same afterwards. Thank you for being such an extraordinary teacher.

The treatment of addictions has been a central focus of my life and work. The late Dr. Alan Marlatt wrote "Relapse Prevention" in 1985 and this work has been and continues to be a foundational component of my addiction practice. Whenever I am working with addicted patients, your creative energy is always present. All of us who wrestle with the tragedy of addiction are in your debt.

I had the privilege of working with Dr. Mary Jeanne Kreek in the Laboratory on the Biology of Addictive Diseases at The Rockefeller University for seven years. Dr. Kreek—I am grateful for all that I learned while being a member of your lab and I am especially appreciative of the freedom and opportunities you gave me to pursue my own passions and callings.

For nearly two decades, I have been a member of the Executive Committee of the Division on Addictions of the New York State Psychological Association. This group has been an incredible source of community and creative inspiration. The many dynamic encounters that I have had with my colleagues on the committee (past and present) have helped me to discover more effective ways of treating addictions and I acknowledge this with pleasure.

Over the last six years, I have had a number opportunities to do Transformational Chairwork trainings throughout the world. This has been centrally due to the generosity of colleagues both within the Schema Therapy community and outside of it. My gratitude goes out to Erlend Aschehoug, PhD; Martin Bamber, BA (Hons), RMN, MA, MPhil, DPsychol, CPsychol, AFBPsS; Wendy Behary, LCSW; Tim Bingham, BA (Hons); Michler Bishop, PhD; Marsha Blank, LCSW; Philip Brownell, MDiv, PsyD; Anthony Cichello, MA; Noah Clyman, LCSW, ACT; Dov Finkelstein, LCSW; Iris Fodor, PhD; Christoph Furhans, MD; Mícheál Gallagher, PhD; Hannah Gilbert, PhD; Paul Gilbert, PhD; Magdalena Gulcz, AM; Chris Hayes, PhD; Anne Hook; Tracey Hunter, PhD; Thomas Irelan, PhD; Gitta Jacobs, PhD; Kathleen Kelly, LCSW; Chris Lee, PhD; Wendy Levy, PsyD; Reji Mathew, PhD: Lukas Nissen, PhD; Irismar Reis de Oliveira, MD, PhD; Eckhard Roediger, MD; Patricia Escudero Rotman, PhD, LCSW; Constance Salhany, LMHC, PhD, ACT; Susan Simpson, PhD; Mikael Sonne, PhD; Jan Tønnesvang, PhD; and Christina Vallianatou, PhD.

I would like to give special thanks to my colleague and friend, Dr. Andrew Tatarsky. It has been a great joy to dialogue, argue, present, and write with you. The inspiration that has come from these experiences has helped me to clarify and deepen my voice. I look forward to many more years of stimulating collaboration.

The New York University Department of Psychology has been a home for nearly a decade. It has been a privilege to work there and to have been able to teach such extraordinary students.

I would also like to acknowledge the healers who helped me wrestle with the darkness: Vera Michaels, PhD, CSW; Monty Cox, MDiv; Ana Ferreira, PhD; and Susan Jurkowski, LCSW, LP, CGP. Susan—your healing presence and therapeutic gifts have touched me to the quick. Thank you.

On the home front, I wanted to express my appreciation for our core circle of friends: Amy Pretel Gray, Chris Gray, Leslie Goldfarb-Terry, Al Terry, Silvana Vasconcelos, Tom O'Neill, Elizabeth Pretel, and Juan Carlos Carpio. Joquin Brant, my great friend since high school, thank you for all the love and all the adventures; may we have many more.

Within my family, I remember those who have passed on: my mother, Nancy Kellogg Wyckoff; my father, Edward Cummings Kellogg; my step-mother, Barbara Kellogg; my stepfather, James Wyckoff; and my mother-in-law, Frances Samanich. And those remaining: my sister, Jenny Wyckoff; my brother Kevin Kellogg; and my brother-in-law Stewart Pearse. Most of all I send my love to my wife and life partner, Nadine Kellogg, and to our two wonderful children, Chris and Noelle.

Lastly, I would like to thank the late Mrs. Peggy Flinsch who, at an earlier stage of my journey, showed me love and consistently had faith in me.

Scott Kellogg, PhD
August 15, 2014

Chapter 1

Speaking One's Mind

Fritz Perls changed my life. In late 2001, I began my journey with the Gestalt Chairwork technique. In one of my first cases, a patient reported that he had serious problems with authority and that he could not tolerate being told what to do. Through the use of imagery, we were able to connect these emotions to memories of his father oppressively coaching him in golf.[1] The reverberations of these experiences brought up strong feelings of anger—even decades later. To work through and hopefully resolve this issue, I set up an encounter with his father. I invited him to sit in one chair and imagine his parent in the chair opposite. I encouraged him to "speak with" his father and to tell him how deeply distressing those coaching sessions had been for him as a child. After expressing anger about the relentless perfectionism that he had been subjected to, I then invited him to switch chairs and "be" his father. Doing this, he gave voice to his father's concern that he learn how to play the game the "right" way. We alternated chairs and gave voice to both of their perspectives. We then debriefed the experience. The full power of this session became clear a week later when he returned and told me that the dialogue had worked, that he no longer felt a profound resistance to orders and requests and that he had been able to attend and participate in a work meeting without discomfort. It would turn out that this would be a change that lasted. This single session "cure" would inspire me to begin a journey—a journey centered on exploring the healing power of dialogue and encounter (adapted from Kellogg, 2013). Given this, perhaps the best place to start is with the story of Dr. Perls and the development of Chairwork.

FRITZ PERLS AND THE CREATION OF CHAIRWORK

In the 1960s, Dr. Frederick Perls emerged as a major figure in Humanistic Psychology and what would eventually be known as the Human Potential Movement. "Fritz," as he was called, challenged the world of psychotherapy not only with his creative use of *awareness* as a central therapeutic intervention, but also through his astonishing and virtuosic demonstrations using the Chairwork technique. His experiential work with chair dialogues inspired psychotherapists from nearly every school of therapy—with many of them integrating and reinterpreting both the technique and its underlying mechanisms of change. It is this rich and still-developing heritage that is the foundation for this book.

Perls' "overnight success" was, of course, built on a lifetime of effort, exploration, and experimentation. His life was, in many ways, quite extraordinary as he engaged with many of the most tragic and creative forces in 20th Century Western European and American history. It is my intention to briefly touch on some of the key moments in his professional and creative life; for those interested in a deeper exploration, there are a number of excellent biographies available (Clarkson & Mackewn, 1993; Gaines, 1975; Shepard, 1972).

Frederick "Fritz" Perls was born in 1893 into a middle-class family in a Jewish section of Berlin.[2] One of three children, Perls reported that his early childhood was happy, but that things changed as he got older. Over time, his relationship with his father deteriorated to the point of mutual hatred, and, at age ten, he began to "act out"—which eventually led to his being expelled from school.

At fourteen, he was admitted to the *Askanische Gymnasium*. This was a more progressive school than the one that he had attended, and he grew to care deeply about many of the staff members. Fritz always loved the theater and, at age fifteen, he discovered the famous director, Max Reinhardt, the demanding and innovative leader of the *Deutsche Theater*. Perls spent his free time at the theater and, while not a great actor, he was able to fill several walk-on roles, which brought him great pleasure. This early experience in the theater—including that of seeing a great director in action—would stay with him for the rest of his life. The positive environment of his school also helped him to regroup academically and he was able to graduate and enter the University of Berlin where he decided to study Medicine.

Shortly after he began his studies, World War I broke out. Because of medical issues and personal frailties, he was not drafted into the army in 1914; he did, however, volunteer with the Red Cross in 1915. By 1916, there was a growing need for soldiers and the requirements for enlistment were lowered. Fearing that he would be called up, Perls enlisted and became a medic.

As it was for millions of other combatants and civilians, Perls' wartime experiences were deeply traumatic and emotionally damaging. Nonetheless, he won a medal for bravery and was promoted to the rank of Medical Sub-lieutenant, which was an officer rank. After the war, he returned to Medical School and graduated in 1920.

During the early years of Perls' career, he was searching for answers and direction. He began to work as a psychiatrist and started spending his free time with the Bauhaus group and other bohemian circles. A successful doctor, he earned enough to come to New York City in 1923 and was able to get a job in the Hospital for Joint Diseases. He was, however, unhappy with the practice of Psychiatry there and returned to Berlin a few months later. At this time, he was also filled with self-doubt on both personal and professional levels and frequently suffered from bouts of self-criticism and depression.

In 1925, he developed an intense, life-changing relationship with Lucy, who was a sexually-vibrant and married distant relative. This experience served to bolster his sense of masculinity. However, he found the emotionally turbulent nature of his time with her to be deeply disturbing and, in 1926, he decided to begin psychoanalysis with Karen Horney. Karen Horney appears to have seen something in him and she would provide significant assistance to him several times over the next twenty years. After a few months of working with her, he decided to take a job in Frankfurt, and, at Horney's recommendation, he continued his analysis with Clara Happel.

In Frankfurt, Perls was able to procure an Assistantship with Kurt Goldstein at the Institute for Brain Damaged Soldiers. This would be significant not only because it meant that he was working with one of the leading advocates of Gestalt Psychology, but also because it was here that he met Lore Posner, a graduate student. They would eventually marry and she would later become known as "Laura Perls," a world-famous therapist in her own right.

After what appears to have been an unsuccessful analysis, Happel announced that he was "cured" and that he could now do supervised work as a psychoanalyst. Perls then went to Vienna and treated patients under the direction of Helene Deutsch and Edward Hitschmann. With Hitschmann, he began, for the first time, to open up about his fears and insecurities. He returned to Berlin and underwent another deeply unsuccessful analysis with Eugen Harnik. This treatment lasted for a year-and-a-half.

In 1929, he married Lore Posner and by 1932, he was a trained and certified Freudian psychoanalyst. Still quite unhappy, he again sought out Karen Horney. She said, "The only analyst that I think could get through to you would be Wilhem Reich" (Perls, 1969b, p. 49). Reich would be a major influence on Perls and his work.

In the early 1930s, Fritz and Lore were members of the Anti-Fascist movement. After the Reichstag fire, the Nazis began to hunt down their opponents, and the Perls' were forced to go underground with their young daughter, Renate. This meant that he lost his practice, his home, and his analysis with Reich.

First Fritz, and then Laura and "Ren," escaped to Holland where they were indigent refugees. Eventually, Ernest Jones told him that there was a position in Johannesburg, South Africa; the job was to be the co-founder of the South African Institute for Psychoanalysis. In a later telling of the story, Perls revealed something about his personality and the kind of courage that he had.

> One of the most important moments in my life was after I had escaped Germany and there was a position as a training analyst available in South Africa, and Ernest Jones wanted to know who wanted to go. There were four of us: three wanted guarantees. I said I take a risk. All the other three were caught by the Nazis. I took a risk and I'm still alive. (Perls, 1969b, p. 46)

Perls set sail for South Africa in 1935. After setting up the Institute, Lore and Renate joined him. Both Fritz and Lore, who had earned her doctorate in Psychology, developed very successful practices in Johannesburg, and it was there that they gave birth to their son, Steve. They would have great financial success in South Africa, and they were able to create a lifestyle of comfort and pleasure.

Fritz—influenced by Reich, his own experiences, and conversations with Lore—began to develop his own thoughts on psychoanalytic theory and treatment. In 1936, he went to the International Psychoanalytic Association Congress in Marienbad, Czechoslovakia to present his paper on "oral resistances." This turned out to be a devastating and life-altering experience in three ways.

The initial shock took place when Perls went to meet Freud for the first time. Freud, for whatever reason, was very cool to him. He stood in his doorway and did not invite Perls into his room. When Perls told him that he had just come from South Africa, Freud asked him when he was returning, and, after three or four minutes, ended the conversation.

The second disappointment came when the paper he presented was poorly received; and the third involved Wilhelm Reich. "Fritz was greatly disheartened to find Wilhelm Reich, the analyst who had given him so much, withdrawn, morose, and barely capable of recognizing Fritz" (Shepard, 1972, p. 45).

This rejection by Freud would haunt Perls for the rest of his life; in some ways, much of his later work was a kind ongoing dialogue or debate with the Master. There is a telling and poignant incident in *The Gestalt Approach/ Eyewitness to Therapy* (Perls, 1973). Perls is working with Barbara, a woman who is wrestling with self-esteem and competence issues. I suspect that he understood her to be someone who had basically disavowed her sense of personal competence and had projected it on to others (see chapter 7). Beginning in a slightly playful manner, Perls proposed that they switch roles, that she be the therapist—that she be "Fritz"—and he be the patient. After making a disparaging comment about Freud, she invited him to have a dialogue with Freud.

In a compelling example of the power of the technique, the session soon got quite serious for Perls. As he brought Freud into awareness, Barbara asked him what he was feeling. Perls said quite seriously, "A great sorrow that Freud is dead because I could really talk man to man with him" (p. 205). She then invited him to speak with Freud directly. Part of what he said included: "Professor Freud. . . . A great man. . . . But very sick. . . . You can't let anyone touch you. . . . I wish you would listen to me. In a certain way I know more than you do."

After saying a few more things and several moments of silence, he turned to Barbara and said, "So, your copy of Fritz wasn't so bad. (Gives Barbara a kiss) You did something for me." To which she replied, "Thank you, Fritz" (p. 206).

Fritz returned to South Africa and began to turn his ideas into a book. After reading a draft of the manuscript in 1940, the analyst Marie Bonaparte said, "If you don't believe in the libido theory anymore, you'd better hand in your resignation" (Shepard, 1972, p. 6). This rebuttal further distanced him from the world of psychoanalysis. In 1942, with assistance from Lore, he published this work in South Africa as *Ego, Hunger, and Aggression* (Perls, 1969a). The volume includes a section called Concentration Therapy which was a first attempt at creating a Reichian-influenced, somatically-integrated psychotherapy. That year, he also joined the English army and served as Medical Officer for the next four years. Despite his admonitions that they should leave Germany, his mother and sister stayed behind and were eventually killed in the Ravenstadt concentration camp.

After the War, he was ready to move again. Despite their financial success, he and Lore had always felt that South Africa was culturally somewhat arid; in addition, the economic situation was changing and their practices were becoming less successful. Lastly, Perls felt that Fascism was now on the rise with the growing movement toward Apartheid. With Karen Horney again serving as his sponsor, Perls came to New York in 1946. He immediately went to New Haven and tried to get a position in the Yale University School of Medicine. They told him that, because of professional requirements, he would have to re-do his medical training. Now in his fifties, he refused to do that.

He went back to New York City and, as things did not appear to be working out, he began to consider returning to South Africa. Erich Fromm, however, told him, "Don't go back. I promise you that within three months you'll have a practice of your own" (Shepard, 1972, p. 55). This turned out to be the case and the whole family relocated to New York City.

Perls had read the writings of Paul Goodman while in South Africa and Goodman, in turn, had read *Ego, Hunger, and Aggression*. When he came to New York, he became friends with Goodman who, in turn, introduce both he and "Laura" to the vibrant bohemian art scene. Over time, he would also become acquainted with Julian Beck and Judith Malina (the founders of the Living Theater), Charlotte Selver (Body Awareness), Dianetics, and Zen (Shepard, 1972).

Laura and Fritz began to attract a group of clinicians and intellectuals who were interested in their therapeutic work. Among these were Elliot Shapiro, Paul Weisz, Isadore From, and Jim Simkin. Paul Goodman became a patient of Laura's as did Ralph Hefferline, the Chairman of the Psychology Department at Columbia University. Fritz invited the two of them to help him in the writing of a new book. This project would have three components: (1) Hefferline would try out the Concentration Therapy techniques with his undergraduates and collect reports of their experiences; (2) Perls would write the theoretical section of the book; and (3) Goodman would edit what he had written. As it turned out, Goodman wrote the theoretical section, building on some of Fritz's ideas while integrating some of his own (Wheeler, 1991). To the consternation of Laura, Fritz called his new therapy, *Gestalt Therapy*. She was particularly upset because she felt that his approach had little to do with the gestalt psychology that she had studied.

Arthur Ceppos, another friend, agreed to publish the work and *Gestalt Therapy: Excitement and Growth in the Human Personality* appeared in 1951. This book, with both its insights and its controversies, would, ironically, come to haunt and hinder the development of the Chairwork technique. Laura also contributed to the volume, but she was not listed as an author. It is important to note that Goodman, while building on Perls' ideas, essentially developed a theoretical framework and foundation that was beyond anything that Perls' had envisioned (Rosenfeld, 1977a; Wheeler, 1991; Wysong, 1985). In fact, the writing in that book does not match the style found in Perls' later writings, such as *The Gestalt Approach*.

The book, which continued his exploration of Reichian, Existential, and Psychoanalytic theories, was divided into two parts. The "first" are the reports of Dr. Hefferline's students who tried various experiments as part of a class they were taking. The "second" part is a dense, complex, and creative theoretical treatise that introduced such core Gestalt concepts as Introjection, Projection, Retroflection, Confluence, the Contact Boundary, and the Contact Cycle.

Following the release of *Gestalt Therapy,* Fritz and Laura, Paul Goodman, and other therapists and supporters formed the *New York Institute for Gestalt*

Therapy in 1952. This was the first training institute and for a long time it centered its work on the study of this seminal volume. After the Institute was founded, Goodman and Perls were increasingly at odds with each other, while Goodman and Laura Perls formed an alliance. Simultaneously, her marriage to Fritz grew increasingly precarious. Perls then began two ventures that would have a serious impact on the development of Chairwork. The first was that he started to travel throughout the United States, training therapists and helping institutes form and develop, notably in Cleveland and, later, California. As he did this, he began to further develop gestalt therapy. This would eventually lead to a model that was strikingly different from the one outlined in the 1951 book and the one practiced at the New York Institute (Kellogg, 2009b; Naranjo, 1993).

The second significant act was that he began to study *Psychodrama* with Dr. Jacob Moreno. Moreno, a Turkish-Jewish psychiatrist who was born in Bulgaria and who had grown up in Vienna, was an amazing, creative, and controversial man in his own right (J. L. Moreno, 1989). He came to the United States in 1925 and, by 1935, he had a sanitarium and training institute in Beacon, New York. During the 1950s, he held weekly seminars at his office on Park Avenue. This New York City gathering was popular among many artists and intellectuals, and a number of social scientists and psychotherapists took part in these experiences and were influenced by what they saw and experienced. These included Gardner Murphy, Theodore Sarbin, and Eric Berne (Clarkson & Mackewn, 1993; Landy, 2008; Leveton, 2001; Moreno, 2012).

Putting the innovative qualities of Moreno's work into perspective, Landy (2008) affirmed: "Moreno . . . was the first to speak of therapy as an encounter between the client and therapist. He was the first to demonstrate the wisdom and power of reworking the past through direct dramatic action, and he was the first to fully transform the clinical consulting room into a therapeutic stage" (pp. 197–198).

Unfortunately for our story, the specific details of their relationship and the work they did together are not clear; although Perls appears to have worked on and off with Moreno throughout the 1950s (Leveton, 2001; Moreno, 1989; Moreno, 2012). "Fritz sat at Moreno's feet at our Psychodrama Institute at 101 Park Avenue, New York City, many times . . . until some time before he moved to California. He was definitely influenced by Moreno. . . ." (Zerka Moreno, Personal Communication, June 3, 2009). It appears, then, that Perls learned Chairwork from Moreno. Strikingly, Chairwork, which was also known as *monodrama*, was a relatively unimportant technique in psychodrama because it emphasizes the use of the group format and of having other participants or *auxiliaries* stand in for significant figures in the patient or protagonist's life.

In terms of Chairwork, Perls expanded the use of this technique in creative and clinically significant ways; the most important of which was that he would invite the patient to enact the different roles him- or herself, rather than having other individuals stand in and play them. "If I let the patient do *all* the roles, we get a clearer picture than when we use Moreno's technique of psychodrama, pulling people in who know very little about you" (Perls, 1992, p. 143). The idea of playing the part of another significant person comes from the psychodramatic technique of *role-reversal* (Dayton, 1994, 2005; Moreno, 2012). This was a radical shift of perspective that greatly increased the therapeutic power of Chairwork and certainly created possibilities for its use in individual therapy that had not existed before (Landy, 2008; Perls, 1973, 1992).

By 1956, Perls had been relegated to a somewhat secondary status in his own institute. As Jim Simkin put it: "Fritz abandoned the Gestalt Institute in New York about '55 to Laura and the two Pauls, Goodman and Weisz" (Gaines, 1979, p. 40). He also began a nomadic period that would last for seven years. He first moved to Miami, where he lived a relatively simple life. Plagued by heart problems, this was a place that he went to heal and recover as swimming was one of the few physical activities left for him to pursue.

In some respects, these were quiet but powerful years for him. Professionally, he kept a fairly low profile, seeing patients, running some groups, and doing road trips to visit the gestalt groups that were developing in Cleveland and elsewhere. On a personal level, he had a love affair with a younger woman that he would come to see as the most important of his life. He also began to use LSD and Psilocybin. Overall, the impact of psychedelics on Perls appears to have been both beneficial (Naranjo, 1993) and debilitating (Shepard, 1972) and by 1959, he started to have experiences of paranoia and, at times, psychosis, from using them.

In 1958, Perls took part in a panel on Psychodrama that was held at the American Psychological Association Convention in San Francisco. His comments as a discussant deeply affected Wilson Van Dusen, a Clinical Psychologist who was in the audience. Impressed by Perls' vision and abilities, he was able to arrange for Perls to be hired as a consultant at the Mendocino State Hospital in California and in 1959 Perls moved to California.

His work in Medocino was generally successful. However, funding for his consultation work at the hospital started to run out and he did not have enough patients for his practice. In 1960, he moved to Los Angeles to join forces with his student, Jim Simkin. Here, he started running groups, groups that included such therapists as Walt Kempler and Everett Shostrom, and did consultations in various hospitals. Jim Simkin was also successful at getting him to dramatically reduce his use of LSD which led to significant improvements in his functioning.

In 1962, Perls decided to go on a "world tour." This trip included two months at the Daitokuji Temple in Kyoto, Japan. This visit provided him with an opportunity to not only study Zen, but also to fall in love with the city of Kyoto. He later went to Elath, Israel, where he lived in an artist colony and took up painting. This was his first encounter with "beatnik" culture, an experience that he greatly enjoyed.

He returned to Los Angeles and resumed working. Taking over a group for Jim Simkin, one evening, he met Bernie Gunther. Gunther was a body worker interested in yoga, body awareness, and weight lifting; he was also immediately drawn to Perls and wanted to promote his work. Fritz, somewhat reluctantly, allowed him to do this and it led to a successful presentation of his work at a bookstore in Los Angeles.

Gene Sagan, a psychologist, then organized a private gathering at Chait's Hot Spring Hotel in Big Sur during Christmas, 1963. The seminar was called "The Psychology of Human Ultimates" and both Gunther and Perls were invited. Bernie loved the place while Fritz was not, initially, impressed. Gunther did, however, persuade Fritz to do a series of seminars there with the argument that it was located half-way between Los Angeles and San Francisco. This was a seminal moment because the other name for Chait's Hot Springs Hotel was the Esalen Institute.

The Esalen Institute, in Big Sur, California, was founded in 1962 by Michael Murphy and Richard Price, and it would play a central role in the development of Humanistic Psychology over the next ten years (Anderson, 1983). Despite his initially negative opinion, Perls would come see Esalen in a different light when he returned in 1964. In discovering Esalen, he found a home; a home that nurtured and helped him heal over the next five years. It was here that he would crystallize Chairwork into what I feel is a psychotherapeutic art form.

As a way of promoting his work in California, he decided to build on the positive reactions that he was getting and created what he would later refer to as his "circuses." These were large, public demonstrations of Gestalt therapy in which he would sit on a stage and work with individuals in front of audiences of hundreds (Clarkson & Mackewn, 1993). These chair-centered performances were particularly effective and they inspired him to center his smaller workshop groups on these dialogical methods. This decision was suited to Perls well as it provided him with a quasi-theatrical venue in which he could demonstrate his extraordinary psychotherapeutic abilities.

The gestalt therapy that developed during the Esalen years included the core components of: (1) awareness; (2) an emphasis on living in the here-and-now; (3) existential responsibility; (4) the integration of polarities; and (5) work with dreams, and the Chairwork-centered group was the vehicle in which many of these ideas were made manifest. Within the context of the time, the work was profoundly innovative and paradigm-shifting. As Claudio Naranjo (1993) put it: "We felt (and by 'we' I mean people like Virginia Satir, Jerry Greenwald, William Golding, Abe Levitsky, and others from my first training group), that we were before something unique, something totally new, and it was. . . ." (p. 294).

For good or for ill, the Esalen years are as much colored by his creativity as his personality. Like other giants in the field of psychotherapy, Perls was a complex man. Deeply wounded and, in many ways, fundamentally unhappy, he could be quite challenging to work with (Shepard, 1975). Miller (1989) wrote that "he was mischievous, vulgar, intimate, bullying, brilliant, seductive, cantankerous, and tender" (p. 6) and Erv Polster, in turn, remembered how extraordinary he was when he said: "He seemed a genius to me" (Wysong, 1978).

His way of working with people was often highly confrontational and, at times, quite impatient. Ironically, the chair next to his was called the "hot seat" and it took courage to go and work with him (Perls, 1969b). Yet, over and over again, he created experiences of profound beauty and power that touched people in ways that would stay with them for years (Gaines, 1975).

The result was that there was no neutrality about Perls as a person or about his work. "The people who loved him, man, *really* loved him! I mean that was deep love" (Julian Silverman in Gaines, 1975, p. 131); "He changed my life. He changed a lot of people's lives" (Tom Shandel in Gaines, 1975, p. 416); or as one participant simply put it, "Thank you, Fritz" (Perls, 1973, p. 206).

Perls became world-famous during his years at the Esalen Institute. Nonetheless, his restlessness and emotional complexities would not allow him to claim this as his final home. In 1969, Perls left Esalen to set up a Gestalt "kibbutz" in Lake Cowichan, British Columbia. This move came both out of a desire to try experiments in Gestalt living and out of a fear that the United States was heading toward Fascism (Baumgardner, 1975; Perls, 1969b). He would die a year-and-a-half later during a trip to Chicago.

INFLUENCES AND DEVELOPMENTS

From this sketch, it is clear that in his professional life, Perls had undertaken an extraordinary journey of clinical and creative transformation. In a frequently repeated phrase, gestalt therapy has been described as "existential, experiential, and experimental" (Rosenfeld, 1977a) and all three of these forces permeate his work. In terms of Chairwork specifically, the three most relevant influences are those of the theater, Existentialism, and Jungian Psychology.

As we have seen, Perls had a long-standing and deep-seated attraction to the theater. In addition to his involvement in the *Deutsche Theatre* of Max

Reinhardt during his teenage years, he had interacted with Julian Beck and Judith Malina, the directors of The Living Theater, in New York City (Clarkson & Mackewn, 1993). Returning again to Moreno and psychodrama, it is clear that Perls drew on the central emphasis on *enactment*. Zimberoff and Hartman (1999) have written that *"enactment . . . is a technique in which the patient is asked to put feelings or thoughts into action"* (p. 101). In turn, Karp (2000) has affirmed: "The difference is in telling a story and reliving it" (p. 82).

In California, Perls also developed a deep connection with Anna Halprin, the dancer. Their first encounter is a story that both captures the flavor of the times and the power of Perls' therapeutic insight. Halprin went to one of his workshops and had a strong reaction to a very "uptight" man who was wearing a suit[3]. In an act that was probably both expressive and aggressive, she slowly began to take off her clothes in front of this man, who began to cry when she was completely naked.

"I was so proud of myself for being so brazen. It didn't startle Fritz at all that I would just take all my clothes off and stand in front of the man. When I sat down, his only comment was, 'So what are your legs crossed for?' I was totally reduced" (Gaines, 1975, p. 199). Looking at this from the outside, it seems possible that he was reflecting back to her that while she was expressing the polarity of freedom and creativity through her dance, her body was expressing the polarity of repression and shame. She resonated with this quite deeply (Ross, 2007).

This was the beginning of a deep friendship. He later did work with the dancers in her company and the two of them worked together in a number of workshops on a dream that she had about a house with many rooms. As she put it, "Every time he worked with somebody, it was like a performance. . . . Fritz loved being the theater director. He loved it" (Anna Halprin in Gaines, 1975, p. 200).

Similarly, in an interview with Edward Rosenfeld, Laura Perls acknowledged and clarified that "Fritz was in theater long before he did anything else. He wanted to be a theater director." Rosenfeld noted that there are aspects of Chairwork that feel like directing. She continued: "But he also did it informed by fifty years of professional experience, which wasn't only theater" (Rosenfeld, 1977a, n.p.).

The second force in the development of Chairwork was Existentialism. Even in the 1951 book, there was a great deal of emphasis on "responsibility," on helping patients claim authority over themselves and their actions (Perls, Hefferline, & Goodman, 1951). This was also manifest in his emphasis on awareness, in the Paradoxical Theory of Change (Beisser, 1970), and in the use of Existential language.

In terms of awareness, Perls at one point said that the essence of his technique could be summed up in three questions" "What are you doing?"

"What are you feeling?" "What do you want?" (Clarkson & Mackewn, 1993, p. 94). "The Paradoxical Theory of Change" was a phrase made famous in a paper by Beisser (1970). Perls (1969b) acknowledged that Beisser had, in fact, captured the essence of much of his work in that chapter. Beisser made the argument that therapists cannot actually get people to change nor can people change themselves directly. In order to change, heal, and transform, it is necessary for the person to more deeply become who they already are. This is why Perls was consistently present-focused and why he repeatedly asked participants in his workshops to give voice to what they were thinking and feeling at that moment. This is also why change is seen as paradoxical. A complex and difficult-to-understand concept, it will be explored at greater length in chapter 7. Lastly, throughout the transcripts, there is a strong emphasis on the use of existential language, of encouraging patients to substitute "I won't" for "I can't" and " I want to" for "I need to" (Baumgardner, 1975) (see also chapter 10). Again, this is a way of taking responsibility for one's self and one's life.

Lastly, Perls connection to Jung was manifested in his work with dreams and polarities. It seems likely that Perls became acquainted with Jung's ideas through the work of Otto Rank.

> Another formulation of Jung's which is relevant to Gestalt therapy was his understanding of the polarities inherent in human nature. He cast these dualities in archetypal characters such as anima and animus, or in the concept of the shadow, the obscure but inevitable companion to the public persona. Otto Rank was influenced by Jung's concept of polarities and it was through his work that Perls became interested. (Polster, 1987, p. 314)

In addition to the focus on polarities, Perls and Jung shared a belief in: (1) the deep potential that lies in the unconscious or the repressed; (2) the importance of integrating the known and the unknown parts of the self; and (3) the usefulness of dreams as a vehicle for doing this work (Bernstein, 1980; Clarkson & Mackewn, 1993; Latner, 1973; Polster & Polster, 1973). This, too, will be discussed at length in chapter 7.

Chairwork After Perls

Chairwork has, in many respects, haunted gestalt therapy (Polster & Polster, 1973). Reading *Gestalt Therapy Verbatim* and other works of that time, it seems clear that Perls was using Chairwork to engage in three major therapeutic tasks: focusing on awareness, resolving unfinished business, and integrating polarities. Chairwork served as a vehicle to help achieve these goals and as a vehicle for Perls to perform. It supported his emphasis on enactment and his stress on doing rather than "talking about." Perls and his colleagues were, however, also very concerned that Chairwork and the other techniques that were developed during this time not be divorced from the underlying philosophy or theory that drove their use.

Despite their apprehensions, the Chairwork technique was and is so powerful that it did overshadow the underlying gestalt theory. The 1951 Gestalt theory was neither easy to understand nor easily integrated with other theories of healing and change. In addition, when practitioners began to use Chairwork on a regular basis, it is likely that they found that a theory of practice emerged from the work itself; that is, Chairwork has its own logic.

A recurring theme in this book is that Chairwork, like psychotherapy more broadly, is an art and a science (Duhl, 1999; Rosenfeld, 1977a). Perls did not, perhaps, fully understand this. In his writings he emphasized the importance of therapists spontaneously creating "experiments" with their patients, and while this may have been possible for a genius like Perls, it seems to be an unrealistic challenge for the rest of us. In fact, there have been no major technical contributions from gestalt therapy since his death. What Perls either did not fully appreciate or acknowledge was the role of practice and work in artistic spontaneity, which is strange for a man who so deeply loved theater, music, and the arts. Zinker (1977) probably came closest to understanding this, but even he did not fully grasp it.

I believe that Chairwork is best understood as a psychotherapeutic art form (Polster & Polster, 1973; Zinker, 1977). It is a way of working that requires study and practice if its true depth and power are to be fully utilized. An analogy might be found in the world of music. For example, with musicians who are famous for their improvisations, it is not uncommon to find that they actually spend a great deal of time working with and further developing their musical ideas. The extraordinary moments that occur in concert actually emerge out of a dialectic between the preparations that they have made and the creative spontaneity of the moment; Chairwork is best understood within this paradigm (Kellogg, 2009b).

Following Perls' death, there was a struggle over the direction and future of gestalt therapy. This battle was crystallized as a struggle between East Coast and West Coast (or California) gestalt therapy, "West Coast Gestalt was developed single-handedly by Fritz Perls. . . . In contrast, eastern Gestalt therapy . . . reflects the interactional, social, and community interests of Laura Perls, Elliot Shapiro, Paul Goodman and the rest of the original New York members and the Cleveland group" (Naranjo, 1973, pp. 214–215). These "East Coast" theorists and practitioners were continuing to center their work on the 1951 book. By and large, they rejected the use of psychodramatic interventions in their efforts, and if they did use them, they did not play the central role that they had in California. Embodying this view, Isadore From

(1984) wrote: "Psychodrama . . . is not consistent with the method of Gestalt therapy" (p. 9).

On the other hand, there were therapists who had attended workshops or had been involved with Perls in other training situations who modeled their work after him and placed a premium on being confrontational. Critics of this group, perhaps fairly, emphasize that many therapists confused Perls' style with the essence of his work. They also pointed out that Perls, a man with extraordinary gifts of intuition and observation, ran his Chairwork groups with a lifetime of clinical experience as a foundation (Clarkson & Mackewn, 1993). Clearly, these were elements that were not easy to replicate.

In turn, the clinically-sophisticated practitioners who championed his Esalen-styled work believed that this represented a major advance over the earlier, 1951 model. "Yet it is also possible to say 'California Gestalt' with dignity, for many of us believe that Fritz's California years were his ripest . . ." (Naranjo, 1993, p. xix). It is my personal belief that Perls, in effect, created a second gestalt therapy. The "1969" model[4] is so different and so rooted in psychodrama, that it bears little resemblance to the "1951" version (Kellogg, 2009b), and this means that attempts at integration, of using all of his ideas and techniques in one coherent model, are likely to fail. This two-therapy position, if more widely adopted, would help practitioners to continue to reap the full creativity of Perls' genius in all of its manifestations.

To be fair, those who had stayed with the 1951 book were also in the process of changing, developing, and growing. "Yontef (1991) has argued that even in the 1960s at least two contrasting styles of Gestalt were already developing—the one theatrical and cathartic and the other hardworking, person to person, dialogic and equally pioneering" (Clarkson & Mackewn, 1993, p. 136). The movement away from the California model occurred as much as a reaction to Perls himself as to his work. Accompanying this, there was a general championing of the 1951 book and a more central emphasis on the roles of Paul Goodman and Laura Perls in creating Gestalt Therapy (Naranjo, 1993). The tragedy here is that much of the creative fire of the Esalen years was lost, and in this process, Chairwork, which had become associated with Perls and emblematic of Gestalt Therapy, was discarded and abandoned.

Chairwork After Perls II

The "orphaning" of Chairwork in the gestalt world continues to this day, and recent major works (i.e., Woldt & Toman, 2005; Yontef & Jacobs, 2013) barely mention it at all. Nonetheless, it does live on. First, in the hands of Gestalt therapists who were trained by Perls and who utilized the West Coast model in their work (Hatcher & Himmelstein, 1983), and second, in the hands of integrative therapists, therapists whose work will inform much of the discussion to come. Perhaps among the first of these integrationists were Robert and Mary Goulding. Students of Eric Berne, they were friends of Perls and they combined Chairwork and imagery practices with transactional analysis. Their approach, called redecision therapy (Goulding & Goulding, 1997) focused on the role of childhood difficulties and trauma as a source of later problems.

Leslie Greenberg, first with his process-experiential therapy (Greenberg, Rice, & Elliott, 1993) and then with his emotion-focused therapy (Watson, Goldman, & Greenberg, 2007), has been the leading researcher and champion of Chairwork dialogues. His emotion-focused therapy is a synthesis of a number of Humanistic therapies including client-centered (Rogers, 1986), focusing (Gendlin, 1984), and Gestalt (Perls, 1992); Chairwork is an essential element in this work. His research has provided empirical support for the power of the Chairwork technique to facilitate the resolution of both past difficulties and internal conflicts (Greenberg, 1979; Paivio & Greenberg, 1995; Greenberg & Malcolm, 2002; Greenberg, Warwar, & Malcolm, 2008). Other researchers who have looked at Chairwork as a vehicle for psychotherapeutic healing and change have frequently used his work as a touchstone (Shahar et al., 2012; Sicoli & Hallberg, 1998; Trachsel, Ferrari, & Holtforth, 2012).

Cognitive and cognitive-behavioral therapists have been drawn to Chairwork as well. Given this, there are several interesting conceptual bridges that can be used to more effectively integrate experiential work into cbt. The first comes from Perls himself who wrote: "The other important discovery of Freud, which he never followed up and which seems to have gotten lost, is his remark, '*Denkin is Probearbiet*' ('Thinking is trial work'). I have reformulated it this way, 'Thinking is rehearsing.' Thinking is rehearsing in fantasy for the role you have to play in society" (Perls, 1970, p. 16). This insight clearly opens the door to treating thoughts in a psychodramatic manner as they can be understood as a form of rehearsal. In a related vein, Bishop (2000), who comes out of an REBT background, has written that thoughts can be understood as "voices." This is another wonderful bridging idea that can help us in our cognitive restructuring efforts as dialogues can now be created between maladaptive and more functional thought patterns.

Beck and colleagues wrote about the use of Chairwork in their book on anxiety (Beck, Emery, & Greenberg, 1985), and Edwards (1989, 1990) made a clear case that imagery and dialogue practice were forms of cognitive restructuring. Marvin Goldfried (1988; 2003), in turn, integrated dialogical work in his cognitive-behavior therapy. Working with the idea that cognitive restructuring was more likely to occur in a state of arousal, he argued that experiential techniques could lead to greater levels of neurobiological activation which would, in turn, facilitate therapeutic shifts in assumptions and schemas. Other practitioners who wrestle with this kind of integration include

Arnkoff (1981) and Lazarus (Lazarus & Messer, 1991). Their efforts have also helped cognitive-behavioral therapists remedy the stereotypic phenomena in which patients say that they understand something but do not feel it.

Lastly, there is Jeffrey Young and his work with schema therapy (Young, Weishaar, & Klosko, 2003). Schema therapy is an empirically-validated treatment for borderline personality disorder (Gisen-Bloo et al., 2006), and it is also used in the treatment of other personality disorders and with "difficult" cases more generally. A synthesis of cognitive, behavioral, psychodynamic, and gestalt therapies, it integrates dialogue techniques for cognitive restructuring, the reworking of traumatic experiences, and the balancing or rebalancing of inner forces (Kellogg, 2009a).

The dialogical possibilities contained within the Chairwork paradigm are vast. As Zerka Moreno (2008) said: "Though often dealing with traumas of the past, it is also concerned with problems in the present and expectations of the future, as rehearsals for living, helping to make alterations as indicated. Role playing can be done as animals, spirits, delusions or hallucinations, voices, body parts, ideas, visions, the departed . . ." (p. ix).

A TAXONOMY OF DIALOGUES

In the classic papers on gestalt therapy, there is repeated mention made of "empty" chair and "two-chair" dialogues. According to Zerka Moreno (Personal Communication, June 3, 2009), Jacob Moreno called it the "auxiliary chair," which became the subject of a paper by Rosemary Lippet (1958). He later added the phrase "empty chair" to allow people to use the technique to dialogue with those who were deceased. Eventually, the terms "two-chair" and "empty" chair were used to describe the basic dialogue paradigms with the first referring to encounters with others and the second incorporating dialogues among parts of the self. I believe, however, that instead of basing our conceptualization of these dialogues on the nature of the furniture involved, it would be more helpful to therapists to use the taxonomy of *External* and *Internal* dialogues (Daniels, 2005; Kellogg, 2004). These would involve, respectively: (1) speaking with forces outside of oneself; and (2) developing, controlling, or integrating inner forces.

In reality, few encounters are pure types. For example, if I speak with "someone" in the other chair about their aggressive behavior, I am both speaking about our relationship and my internal experience. Nonetheless, this can be seen as a predominantly external dialogue. If I do a Decisional Balance and then embody the part that wants to get married and the part that does not want to, I am having a predominantly internal conversation. However, I can also have an *Integrated* dialogue. These are situations that involve starting with one structure and then moving to the other. For example, in a workshop, a therapist played a woman who was wrestling with whether to stay in her marriage. First she did an internal dialogue between the part that wanted to stay and the part that wanted to leave; after this, we reorganized the chairs and she spoke with her husband about her feelings. Switching chairs and roles, she then spoke from his perspective and tried to access his emotional world. After going back and forth between those two perspectives, we stepped out of the dialogue and debriefed. That is, we looked at what had emerged, how she was currently feeling, and what she wanted to do next. In this way, the work embraced and integrated several dimensions of psychic reality.

Another dichotomy of importance is that between the diagnostic and transformational dialogues. Many of the case reports focus on what could be called *transformational* dialogues; that is, encounters in which a trauma is worked through or an inner conflict is resolved in a creative way. These can be powerful and awe-inspiring moments and it is understandable that therapists would want to share them. However, in day-to-day practice, it is not uncommon to have dialogues that may best be described as *diagnostic*. What emerges here is a clearer sense of the dynamics or polarities; that is, the modes are more clearly delineated, the inner tensions and the depth to which a patient is "stuck" is more fully appreciated, and the power of judgment and fear to paralyze and inhibit is revealed. For example, Arnkoff (1981) described a case in which a man was wrestling with the need to choose between work and school. To help him resolve this, they did a Chairwork dialogue. Although he had not made a decision by the end, "it was clear that we had made progress in clarifying and developing the meaning of the conflict" (p. 215). All of this provided a vital understanding of the problem and, perhaps, insight as to what steps to take next. Dialogues of this nature are very valuable and should be seen as holding equal weight with the more dramatic ones that lead to resolution or reorganization.

Therapeutic Stances

A second debate that has informed the use of Chairwork is the therapeutic stance of the practitioner. In an important chapter that looked at the differences between the experiential and the cognitive-behavioral therapies, Greenberg, Safran, and Rice (1989) wrote about facilitating and modifying psychotherapies. "They described the experiential therapies as *facilitating*; the goal was to help the patient grow in awareness so that whatever was unresolved, whatever was necessary for healing and transformation, would emerge from within.[5] The cognitive-behavioral therapies were described as *modifying*; here, the therapist is actively seeking to make changes in the patient's inner world. . . . The differences between the *facilitating* approach, on the one hand, and the *modifying* approach, on the other hand, can be clearly conveyed in the dramatically different perspective on the therapist's role. Greenwald (1976), writing from a Gestalt perspective, described the psychotherapist's work in this way:

> The therapist rejects any kind of authority position toward the person with whom he is working. The therapist does not attempt to lead, guide, advise, or in other ways take away the other person's responsibility for himself [or herself]. Rather, his attitude is that each person knows best what he needs for himself and how to get it; even when he is stuck, he is more capable of finding his solutions than anyone else. (p. 278)

This view stands in stark contrast to that of Goulding and Goulding (1997), who see the therapist in a much more active role, "In redecision therapy, the client is the star and the drama is carefully plotted to end victoriously. . . . The therapist is the director of the drama, writer of some of the lines, and occasionally interpreter. . . . We do not want to produce tragedies—we are interested in happy endings" (p. 177–178). In an earlier passage, Goulding and Goulding (1997) clearly delineated the goal of the therapy when they said, "We are focused exclusively on what the client needs in order to renounce 'victimhood' (p. 168)" (Kellogg, 2004, p. 312).

With contemporary Chairwork, it is not necessary to have to choose between these perspectives; instead, they can both be utilized as clinically appropriate. With situations such as grief, trauma, and cognitive restructuring, it may be more effective to take a modifying approach. With other kinds of conflict (such as in work with relationships where the dynamic is unclear), with the kind of projective work that is done with dreams, and in situations in which the therapist is not yet sure as to which schemas or cognitions are involved, it can be helpful to simply invite the different voices or parts to appear and speak. Perls trusted that when the patient allowed different parts of the self to encounter each other, some kind of creative solution would emerge.

Affect and Cognition

An additional point of tension has been the optimal balance between the emotional and cognitive contents of the work. In the West Coast Gestalt culture of the 1960s and early 1970s as well as in the Encounter movement in general (Schutz, 1972), there was a strong emphasis on emotional, and even cathartic, expression. As Latner (1973) maintained, "Emotions are the meaning of our experiences. Gestalt therapy encourages experiencing and expressing intense emotions, because they make our existence understandable and satisfying. We must abandon ourselves to them if we are to embrace all of ourselves, and if we are to come to workable solutions" (p. 173). It seems now that this made sense within the zeitgeist of the time which emphasized the throwing off of the old and the creation of the new, and which favored freedom over repression and restraint. Clearly, the experience of deep emotional expression was and continues to be healing for some; however, it is not sufficient to lead to deep or lasting change in all cases.

The Gouldings (1997), even in the 1960s and 1970s, emphasized that experiential techniques needed to be anchored within a cognitive structure and framework. For most patients, the meaning of the experience is as important as the experience itself. In the decision-oriented Chairwork discussed earlier, Arnkoff also discussed the cognitive implications of what might have been seen as a primarily emotive technique. "The artificial separation of each side set the stage for an uncovering of a complex network of beliefs and assumptions" (Arnkoff, 1981, p. 216).

Young, in his schema therapy work, envisioned the use of Chairwork in two different ways. When challenging an entrenched maladaptive schema with a healthy alternative, he understand the dialogue to be a primarily cognitive intervention. When reworking scenes of mistreatment, he saw it as an emotion-focused technique (Rafaeli, Bernstein, & Young, 2010; Young et al., 2003). Greenberg, Safran, & Rice (1989), in turn, have focused on the fused nature of cognition and affect. This has led them to speak of "affect-laden appraisals" and "meaning-laden feelings" (p. 172). The implication here is that not only does cognitive-restructuring change affect, but also affective experience changes cognition.

In any case, most contemporary practitioners see Chairwork as always combining emotive and cognitive elements. In some instances, language will be at the forefront, in others, the affective qualities will be sought, and in yet others the fused nature of the two will be present. Landy (2008) focused his efforts on the relationship between affect and cognition and on the expression and structural containment of emotion. This search for balance was what he called *aesthetic distance*—"the optimal balance between feeling and thought, experience and reflection" (p. 203). In his drama therapy work, he invites patients to engage with their pain through the use of storied enactment. "Rather than tell me the issue, could you think of it as a story and give the story a title? . . . You can go wherever you want to with it, but make it somewhat of a fairy tale. Would you start: Once upon a time there was . . ." (p. 116).

The Chairwork dialogues emerge out of this narrative. In his vision, this method allows for powerful emotional expression while also providing the patient with a container through the use of a role. In short, they are saying strong things, but they are saying them for someone else.

While Landy is working in contrast to the high levels of affect engendered by some of the gestalt therapist in the 1960s, I believe that there is no one right answer and the middle is not always the best place to be. For patients who are very intellectual, it may be useful to favor emotion; for those who are highly emotional, cognitive-centered dialogues could be helpful; for those who are fragile, brief and low-intensity encounters may be the best way to start; and, lastly, for those dealing with very difficult issues, the drama therapy approach of being one-removed from the actual experience may be a very useful place to begin. As the work develops and the patient changes, a different emotive/cognitive calculus may be more appropriate. It is, however, certainly useful that we have these many options.

A CHAPTER OVERVIEW

My goal, in the chapters ahead, is to introduce you, step-by-step, to the many clinical opportunities for change and healing that can be created through the use of Chairwork dialogues. The use of dialogues, whether scripted or transcribed, has a long tradition in gestalt therapy. Perls was one of the first psychotherapists to extensively film and share his work. *Gestalt Therapy Verbatim* (Perls, 1992), *The Gestalt Approach/Eyewitness to Therapy* (Perls, 1973), and *Legacy from Fritz* (Perls, 1975a) contain extensive transcripts of his work. Passons' (1975) *Gestalt Approaches in Counseling* is filled with scripted examples of a wide array of gestalt therapy techniques and interventions. This book has, in fact, been an important influence on the scripts that I have developed for this volume.

Beginning with the external encounters, the problems of grief, loss, and unfinished business are explored in chapter 2. Chapter 3 continues in this vein with the detailing of strategies for working with trauma and difficult relationships. It also includes an exercise on working through countertransferential feelings toward "difficult" patients. Chapter 4 draws on the behavioral tradition and will focus on empowerment through work with assertiveness and behavioral rehearsal.

In chapter 5, the focus moves to dialogues that are distinctly internal in nature. In this chapter, we will look at such key concepts as multiplicity, inner conflict, and decision making. Chapter 6 continues in this direction and focuses specifically on the issue of the inner critic and a number of strategies for addressing self-hatred, self-attack, and problematically high standards. It also includes a dialogue that draws on Neff's (2011) important work with self-kindness and self-compassion. Chapter 7 re-visits the extraordinary work that Perls did with polarities in the 1960s; the relevance of this model for contemporary psychotherapeutic work is explored as well.

Chapter 8 is dedicated to the use of Chairwork paradigms with addictive disorders. Here, Chairwork is clearly anchored within contemporary developments in the treatment of drug and alcohol problems. This chapter includes both a motivational dialogue and one that looks at the patient's relationship with his or her substance of choice. Building on models and issues addressed earlier, chapter 9 more briefly reviews the use of Chairwork in four disparate clinical areas: feminist therapy, internalized oppression, somatic concerns and illnesses, and psychotic disorders.

The book concludes in chapter 10 with an exploration of how to add power and depth to one's practice. The deepening techniques, which have been used throughout the various dialogues, are now more formally presented. The chapter also includes an examination of therapeutic stances, ways of working with resistant patients, and the important subtleties of chair placement. It is the judicious use of these techniques and interventions that constitute the art of Chairwork while the basic dialogue structures that inform the clinical presentations that make up the science. Putting these together, the psychotherapist will have the tools necessary to effectively help people heal and change.

NOTES

1. Some of the details of this case and others presented in the book have been changed in order to protect the confidentiality of the patients.

2. Except when otherwise referenced, this biographical sketch is drawn from Shepard (1972).

3. This "man," it would turn out, was Dr. John Enright, a psychologist, who also went on to become a prominent gestalt therapist (Shepard, 1975).

4. I have called this the "1969 Model" not only because that was the year that *Gestalt Therapy Verbatim* was first published, but also because the book captured much of the spirit of his work at Esalen.

5. This quoted section is taken from Kellogg (2004) and is used with permission.

Chapter 2

External Dialogues

Grief, Loss, and Unfinished Business

Patients enter therapy with a wide range of problems. The work may need to focus on the past (which may involve trauma and loss), the present (which may involve depression and anxiety), or the future (which may involve existential choice and life creation) (Dayton, 2005), and the encounters and enactments may be primarily internal, external, or both (Kellogg, 2004). Starting with the external dialogues, we will take up the issue of working through grief. The chapters that follow will address three other external dialogue structures: resolving trauma, changing the dynamics of problematic relationships, and assertiveness.

An essential part of the external dialogues is the use of an approach known as *role-reversal*. A central technique in psychodrama (Dayton, 1994, 2005; Moreno, 2012), it involves playing the role of another in such an empathic way that we can understand their perspective as if it were our own. This, in turn, can lead to an increased sense of compassion and an experience of resolution and healing.

UNFINISHED BUSINESS

Resolving "Unfinished Business" was a central focus of Perls' work. Simply put, it brings to the fore "unexpressed and unintegrated . . . thoughts and feelings relative to a person" or situation (Applebaum, 1993, p. 491). Clearly, this is a common and universal part of the human experience; it becomes problematic, however, when there is so much emotional energy tied up in these situations that it blocks the person's growth.

In therapy, these unresolved memories can be revisited and resolved. Perls wrote: "You can begin to finish them by repeatedly re-experiencing them in

fantasy. Each time you go through one of these painful episodes you will
be able to recover additional details and to tolerate in awareness more and
more of the blocked-off emotion which they contain" (Perls et al., 1951,
pp. 102–103).

Loss and Grief

Loss and grief are a painful and unavoidable part of the human condition.
Often these experiences are successfully mourned and released, but sometimes they are not and people are left carrying the weight of the past. Given
this, it is not uncommon to find that patients may need to say goodbye to
former romantic partners, to relationships that have ended through divorce or
maturation, and to those who have died. In a remembrance of the anguish she
felt over a romantic loss, bell hooks, wrote: "At the time, . . . I was often overwhelmed by grief so profound it seemed as though an immense sea of pain
was washing my heart and soul away. . . . In my head I engaged in imaginary
conversations about the meaning of love with him" (hooks, 2000, xv–xvi).
One of the things that is striking here is that she is engaging in dialogue work
in an organic fashion.

People may also need to mourn other kinds of losses such as those connected to immigration or emigration or desired careers or personal dreams
that they were unable to fulfill (Goulding and Goulding, 1997). For example,
a man comes to New York from California to work. The original plan may
have been that he would stay for a few years and then go back West, but as
the years go by, he has neither returned to the West Coast nor has he fully
invested in a life in New York City. To resolve this dilemma, he may want
to do some grief work in which "California" is put in a chair and a dialogue
is held in which he ultimately says goodbye to his old home and claims and
affirms New York City as his new one. Similarly, a college student who
always thought that she would become a doctor may find that the classes are
too difficult or that she is just not as interested in pursuing medicine as originally thought. The work may involve releasing and mourning a dream that
was a defining part of who they were for many years.

Tobin (1976) has outlined a classic gestalt approach to using chairs to
facilitate the mourning process. The patient is first invited to imagine the
absent individual in the "empty chair" opposite them. To deepen the experience, the patient is encouraged to first describe the person's appearance (age,
appearance, emotional state, expression) and then to clarify what they are
experiencing emotionally as they "see" them.

Gestalt work emphasizes giving voice to everything and integrating opposites. This means that patients will be encouraged to go through the *cycle
of emotions*; that is, to express their love, anger, grief, and, if appropriate,

fear, when they engage with the absent person. It is also a part of the gestalt approach to begin where the patient is, which means that the dialogue would start with the expression of the emotion that is most figural or salient. If it were anger, they would speak from that; if love, they would start there (Tobin, 1976).

To do this effectively, patients should be encouraged to express their feelings in forceful and powerful ways (see chapter 10). This can include bringing up memories and/or putting photographs or other mementoes on the chair to evoke as much emotion as possible. Therapists may need to give patients permission to share their anger and disappointment as this may violate cultural or subcultural norms. One way to do this is to point out that the expression of "negative" emotions can help in the healing and ultimately lead to a deeper sense of love for the deceased person (Neimeyer, 2012).

The patient may, but need not, switch roles and speak from the perspective of the deceased or missing person. This can, however, be an illuminating experience as ideas, beliefs, and perspectives emerge that were not anticipated and perhaps not even imagined. For example, in a session that took place at Perls' "Kibbutz" at Lake Cowichan, a woman did work on the death of her child. Her baby had a bad heart and, following the advice of their doctor, she and her husband decided to have the child undergo an operation when a year old. The operation was, however, unsuccessful, and the baby died. The woman had felt guilty and depressed about this for sixteen years.

The therapist asked her to imagine her baby in the opposite chair and to share her feelings of guilt, love, and depression. After she was finished, the woman was invited to switch roles and to play the baby. When the "baby" spoke what emerged was that the baby had wanted a full life and that he or she would have made the same decision and taken the chance. The patient then switched back to her original seat. With this new perspective, she was able to: (1) begin to understand that she had not done something terrible to her child; and (2) start to say goodbye to the baby (Stevens, 1970).

This case is a good example of role-reversal. When playing the role of her child, the mother was able to come to a perspective and understanding of the death in a way that she had not been able to achieve on her own. This is also an example of a transformative dialogue. Here we see a patient who, having been stuck for over a decade-and-a-half, was able to profoundly reorganize herself after one session of work. Might there be more work to do? Of course. Chairwork does not have to provide "miracles" nor does it rule out the central importance of empathic sharing with the therapist. Nonetheless, something quite extraordinary happened here, something that deeply affected both the woman involved and those who were watching (Stevens, 1970).

In clinical practice, working through loss may involve one powerful encounter or it may require work extending over several weeks or months.

At some point, however, it will be time to invite the patient to make a decision. They will be called on to decide: "Are you now prepared to let go and say goodbye to the person or do you want to keep holding on to this figure from the past?" It is likely that most therapists will favor the patient's letting go of the past and moving forward with his or her life, but this is, of course, the patient's decision. After doing the dialogues, telling the stories, and releasing the emotions, there will be some patients who still do not want to move forward and say goodbye. These patients can be told that they have every right to do this and that they may feel that it makes sense to do so; however, they are also told, in a gentle yet clarifying manner, that they are now making an existential decision, a choice to remain tied to the past and to commit their cognitive and emotional energies to someone who is no longer present in their life.

Blatner (1999) has used this same approach with patients who have had multiple losses. Here a number of "empty" chairs can be used and patients can speak to those they have lost individually or as a group. Moving beyond the individual therapy format, Leveton (2001) has used it in a family therapy situation as a way of enabling family members to speak with and about someone who is not there, regardless of the reason for the absence. Lowe (2000) has recommended the use of this technique when treating African-American families. As a result of racism, cultural oppression, and the War on Drugs, many families have lost grandfathers, fathers, husbands, and sons, frequently to drugs, prison, and murder. The "empty" chair provides an opportunity to uncover fantasies and to express anger, grief, love, and longing.

Lastly, moving to a realm beyond the therapeutic office, Blatner (1999) has used the chair in memorial services. Here a dialogue can take place in which an entire group can "see" the person before them and express their love and grief and, perhaps, anger to the departed. Especially with difficult deaths, such as a suicide, this can help further the process of reconciliation and healing.

WAYS TO USE THE SCRIPTS

The scripts are the heart of this book. They were written with the intent of giving psychotherapists an experience of "doing" Chairwork. While all of the dialogues share common features, they each have unique qualities. This is the case not only because some clinical situations call for certain ways of responding, but also as a way of increasing therapists' comfort with a wide range of techniques and dialogue structures. Given this, it will be fruitful for therapists to read, study, and enact these dialogues on their own. Another dimension can be added to this experience if the role-plays can be shared with a partner.

The Deepening Techniques

Throughout the script there will be places where the therapist will use the deepening techniques (see chapter 10). The intention is to: (1) encourage the patient to voice his or her thoughts, fears, and desires as directly and clearly as possible; (2) invite the patient to significantly increase or decrease their level of emotional expression, as appropriate; (3) enable the therapist to demonstrate an empathic connection with the patient by providing or suggesting statements that resonate with the truth of the patient's situation; (4) have the therapist guide the dialogue process so that all of the relevant parts are invited to speak and an opportunity is provided for a full emotional encounter; and (5) encourage the patient to use existential language so that they may speak more powerfully and claim ownership of what they say. Again, this way of developing the dialogue constitutes the *art* of Chairwork. Through practice and study, therapists can begin to develop their own way of using these techniques. It should be acknowledged that some patients will require more direction than others, and even with the same patient, some problems will call for more coaching while others will require less. In the latter, the therapist's primary healing work may be that of serving as a witness.

Loss and Grief Dialogue

In this scenario, the patient is in conflict. They have met someone that they would like to have a future with, but they feel that their heart is still tied up with someone from the past. This earlier relationship had a period of intense romance, passion, love, and connectedness; unfortunately, something went wrong and things came to an end. This brought great distress to the patient, and they went through a period of partial mourning after the loss; they also shut themselves down to new possibilities for a while. With the new person that they have met, they are not only confronted with an opportunity to love, but also with the reality of having to truly and finally release this former relationship.

In terms of chair placement, the set-up is fairly straight forward. The patient and therapist will begin by speaking in a normal face-to-face set-up. After the patient agrees to engage in a dialogue, the therapist will bring over another chair and the patient will move their chair from its original spot to one where he or she can face the person from the past (see figure 2.1). In this case, it will be a direct, one-way conversation and the patient will not need to switch seats. At the end of the dialogue, the chair will be brought back to its original location and the patient will debrief the experience with the therapist. An alternative approach is to have two additional chairs located in a different part of the room or therapy space. The patient and therapist can start in the normal place and then move to this second space during then dialogue and the back to their original location afterwards.

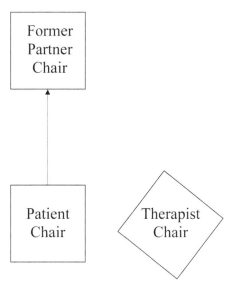

Figure 2.1   Romantic Loss Dialogue

There are a few technical considerations at work here. It is important for the therapist to sit on the patient's side. It is probably best if he or she is at an angle in which both the patient and the person from the past can be clearly seen. In the scripted dialogue, the therapist stays back to some degree, but he or she does use a number of deepening techniques. In addition to directing the patient to identify their emotional state and explore anger, love, and grief, the therapist will: (1) ask him or her to describe the person they are seeing in the opposite chair; (2) encourage the patient to use repetition; (3) provide positive reinforcement; (4) invite further comment; (5) "feed" them lines; and (6) re-orient the patient to direct their comments to the other. There is a brief, mild, and optional erotic passage in the script. While this can be used or ignored as the participants see fit, in a real therapeutic situation it is important to provide the patient with the opportunity to speak openly about all aspects of the relationship. In a sense, this work is similar to that of cleaning out a wound so that the healing can proceed.

The dialogue begins with the patient making contact with the person from the past. They explain why they are there, that they have met a new person and that the memories from the past are stopping them from making a new connection. After they are invited to express anger, love, and grief, the therapist will ask the patient if they are ready to say goodbye and release this figure from the past. At this point, there will be a split in the dialogue. For those who want to say goodbye, the dialogue continues. For those who do not, the dialogue will jump to page 33 where they will express their desire to hold on to the past. After this, they will both go back to their original chairs and debrief, as outlined on page 33.

Background Information

Before doing this as a role-play with a partner, the Therapist should ask the Patient for:

The name of the person in old relationship:

The name of the person who being considered for the new relationship:

Romantic Loss Dialogue

Patient: The issue that I have been wrestling with is that, after a long time, I have met a new person. His/her name is [ ]. There are a lot of good qualities about her/him, and it looks like things have the potential to get serious.

   As you know, I had that powerful relationship with [ ]. Even though it ended, I have always thought of [ ] as the great love of my life. My dilemma is that when I look into my heart, I know that I'm still very connected. I don't feel emotionally free to fully pursue this new relationship, yet it doesn't seem to make too much sense to hold onto someone who isn't there.

Therapist: One way to work with this, if you are willing, is to have a kind of imaginary conversation with [ ]. What I would like to do is to have you imagine him/her sitting in that chair. I would then invite you to talk to [ ] and express your feelings about the relationship and where things are now. How does that sound?

Patient: Sounds good.

Therapist: (The Therapist moves the chairs so that the Patient is now facing the empty chair. The Therapist is seated by the Patient, but at a diagonal so that he or she is facing both the Patient and the figure in the opposite chair.) (See figure 2.1) The first thing that I would like you to do is to try to see [ ] sitting over there, as best you can. Once they come into view and you have a sense of them, I would like you to describe what you see: what they look like, the clothes they are wearing, how old they are, and the expression on their face.

Patient: (Takes a moment to imagine the person and then describe him or her.)

Therapist: Now I would like you to tell [ ] what is going on with you and why you want to speak to her/him.

Patient: I know it's been a long time since we saw each other or spoke. It seems ridiculous that I'm still carrying you inside of me, that you are still in my heart, when you have moved on. I now have the chance to be with [ ]. He/she's good. I think we have the chance to have a great life together, but I feel myself holding back. A part of me is holding back because I'm still tied to you. I'm working on this today because it's time to let you go, to say goodbye. I don't want our past to stop me from having a future.

Therapist: When you look at [ ], what do you feel?

Patient: I feel a lot of anger.

Therapist: Tell him/her about that.

Anger/Resentment

Patient: When I think of the pain our break up caused me, I'm just so angry. Losing you was a kind of a death. It was awful. The grief seemed never-ending, and I just wanted to cry all the time. It was embarrassing, I would be out doing errands or hanging out with friends, and I would feel the tears coming on.

I used to feel it in my chest and my heart all the time. It was hard to breathe. I couldn't sleep, I couldn't focus, I didn't want to be around anyone, I didn't want to do anything. Nothing worked. I just wanted you back, and you weren't coming back.

I remember the first time I saw you with him/her. You didn't see me. I thought that it was going to kill me. I wanted to call you up so badly, but I didn't. It seemed so unfair—how could you be with him/her and not me? I hated you for that.

Therapist: Say that again.

Patient: I hated you for that! I hated having to put on a good face, to go out and pretend that everything was fine. As the months went on, people assumed that I was over it; I wasn't. I wasn't over it. But I would smile and look engaged, while I was bleeding on the inside. I hated you for putting me through this. Eventually, I just shut myself down. I didn't feel anything for anybody, I didn't allow myself to feel. I wasn't living; I was just going through the motions. As you can see, I have been like that for a long time. It's only with [ ] that I have begun to feel again. That's why I'm talking with you today—I need to be free of you, I want to be free of you.

Therapist: Tell her/him again.

Patient: I want to be free of you.

Therapist: Again.

Patient: I want to be free of you. I want to be done with this.

Therapist: Good. *(Pause)*

Appreciations/Love

Therapist: I would like to shift you. I would like you to look at [ ] sitting over there, and I would like you to speak to her/him about the love you had or still have for her/him. The more you can say, the more you can get out, the better.

Patient: Given all the pain that you've caused me, it's weird to have these positive memories. The memories of the early days when things were good between us haunt me at times. Despite myself, I find myself smiling and even laughing about them.

I remember when we first started. It was like everything in my life was special. I know it's a cliché, but the world seemed changed in our early days together—I know that you remember that. It's funny how the small moments seem to dominate in my mind—laughing together at our little jokes, being in that café we used to visit, getting lost for hours at Barnes and Noble, holding your hand in public.

That first trip to Costa Rica was amazing; neither of us had done anything like that before. Being in the rainforest was a kind of spiritual experience for both of us. Whenever I hear that song, I'm still filled with longing for you, like Pavlov's dog.

I was so proud to be with you. You were so handsome/beautiful. And you were great with people. All my friends liked you—I loved that.

It was exciting when your career took off; it was an adventure that we both shared. We had a great weekend in that hotel in Idaho when you were at the convention. It was also great when things began to happen for me. I was so happy that you were there to share it with me.

I trusted you like I had never trusted anyone before. I told you some of my secrets. I know that you felt the same way about me, especially when you shared some of those things that you had been through. I felt honored that you trusted me enough to reveal those things.

(Erotic Life—Optional Passage) Of course, memories and images of some of those private times still haunt me as well. I wanted to be with you all the time during those early days. I loved your skin and I loved the way you felt. I loved you for wanting to be with me. It was like we were safe in our own little world. The thought of you being like that with someone else still kills me. *(Pause)*

Therapist: What are you feeling right now?

Patient: A mixture of being happy and being sad.

Therapist: Is there anything else you would like to say about love?

Patient: No, I'm done.

Grief and Sorrow

Therapist: Now I would like you to shift and speak to [ ] about your grief and sorrow over what happened.

Patient: Saying these things, remembering these things, brings up so much sadness. I'm sorry that the early days are gone and I'm sorry that things turned bad and that we lost our way with each other. I'm sorry that we couldn't find a way a back.

I'm pained beyond words that you will not be in my life, that you will not be in my future, that the dreams will never come true. That loneliness and exhaustion, it's there inside of me again.

Therapist: I just feel exhausted.

Patient: I just feel exhausted.

Holding On or Letting Go

Therapist: You've said a lot of things to [ ]. At this point, are you willing to say goodbye and release him/her from your past or do you want to hold onto this connection with [ ]?

[Here the Patient needs to make a choice. If they decide to hold on, it is an existential decision and they are no longer a victim; if they decide to let go, they can speak to the person and say goodbye. The script for Saying Goodbye is on this page; the one for Holding Onto the Past is on page 33.]

Saying Goodbye

Patient: I want to release *him/her*, I want to let go. I want to move on with my life.

Therapist: Please tell [ ] that.

Patient: I need to release you; I need to accept the fact, to make the decision that it's over . . . that it's done. I need to turn away from you.

Therapist: I *want* to turn away from you.

Patient: Yes, I want to turn away from you. As sweet as it was at times, there is nothing for me here. You've moved on and I know that you're not coming back.

Therapist: There is nothing for me here—say it again.

Patient: There is nothing for me here. *(Pause)*
You cost me too much—time, possibilities, life, happiness. I'm holding onto a dream. Actually, a fantasy. I'm wasting myself over this. Too many months, just too many. I want to turn away. It hurts me to say this but I want you out of my life. I want you out of my mind. I want you out of my heart. I don't want to think about you; I don't want to remember you. I want you to be gone.

Therapist: You moved on and you left me behind.

Patient: You've moved on. You burned the bridge. Enough is enough. I want to say goodbye. I just want to say goodbye.

Therapist: I want to turn away from you.

Patient: Yes.

Therapist: Tell [ ] it's over; Say goodbye one more time.

Patient: Goodbye. I'm saying goodbye. It's over; I'm done.

[Go to Debrief below.]

Holding Onto the Past

Patient: I don't want to let go. I'm just not ready to do it.

Therapist: Please let her/him know.

Patient: I know that I should say goodbye to you, that it makes no sense to keep holding on to someone who is not in my life anymore, but I don't want to. I don't feel ready to, and I just don't want to.

Therapist: Again, I just don't want to.

Patient: Yes, I don't want to. My memories of being with you are still some of the happiest of my life; if I say goodbye to them, if I let them go, what will I be left with? [ ] is great, but he/she doesn't compare with you. I can't stand the thought that it would all be gone, that it would all really be over. I don't want it to be over. I don't want to say goodbye, whatever it costs me. I don't want to say goodbye.

Debrief

Therapist: Let's move back over here. *(They go back to their original places.)* So . . . how was that? What are you feeling? What are you thinking?

The Patient speaks about the experience and shares his or her sense of where they are in terms of the relationships.

Reflections

This dialogue followed the basic cycle of emotions structure. The patient was invited to speak about anger, love, and grief. Fear was not included because it was not appropriate in this scenario. The existential aspects of the work not only include using "want" instead of "need," but also encouraging the patient to take a clear stance. The deepening techniques of replication and simplification were used to clarify the voice and heightened the emotional intensity.

Chapter 3

External Dialogues

The Treatment of Trauma and Difficult Relationships

The treatment of trauma, abuse, and interpersonal violence is, tragically, an all-too-common occurrence in psychotherapuetic practice. Whether it meets the formal criteria of a Post-Traumatic Stress Disorder (PTSD) diagnosis or not, many patients report histories of emotional, physical, and sexual abuse and mistreatment. Some have also had experiences of cruelty and humiliation, all of which have left them with inner pain and stories to tell.

Psychodrama is a powerful approach for working with trauma (Kellerman & Hudgins, 2000). Moreno stressed the importance of reliving traumatic experiences as a way to heal (Dayton, 2005). As he put it, "every true second time is a liberation from the first" (Moreno, 1947, pp. 90–91, as cited in Marineau, 1989, p. 80). He also pointed out that it may be necessary to have patients relive their traumatic experiences several times before they achieve a "true second" (Kellerman, 2000). Perls grouped traumatic experiences under the general heading of "unfinished business" (Hardie, 2004; Perls et al., 1951). In fact, many of his technical innovations have become staples of trauma treatment. As Hardie (2004) pointed out: "Fantasy and visualization, creative enactments of body language, two-chair work, graded experiments, psychodrama and enactment were therapeutic techniques used by Perls and are currently used with people who are experiencing trauma" (n.p.).

As discussed earlier, Robert and Mary Goulding, the creators of redecision therapy, integrated transactional analysis and gestalt therapy to develop a trauma-centered model of psychotherapy (Goulding & Goulding, 1997). In their view, many patients have had difficult, problematic, troubling, and sometimes abusive experiences early in life. As a result, they made decisions about themselves and the nature of the world that have resulted in various kinds of problematic behaviors and psychopathology. Using visualizations and chair dialogues, they took patients through what can be envisioned as a five-step process.

The patient begins by imagining the abusive figure in the chair opposite. The first step in the process is to speak to the figure and say as clearly and directly as possible what actually occurred between them, being as specific as possible about the details of the abuse or mistreatment. In short, they are asked to tell the story and to say what occurred.

Next, they are asked to speak about how they were changed at that time by what had happened. This might include such experiences as: "I felt tainted"; "I was really afraid for the first time in my life"; "I now had the burden of a secret"; or "My innocence was gone." The third step is to describe how they have lived their life as a consequence of what happened. "I have been angry"; "I have not trusted others"; "I have suffered depression and I have blamed myself"; "I cut myself"; or "I started smoking pot every day." These three steps form the heart of the early Chairwork dialogues; for some, this work will be sufficient to facilitate healing. The final two steps of the model are centered on existential empowerment.

Called "redecisions" by the Gouldings, the fourth step invites the patient to make the decision that they are no longer going to live in the shadow of the trauma and that they are going to heal from the damage. The fifth step, which flows from the previous one, is an affirmation that they are going to live in healthier ways and that they are choosing specific actions that they could take to symbolize and manifest this new life direction. The Gouldings provided three examples from women who imaginally confronted those who mistreated them: "From now on, I am going to find trustworthy people, and I will trust them. Everyone is not like you." "I enjoy sex today in spite of what you did to me. You are no longer in my bed." "I can laugh and jump and dance without guilt, because my fun didn't cause you to rape me! It was your perversity!" (Goulding & Goulding, 1997, p. 248). Here we see excellent examples of patients claiming power and reclaiming authorship of their lives.

To be clear, this is a process that may take place over a span of sessions. It is also possible that any one of these steps could lead to fruitful explorations of related areas. This means that therapists will need to be flexible in their efforts. Regardless, the Gouldings have provided a valuable structure to the guide the work.

Mainstream cognitive-behavioral treatments for PTSD often include elements of exposure and cognitive restructuring. The first might include protocols in which patients write out the story of the traumatic event, including the details of what took place, how they were feeling, and the thoughts and beliefs that they were having. This narrative is then read aloud in the session and at home on a daily basis (Bryant et al., 2008).

Social Processing Therapy (Resick, 2001; Resick, Monson, & Rizvi, 2008) emphasizes the challenge to core schemas that take place in the context of trauma. The understanding is that trauma-driven alterations to the core beliefs that are made by the patient may actually fuel the PTSD symptoms themselves (Resick, 2001). For example, if the individual is operating under an assumption that the world is a relatively safe and predictable place and that they are a fundamentally good or slightly mixed person, an unexpected violent attack or assault may challenge their faith in the predictable nature of the world. It may also lead to a split—the world before the attack and the world after it. As they seek to make sense of the experience, they may look at their own behavior to see if there were some things they did that contributed to the event and/or if they could have done something differently. The positive value of this attribution is that it may allow them to feel some sense of control and mastery over their life; the negative aspect is that it may make them vulnerable to experiences of self-blame and guilt. ("If only I had not walked down that street! How could I be so stupid.") This will be greatly compounded if others also blame them for being hurt or say things about them that are demeaning and derogatory.

Resick emphasizes the importance of integrating the schemas. One Chairwork dialogue that could be developed for this involves using one chair to give voice to how they saw themselves and the world after the event while using the other chair to embody their life perspective before the event. The encounter between these two viewpoints could help lead to a healthy and personally meaningful integration. It could also help the patient regain access to some of the strengths that they had before the trauma.

To be clear, when working with these kinds of experiences, we can use many chairs, not just two, and both the patient and the therapist can speak to the various figures in the story. Dialogues can also be created in such a way that there is some titration of the intensity. In turn, patients can have internal dialogues where they give voice to their fear in one chair and their anger in another. It is important that they go back and forth as a way of fully giving voice to these two parts. A third chair can be added in which the patient speaks to the anger and the fear and honors both. In this way, the patient may be able to get some distance from their emotions.

In cases of interpersonal violence, one chair can be used to represent the perpetrator and another chair can be used to represent the patient. Here the clinician speaks and the patient listens. The therapist confronts the attacker and clearly makes the case that what they did was wrong. The clinician also speaks to the patient to affirm that they are not at fault. Before doing this, it may be helpful to clarify the patient's beliefs about their own responsibility for the events. When the therapist says thing like "It doesn't matter how you dressed and doesn't matter how much you had to drink, he still had no right to touch you or hurt you," he or she is challenging the patient's maladaptive cognitions and schemas. This is a form of modeling and, in schema therapy terms, a form of reparenting. The patient, with support from the therapist, can then do the same thing, confronting the abuser while nurturing and defending him- or herself in a third chair.

Moving to a level of greater intensity, the patient can confront the abuser in the opposite chair. I frequently like to have the patient stand behind the chair when doing trauma work as it is a more powerful stance and it allows them to move. Working with the patient, we can decide how far away to put the "abuser" chair; that is, how much "distance" there should be between the two of them. Some patients are quite frightened to be in the same room with such figures and we can use other chairs to build a protective barrier or "wall" between them. In this setting, the patient can engage with the five steps of the Goulding model.

When the trauma has occurred within the context of the family or a long-term relationship, the work can be particularly complex. The patient may not only have memories of abuse and pain, but also those of love and happiness. This is deeply confusing; it also makes it difficult for the patient to have a clear voice. Given this, I have found a three-chair model to be helpful. The patient sits in a chair and one chair is placed, a few feet away, 45 degrees to the left and another is placed at similar distance, 45 degrees to the right. One chair embodies the bad or abusive experiences while the other contains the good ones. Working this way can be a relief to patients; since they feel less conflicted or guilty, they can speak more clearly.

Engle, Beutler, and Dalup (1991) report a case in which a woman confronted her grandmother in the opposite chair. The grandmother had treated her badly as a teenager. In this dialogue, the patient confronted the grandmother and said: "You are so mean, I hate you. I do love you, but I hate you. . . . I hate being here with you. You constantly talk about dying and death, death, that's it, every day, every day. . . . I resent the times you called me a tramp. . . . I was never a tramp! You always said, 'You'll become pregnant.' I never did things like that. But you always said I was no good, a slut. . . . I resent you for not trusting me, for not letting me be a young person. I resent you for dragging me to cemeteries to see dead graves. . . . I resent that . . ." (Engle, Beutler, & Dalup, 1991, pp. 180–182).

Here we can see an example of a woman expressing an anger that, most likely, was not permitted when she was living in her grandmother's house. It is also worth noting that at the start, she spoke about having both anger and love for her grandmother, which again demonstrates that those who were abused by people they were in relationship with may have deeply conflicting feelings about them. Again, this may be because they had a variety of experiences with the abuser, some fun and caring and others dreadful and damaging; it may also be because they have undergone an experience of traumatic bonding.

Lastly, there is an important technical issue that needs to be addressed in any discussion around creating dialogues with abusers. Whenever a patient engages in a role-reversal and gives voice to the perspectives of another, there is a chance that they will experience an increase in empathy for that person. While this can be a boon, it can also be a problem. Since we want the patient to have the freedom to tell the story of what happened to them and to express their outrage and pain, empathy can actually interfere with this process. Given this, I do not invite patients to speak from the perspective of the abuser and I advise therapists to refrain from doing so. Nonetheless, if therapists are contemplating taking this step, there are two guidelines to keep in mind. The first is that they need to realize that they are making a major intervention which will probably have a lasting impact on the therapy work to follow—so they should do it with a sense of conscious awareness, not mindlessly or as a matter of course. The second is that if they want to do this, it would be prudent if if they waited until the patient had an opportunity to tell the story repeatedly and go through the cycle of emotions. With this work accomplished, it would then be acceptable to proceed in this way if the therapist still believes it is in the best interests of the patient.

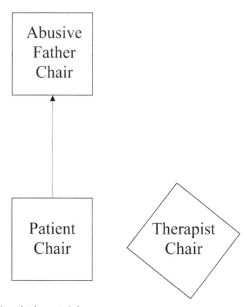

Figure 3.1   Emotional Abuse Dialogue

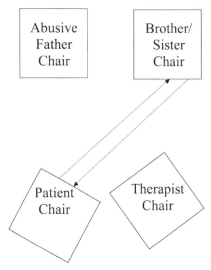

Figure 3.2   Emotional Abuse Sibling Dialogue

CONFRONTING EMOTIONAL ABUSE

In this dialogue, the patient confronts a father who was emotionally cruel and abusive. This is a one-way dialogue in which the patient talks to the father about what he did. The therapist works to increase the emotional intensity of what the patient is saying.

Emotional Abuse Dialogue

Patient: I know that over the past few months, I have mentioned that growing up with my father was really terrible. I never really told you what it was like. I have so much rage at him that I think that it is time to confront it.

Therapist: I appreciate your courage in choosing to do this. One way to approach it, if you're willing, is to have an imaginary conversation with your father. What we can do is imagine him sitting in this chair over here. You can tell the story and confront him and say the things that you couldn't say when you were young.

Patient: Sounds good.

Therapist: (The Therapist moves the chair so that the Patient is facing his/her father. The Therapist sits, at a diagonal, by the Patient's side. The Therapist see both the Patient and the father.) (See figure 3.1) I would like you to imagine him sitting in that chair. When you get an image, can you tell me what you see? What does he look like? How old is he? What is he wearing? What's the expression on his face?

Patient: (Patient does that and describes what is seen.)

Therapist: Talk to him. Talk to him about what happened, what he did, and tell him how you feel about it.

Patient: I hated growing up with you. I hated living with you. You were so sick and so cruel to me, to my brother and my sister. *(Pause)*

Therapist: It looks like you're feeling something.

Patient: Yeah.

Therapist: Just take your time. Breathe. Start again in a minute.

Patient: (Pause) I hated our so-called family dinners. You insisted that we all had to eat together and that no one could leave the table until you said so. You would give us those lectures about life, politics, religion, and whatever crazy ideas you had in your head. We all had to sit there until you were done talking.

Therapist: (Slowly) You held us captive.

Patient: Yes. You held us captive. I remember that we would sometimes be stuck there for an hour after we had finished eating. I remember staring at the empty plates in front of us while you ranted and raved. You were so mean to the little ones. If they fidgeted or got restless, you would go up to them and scream at them and wave your finger in their face. You terrified them.

Therapist: Tell him he was a bully.

Patient: You were a bully; a cruel, mean, cowardly bully!

Therapist: Tell him again.

Patient: You were nothing but a [ ] bully!! *(Pause)* And the way that you gave us all nicknames was horrible. You called John "Stupid." I know now that he must have had some kind of a learning disability and that school was hard for him, but you called him "stupid, stupid, stupid" all the time. Even worse, you would do this in front of other people, people we knew and total strangers. I used to feel so mortified that I wanted to die.

And Suzie, you always called her "Ugly Duckling" or "The Ugly One" or just "Ugly." You were relentless about teasing her and criticizing her about her weight. I especially hated you that time, that rare time, when we went to the ice cream store. You were so cheap! You bought ice cream for everyone except Suzie and she was just five. You gave her a lecture in front of the people in the store and told her that she couldn't have any because she was already too fat, and that she could only have some when she lost some weight.

She looked so sad. She wanted to cry but held it back. And then you kept asking the rest of us how we were enjoying our ice cream. All I wanted to do was give her mine, but I knew that would just make things worse, that you would really go crazy. I was torn between wanting to throw the ice cream up and throw it at you, bastard.

Therapist: I just wanted to smash it in your face.

Patient: I wanted to shove it down your throat. *(Pause)*

Therapist: Did he have a name for you?

Patient: He used to call me "Smarty Pants." I hated that. It was a good thing that I was smart because it helped me to get out of there.

Therapist: Tell him.

Patient: It was a good thing that I was smart or at least good at school because it helped me to finally get away from you and your sickness. The "Smarty Pants" things, the sarcasm part, I realize now that you were jealous of me, that you knew in some way that I *was* smarter than you were and ever will be. But you worked it both ways.

Even though I generally did well, it was never good enough; everything had to be perfect. If I got a B+, you would give me the endless lectures about trying harder. I was smart, but I wasn't a genius. Some of those classes were difficult and I wanted to do other things and not just study all the time.

You used to embarrass me on those meet-the-teacher days. Sometimes they would say what a good student I was, and then you would start telling them how good a student you had been and how everything that I did well I got from you. I didn't get anything from you.

Therapist: Say it louder.

Patient: I didn't get anything from you!

Therapist: Again. Slowly

Patient: (Slowly) I did not get anything from you.

Therapist: (Pause) Where was Mom in all of this?

Patient: She was completely dominated by him.

Therapist: Speak to him about it.

Patient: Then there would be the times that something would go wrong, and you would stop talking; that used to get Mom so upset. She really couldn't stand it. You would go in your room and refuse to come out. You would go on for days giving her and us the silent treatment. She felt so desperate because she didn't have any money and there were all these small kids. She would come and ask us to go apologize to you, even if we hadn't done anything wrong. She just wanted to get you to start talking again. It was torture for her when you behaved that way.

(Pause) One of my last negative memories was when I was a teenager. I always tried to keep the boys/girls that I was interested in far away from you. Once you did catch up with me when I was with Henry/Emma. I warned her/him about how crazy you were, but he/she was just being polite and allowed you to start talking. Right there, you started telling embarrassing stories about

me from my childhood. You even said unpleasant things about my body to her/him. How could you do that? Things were difficult and awkward enough for me at that time—how could you humiliate and shame me like that?

I remember thinking that I had reached a new level of hatred for you that day. *(Pause)*

Therapist: Talk about getting out of there.

Patient: The day after graduation from high school I moved out. First, I went to live with my boyfriend/girlfriend's family. They somehow sensed the insanity that I lived with and gave me some shelter. Then I went off to college, not that he ever paid a cent of it.

I felt very guilty that I was leaving Suzie and John behind. I didn't know what to do. They were still young. I couldn't take care of them; I was trying to escape myself.

Therapist: (The Therapist gets up and brings over a third chair. He/She puts the chair a few feet in front of the Patient, to the right of the father.) (See figure 3.2) I would like to have this chair symbolize your brother and sister at the time you left the house. I would like you to talk to them about the dilemma that you were facing.

Patient: (Looking at the new chair) I'm so sorry. I didn't know what to do. I had to get out of there. I had an opportunity and I had to take it.

Therapist: I wanted to take it.

Patient: I wanted to take it. I didn't know if I would've another chance.

I didn't want to leave you. I want you to know that. If I could've taken you with me then I would have. I was just 18; I didn't have the resources.

Therapist: Tell them again. I would have taken you with me if I could.

Patient: I would have taken you with me if I could.

Therapist: Again.

Patient: I would have taken you with me if I could. I wanted to. I just wasn't able to. I hated leaving you there. I felt so guilty. I still feel guilty. *(Pause)*

Therapist: I would like you to switch chairs and sit in the chair where Suzie and Johnny are. I am going to ask you to speak from their perspective. Can we put them both in one chair or do you think we should give each of them a chair?

Patient: I think that they can share a chair.

Therapist: Good. *(Points to the Sibling chair.)* Would you go over there.

Patient: Okay. *(The Patient goes over and sits on the Sibling chair; the Therapist stays where he/she was.)*

Therapist: Suzie and Johnny, thank you for being willing to join us today. I've been working with [ ] about the childhood the three of you had and about the terrible experiences you had with your father. He/She still feels quite guilty about leaving the two of you behind when he/she was eighteen. Would you speak to him/her about that?

Patient (as Siblings): [ ], don't feel bad. Don't feel guilty. We know that you had to leave. We know that you had to get out of there. We know that you loved us . . . but there was nothing that you could have done. Dad was too strong.

Therapist: Would you repeat that? I think [ ] really need to hear it. Would you tell him/her: there was nothing you could've done, Dad was too strong?

Patient (as Siblings): There was nothing you could have done. Dad was too strong. You did the right thing to get out.

Therapist: Again.

Patient (as Siblings): You did the right thing. Don't feel bad. Don't feel bad. Don't feel guilty. Dad was too strong. There was nothing you could've done.

Therapist: This is good. [ ] still feels very upset. He/she wants you to know that he/she loved you and still loves you. Can you speak to him/her about that?

Patient (as Siblings): Don't worry, we love you. You did the right thing to save yourself.

Therapist: Say this, if it feels right. We want you to live; we want you to be happy. Don't feel guilty. We love you.

Patient (as Siblings): Yes. We love you. Be happy. Don't waste your life feeling guilty. Dad was the bad one. Be happy. Live a full life. You did the right thing. You loved us and protected us as much as you could when we were children. Thank you for that. Thank you. We are grateful. We love you. *(Pause).*

Therapist: Is there anything else you want to say to [ ].

Patient (as Siblings): No, I think we said everything.

Therapist: (Pause) Please come back over here. *(Patient moves back his/her original chair.)* I would like you sit here for a moment and take in whatever you are open to letting in. *(The Therapist pauses while the Patient takes a moment or two to internalize the experience.)* Is there anything you would like to say to your siblings?

Patient: (Turning to the Sibling Chair) Thank you. I feel a lot better. I feel lighter. Thank you for that. You've taken a burden off of my shoulders. I'm grateful.

Therapist: Is there anything else you want to say to them.

Patient: No, I'm good

Therapist: Let's go back to our original chairs and debrief. *(Patient and Therapist go back to their original chairs.)* As you sit there now, how are you feeling? How was that for you?

Patient: I feel like I have been through a real journey. So many emotions.

Therapist: What were some of the things that struck you?

Patient: I was glad to speak to my father like that. I have never really expressed my anger or confronted him like that. I have to admit that things came out when I was speaking that I did not expect.

Therapist: I was struck by the love that your brother and sister had for you.

Patient: Yes. That was great. I've been afraid to talk to them about what happened. I was afraid that they would condemn me. Maybe now I have a bit more courage to do that.

Therapist: That could be good.

Patient: Yes.

Reflections

The dialogue began with a focus on an abusive parent. Here, the goal was to tell the story in a witnessed manner and to empower the patient to move from a victimized young person to a healthy adult state. Along the way, it became clear that her experiences of abuse were complicated by feelings of guilt related to her sense of responsibility for others in this situation. While this is not always the case, it is not uncommon. As was the case here, it is an issue that may require specific attention if the person is to heal. Again, this just speaks to the complex nature of trauma work.

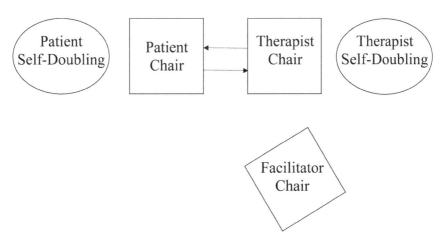

Figure 3.3   Self-Doubling Dialogue

WORKING WITH DIFFICULT RELATIONSHIPS

Above and beyond abusive relationships, many patients have ongoing connections and interactions with people whom they find to be problematic,
frustrating, irritating, anxiety-provoking, or disappointing. Out of necessity
or choice, they may decide that they will continue to keep these people in
their lives.

As discussed earlier, playing the role of the abuser, enacting and giving
them voice, is very likely to increase one's empathy for them and this can be
problematic. With difficult relationships and problematic people, however, it
may, in fact, make sense to become more empathic. This can be facilitated
by gaining a greater understanding of what they are going through; within a
broader dialogue structure that allows for the free expression of anger, frustration, disappointment, despair, affection, and hopefulness.

One of the more powerful moments in my workshops occurs when therapists engage in dialogues with "difficult" patients. This exercise in counter-
transference allows therapists to speak freely and safely while also allowing
them to put down the burden of being a "therapist" for a few moments. They
also have the opportunity to give voice to the "patient" and allow him or her
to speak freely, to say things that might not normally be shared in the session. If the therapist can express themselves openly and with deep honesty,
a frequent outcome is that they feel less angry at the patient and have more
understanding of their situation. They also feel more empowered and excited
about working with them.

The Self-Doubling Technique is a particularly wonderful way to do this.
Originating in the Psychodrama tradition as *Doubling* (Dayton, 1994, 2005),
Self-Doubling is a version of this that seems particularly suited to Chairwork
as it allows the patient to access and speak from a number of different perspectives (Kim & Daniels, 2008; Walters & Swallow, May 2009) .

Normally, the roles would be therapist, patient, and "difficult person."
In this case, we will use the roles of Facilitator, Therapist, and Patient. The
Facilitator will conduct the dialogue between the therapist and his or her
"patient."

Self-Doubling/Countertransference Dialogue

Facilitator: I remember that we were speaking about that patient Trevor last
week. How's it going?

Therapist: I am still having a terrible time with him. It's uncomfortable and I
just feel stuck in the process.

Facilitator: We did discuss having a dialogue with him as a way of possibly
working this through. How are you feeling about that?

Therapist: I was thinking about that this week. While part of me thinks that it would be a good idea, I'm also really uncomfortable about doing it. I don't want to be so exposed. I'm afraid that I will be judged, that you'll think of me as a bad therapist.

Facilitator: Let's make something clear from the get go. All therapists have patients that they cannot help, patients that make them feel frustrated, anxious, or even frightened. We have all had times when we wished they would cancel the session; times when we felt trapped and unhappy. I want you to know that this is difficult work and that the kind of difficulties that you are having are normal. Unpleasant, but normal.

Therapist: That is good to hear. Sometimes I get really upset about this situation and think that maybe I went into the wrong profession. I feel like I just should not be feeling this way about the people that I am supposed to be helping.

Facilitator: That's a tough one.

Therapist: Definitely.

Facilitator: If you're willing to proceed, I would like to set up the chairs so that we can do a two-chair dialogue.

Therapist: That's fine. Let's do it.

Facilitator: To be clear, I'm going to want you to speak as freely and deeply as possible. The things that you say here are private; they are not things that you will say to the patient. This is not a rehearsal for speaking to Trevor. This is a situation in which you can speak freely and honestly and safely. I just wanted to be sure that we were clear about this.

Therapist: Thanks. I am glad you clarified that. I feel a little more comfortable.

Facilitator: (The Facilitator sets up the two chairs so that they face each other. The Facilitator will sit on the Therapist's side. The Facilitator will not switch sides when the Therapist plays the Patient.) (See figure 3.3) I want you to sit in this chair *(pointing to one of the chairs; the Patient moves to that chair)* and I would like you to imagine Trevor sitting over there. I would like you to take a moment to try to imagine him sitting there. When you are ready, please describe him to me. I want you to tell me what he is wearing, how old he is, what the expression on his face is, and how you are feeling as you look at him. If you can't see him clearly or if you can only get a sense of his energy in the chair, that is fine also.

Therapist: (Long pause) I see him there. He's in his late thirties. He's wearing jeans, a tee shirt, and sneakers. He looks kind of irritated and restless.

Facilitator: What are you feeling as you look at him?

Therapist: Frustrated.

Facilitator: Tell him about your frustration.

Therapist: Trevor, it's really frustrating to work with you.

Facilitator: It's really frustrating for *me* to work with you.

Therapist: Yes, it's really frustrating for me to work with you. You don't want to cooperate with me. I am trying to help you get better and you treat the therapy like it's a joke.

Facilitator: It's not fair . . .

Therapist: That's right. It's not fair. It's not fair that I am struggling so hard here and that you are mocking me and not taking this seriously. I'm trying to do a good job, I'm trying to get you better, but you just won't cooperate. It's very stressful.

Facilitator: Say more about the stress that you are under.

Therapist: I'm under a lot of stress because I'm trying to do a good job and be a good therapist and I am also under a lot of stress because I have a supervisor that I have to report to. The fact that this case is not going well is embarrassing. It puts me in an awkward position.

Facilitator: Tell Trevor about this.

Therapist: You are putting me in an awkward situation. I don't like it. And I don't like you for doing that.

Facilitator: It sounds like you are stuck between a rock and a hard place.

Therapist: I am stuck and I feel trapped.

Facilitator: Trapped. Good. Say that a couple of times.

Therapist: (Slowly) I feel trapped. I am trapped.

Facilitator: Between you and the Supervisor, I feel trapped and I really don't like it.

Therapist: Yes. I really don't like it. I don't like being stuck between the two of you. *(Pause)*

Facilitator: Tell Trevor about some specific things that he has done that got you angry and upset.

Therapist: I think that you mock me. I feel like you don't take me seriously in the sessions. You look bored and sometimes you make fun of the things I say. And I was really very upset when you made that comment in the waiting room in front of the other patients.

Facilitator: What did he say? Tell him.

Therapist: You really embarrassed me when you made that joke about me in front of the other patients. I acted professionally and was stoic about it, but you really hurt my feelings. I hated that.

Facilitator: I hated you for doing that.

Therapist: Yes, I hated you for doing that. You hurt me in a deep place. I don't like that feeling and I don't like you for doing that.

Facilitator: How are you feeling?

Therapist: I am feeling distressed.

Facilitator: Try this, I wish you would go away and not come back.

Therapist: Yes, I wish you would go away and not come. You make me unhappy. My other cases are going okay, but it's always difficult with you. I don't want to see you, I don't want to work with you, I don't like you. I just want you to go away.

Facilitator: Try this. You can use your own words. I look at you and I feel angry and upset. You frustrate me and you hurt my feelings and I just don't like you.

Therapist: Yes. I feel so upset when I look at you. You embarrassed me. You made me feel ashamed. It's so unfair. I'm working hard. It's not easy. I am trying to get this right. I have a supervisor who's on my case and you are making me look incompetent. I hate that and I hate you.

Facilitator: (Pause) Anything else?

Therapist: No.

Facilitator: (Pause) Now I would like you to get up and stand behind your chair. I would like to you to speak about how things look and feel from that perspective. *(Facilitator stands up also.)*

Therapist: (Standing behind the chair) Wow, it seems so different from up here.

Facilitator: What do you see going on between the two of them?

Therapist: The first thing is that Trevor seems much smaller from up here. He looks weaker and a little pathetic. From this distance everything seems different.

Facilitator: What do you see going on between yourself in the chair and Trevor?

Therapist: I see a lot of tension. When I look at myself, I feel like I am working very hard, very hard. It seems stressful.

Facilitator: I want you to say the things that you are thinking and feeling about Trevor and your work with him that you did not say while sitting down. I would like you to say the things that you are afraid to say. I am not asking you to actually say them to him in real life; I just want you to do it here. It's safe to do it here.

Therapist: Now you are really pushing me.

Facilitator: Yes.

Therapist: (Pause) I would never say this to him but . . . Trevor, I really hate working with you.

Facilitator: Good; again.

Therapist: I really hate working with you. You ruin things for me. You just ruin things for me. *(Pause)*

Facilitator: Anything else?

Therapist: No. That's it.

Facilitator: I would like you to sit down in the chair in front of you.

(Both the Therapist and the Patient sit down.)

Facilitator: Now I would like you to move to the chair opposite.

Therapist: (Therapist moves into the "Patient" chair.)

Facilitator: Now I'd like you to "be" Trevor. I'd like you to speak from *his* perspective.

Therapist as Patient: Oh, that's going to be a problem as all he does is fight me.

Facilitator: I want you to speak his "truth"; I want you to say what is in his heart. I want you to say the things that he is not saying or not saying yet. Just feel your way into it.

Therapist as Patient: Okay, I'll try. *(Pause)* I don't want to be here. I hate being here. I don't want to talk to you.

Facilitator: (Speaking to the Therapist as the Patient) Tell him/her why you don't want to talk to him/her.

Therapist as Patient: You want me to be really honest.

Facilitator: Yes. Be honest. I want you to really speak from Trevor's truth. I want to hear what he has to say.

Therapist as Patient: Okay. *(Pause)* I don't want to be here. I don't want to work with you because I am ashamed to be here. I am ashamed to have to sit here and have you look at me. I just don't want to be here.

Facilitator: Trevor, I know this is hard but please tell [ ] why you're ashamed, why it is so hard to be in therapy.

Therapist as Patient: When I come to session and look at you, it makes me think about how much I have messed things up. My life was not supposed to end up like this. I was supposed to be sitting where you are. There were people who loved me growing up. There were problems, for sure, but there were people who loved me. I let them down. They wanted me to do something with my life and I went the wrong way.

Facilitator: Trevor, [ ] thinks that he/she is doing something wrong or that he/she is a bad Therapist. Is that how you feel?

Therapist as Patient: No. He/she's fine. I am just fighting because I don't want to be here and I don't want him/her to see me. I hate being looked at by shrinks.

Facilitator: Would you tell him/her that? I think he/she really needs to know that.

Therapist as Patient: Okay. . . . Listen, it's not about you. I am ashamed. It's a front. I do it to protect myself. I know you're trying to help me; I just don't want to show any weakness. I want to come to the clinic to get the things I need and then get out. When I was doing the drugs, when I was in that world, I did all kinds of things, things that I am not proud of. I'm afraid you might ask me about them. . . . I think that if you knew about what happened that you would judge me. . . . I don't want that. I don't want to be judged by you.

Facilitator: Tell him/her again. I don't think he/she got it. He/she needs to hear it again.

Therapist as Patient: It's not about you. It's not about you. It's about protecting myself. You're fine. It's just embarrassing to be here . . . to talk about stuff . . . to be exposed.

Facilitator: (Pause) Is there anything else that you want to tell him/her? Anything else that you think he/she needs to know?

Therapist as Patient: No. I think that's it.

Facilitator: (Pause) Now, I would like you to stand behind this chair, like you did on the other side. *(The "Patient" gets up and stands behind the chair; the Facilitator stands up also.)* First, how do things look as you stand there?

Therapist as Patient: Well, I feel a little more distanced from it. I can see that [ ] is trying to help and I can see that I am trying to keep him/her at bay

Facilitator: Good. Now, I would like you to give voice to the thoughts and feelings that you did not share when you were sitting down and talking to [ ].

Therapist as Patient: (Pause) I am just really sad. I am really sad about my life. I feel like I have ruined everything and there is no way back, there is just no way back. I am so guilt-stricken I can barely stand myself. I hate you looking at me because I am just so ashamed. *(Pause)* I guess that's it. *(Pause)*

Facilitator: Anything else?

Therapist as Patient: No, I think I'm good.

Facilitator: (Pause) Okay, please come around and sit in this chair again. *(The "Patient" sits back down in the chair; the Facilitator sits back down as well.)* *(Pause)* Now I would like you to come back to this seat *(pointing to the Therapist's seat)* and I would like you to become yourself again.

Therapist: (Goes back to the opposite chair.)

Facilitator: How are you feeling? How was it to play Trevor?

Therapist: (To the Facilitator) Once I got into it, it was very powerful. In a way, I knew all those things already, but to actually sit there and say them got me much more connected to him emotionally. I think that I got a much deeper sense of how difficult it is for him to be here and to be in therapy.

Facilitator: How do you feel about your own therapy work?

Therapist: I actually feel better about it. I realize that I am really under a lot of pressure. I pressure myself with all of the "shoulds" in my head and I get pressured by my supervisor as well. I can see that this is not really helping.

Facilitator: Do you think that you might want to do things differently when you see him next?

Therapist: Definitely! I want to slow it down. Let me try to connect with him more. I think that I need to do some motivational work. I've been pushing hard to get him to do things and I can see now that he is really quite frightened. I want to work on that first. . . . I want to work on the shame issues. Then we can go forward.

Facilitator: Would you tell him that directly?

Therapist: (Turning to the Patient chair) Trevor . . . I am experiencing you in a different way. I get it. I understand that you're frightened and ashamed. I will slow it down and try to connect with you more. Maybe we can do some work around the shame. I know that you are uncomfortable and I respect that. I also know that if we can do some work, that you will get better and be happier. I am not willing to give up; I'm a fighter. I see that I need to relax and approach this differently.

Facilitator: That is very good. Is there anything else that you want to say to Trevor right now?

Therapist: No, I think I'm good.

Facilitator: How are you feeling as you sit there?

Therapist: I am feeling more relaxed and I am feeling more hopeful. I feel like I can do something here; it seems less hopeless.

Facilitator: You said that you are going to stand up to your supervisor. Do you need help with that or is that something you can manage?

Therapist: I feel like I can manage it. I am realizing that I need to claim power in this situation. I am going to do that. I'll be fine with the supervisor.

Facilitator: This is good. *(Pause)* Now I would like you to get up again and stand behind the chair again.

(The Therapist gets up and stands behind the chair; the Facilitator stands up as well.)

Facilitator: How do things seem now? How are things as you look at the two of them?

Therapist: (Pause) I can really sense the difference as I stand here. Things are much less tense between the two of them.

Facilitator: How do you seem to yourself?

Therapist: He/she is definitely more relaxed. As I stand here I can feel the energy shift. There is a lot more excitement here.

Facilitator: How are you feeling toward him and how are you feeling about going back to work with him?

Therapist: Amazingly, I am feeling much more empathy for him. He's still a pain in the neck but I sense that he is suffering more. I feel like there has been a shift in the balance of power. I feel stronger now, he seems smaller and more in pain. I feel more up for working with him.

Facilitator: Wow. That is quite a shift. Something really happened when you did that.

Therapist: It really did.

Facilitator: (Pause) Now I would like to shift things. I would like you to speak to the therapist who is sitting in the chair in front of you. I would like you to take the role of supporter and friend to yourself. I would like you to just be positive to yourself and say your version of the things that I am saying. Okay?

Therapist: I'll try.

Facilitator: I know that you are having a difficult time with Trevor but I want you to remember, and know, and understand that you are a very good therapist.

Therapist: That's a tough one. *(Pause)* Okay. I want to let you know that I understand that you are having a lot of difficulty with this case. I also want to say that I know that you have been successful with other patients and that this is not typically what happens when you work with patients. He's difficult and you are a good therapist.

Facilitator: Say that again.

Therapist: He's a difficult patient and you are a good therapist.

Facilitator: I would like you to imagine that you are putting your hands on his/her shoulders. I want him/her to really feel your presence. And I want you to say this or something like it—I love you, I admire you, I respect you. You are a very good therapist. He's not cooperating. I am on your side. I know what is going on; I know how hard you work and how much you want this to go well. I want you to take me in and know that I am with you in this.

Therapist: Again . . . a tough one. I am usually very hard on myself so it is difficult to say these kinds of things to myself.

Facilitator: We know there is a Critic there, now we want an Affirmer.

Therapist: Okay. *(Puts hands on the shoulders of imagined "self" sitting in the chair in front.)* I want you to know that I like you.

Facilitator: That I love you.

Therapist: That I love you. I want you to know that I know how hard you have worked to be a therapist. I know about the long hours and how you have wrestled to find techniques and ideas that would help your patients.

Facilitator: I admire and I respect you for this.

Therapist: Yes, I admire and I respect you for this. Let's be honest. He's not cooperating; he's giving you a hard time.

Facilitator: Everyone would have trouble with a patient like this one, even your supervisor.

Therapist: Yes. He's really impossible. Even our supervisor would not be able to work with him. These are difficult cases and sometimes we just can't get through. I want you to understand this and I want you to accept it. I want you to know that it's true. Regardless of how hard you work, sometimes you just can't get them better. I also want you to know that this is not a reflection on you. I want you to know that I am on your side. I know better than anyone what you have gone through and what you are going through and I want you to take me in.

Facilitator: I want you to let me in. I want you to let me in so I can support you, so that I can support you when things get tough.

Therapist: I want you to let me in so that I can support you, so that I can support you when it gets difficult.

Facilitator: And I want you to relax and breathe.

Therapist: I want you to relax and breathe.

Facilitator: (Pause) How are you feeling now as you're standing there?

Therapist: I am feeling more relaxed and I am feeling more connected to the part of me that is sitting in the chair.

Facilitator: How is he/she doing?

Therapist: He/she is taking in what I have said. It's true. *(Pointing to the other chair)* He's behaving badly and we're doing the best we can.

Facilitator: I would like you to speak to yourself again. I would like you to support and affirm him/her again.

Therapist: Okay. . . . That was good, what you just did. I think that you're on to something and that you will be able to work this through.

Facilitator: You are a very good therapist.

Therapist: You are a good therapist. A very good therapist. Hold onto that.

Facilitator: I want you to hold onto that.

Therapist: I want you to hold onto that. Sometimes it is going to be difficult, that's just the way it is with some of these patients.

Facilitator: I'm on your side.

Therapist: I'm on your side. I love and respect you. I think that you've shifted and that things will be better.

Facilitator: I want you to take in what I'm saying.

Therapist: I want you to take in what I'm saying. Relax and breathe. We'll be fine. . . . And he'll be fine also. *(Pause)*

Facilitator: Is there anything else that you would like to tell [ ]?

Therapist: No, I think I'm good.

Facilitator: Now I would like you to sit back down in the chair one more time.

(Therapist sits down in the chair.)

Facilitator: I would like you to take a minute. I would like you to take in what the Affirmer just said. Whatever you're open to.

Therapist: (Pause) I think I can take in some of it. It was hard earlier, but I think at this point I can take some of it in.

Facilitator: Do you think that you can bring it with you into your sessions?

Therapist: Yes. I think I can.

Facilitator: Good. I'd like to move our chairs back to where they originally were so that we can debrief.

Debrief

The Facilitator and the Therapist move their chairs back to the original place. Now facing each other, they can explore some specific strategies for engaging with Trevor that build on the work that was just done.

Reflections

Self-Doubling invites people to work on at least two dimensions at the same time. It involves different ways of sharing and revealing. It allows the individual to go past their persona and express their very intimate thoughts and feelings in a manner that is safe. The physical shifting from a sitting to a standing position helps to facilitate a change in perspective that is cognitive and emotional, as well as postural. The end result is that the patient feels less distressed and more empathic toward the other person. It is because of this, that I recommend that this technique be used for difficult relationships but not for those that are centered on abuse and mistreatment.

Chapter 4

External Dialogues

Assertiveness and Behavioral Rehearsal

Assertiveness Training, a form of Behavioral Rehearsal, is a quintessential American therapy. The goal of this work is to empower patients to engage in "direct, open, honest communication that is self-expressive, but respectful of the other" (Fodor & Collier, 2001, p. 223). Strikingly, it reflects and manifests some of the most cherished values of those who live in the United States. Kohls (1984), in his essay "The Values Americans Live By," included "directness, openness, and honesty" as well as "equality/egalitarianism" in his list of thirteen core values, and these are some of the central principles of assertiveness training. Assertiveness training was a major contribution of the Behavioral tradition to psychotherapy, in general, and to Chairwork, more specifically. Originally called "behavioristic psychodrama" by Wolpe (1982) and also known as role-playing, it was especially popular in the 1970s. The book, *You're Perfect Right* (Alberti & Emmons, 1986) was a major bestseller at that time and it served to popularize this approach. Its relevance to the needs of most patients, however, has not diminished over time.

Embedded in the assertiveness perspective is a belief that this is, generally, the emotionally and psychologically healthiest way of interacting with others (Fodor & Collier, 2001) Alternative communication styles include aggressive, where I am directly disrespectful and violate the boundaries of others; passive, where I inhibit my self-expression, allow myself to be disrespected, and acquiesce to the violation of my personal boundaries; and passive-aggressive, where I am aggressive in indirect ways.

In reality, there are, of course, times when it is appropriate to behave in a passive, passive-aggressive, or aggressive manner. For example, when faced with a bullying or oppressive force that is overwhelmingly stronger, passive or passive-aggressive behavior may be, at least initially, an appropriate way of responding. In the geopolitical arena, guerilla warfare can be seen as a

passive-aggressive response in the face of a military force that is too strong
to be met head on.

On the other hand, in the face on an attack on loved ones, it may be best to
act in a direct, purposeful, and aggressive manner to protect life and limb. A
mixing of the assertive and the aggressive would be manifest in the Warrior
archetype:

> As Colonel Frank Reed, a combat infantry commander in Korea, once said, "the
> first rule of war is to know it when you're in one." Then comes the courage to
> act, and then the judgment to act appropriately. Whatever you do must be effec-
> tive and not excessive. Finally, the action must be thorough and decisive so it
> does not have to be repeated, locally or elsewhere. Judgment, restraint, courage,
> and skill. (Redmoon, 1994, pp. 23–24)

Working with patients on issues of assertiveness and self-empowerment
involves covering a number of philosophical, pragmatic, and capability
issues. The order and intensity may vary from patient to patient, but most will
need to engage with each of these dimensions to some degree.

One of the more essential issues with assertiveness is that both the patient
and the therapist need to accept the philosophy that undergirds it. This
includes seeing all people as fundamentally equal and worthy of respect,
regardless of position, title, or background. It also includes the idea that each
individual has the right to express him- or herself freely, as long as they do
not violate the rights of others. While this may seem rational and democratic,
it is by no means intuitive. Few people, if any, are taught to be assertive and
it is not a general part of school curriculums (although it may emerge in some
drug prevention programs). While some of the moral edicts of our culture
promote a rough equality (e.g., the Golden Rule), the importance of obedi-
ence to authority is a more common message. When working with patients
from other cultures, especially cultures where strong family ties and obedi-
ence to authority are deeply cherished values, the philosophical work may
be even more important. First generation Americans, individuals wrestling
with two value systems, may want to be assertive in some settings and more
traditional in others. Therapists would do well to review the assertiveness
literature (e.g., Alberti & Emmons, 1986) and work out their own conflicts
and misgivings before trying to teach it to patients.

The second issue is that of safety and consequences. All things being equal,
assertive behavior should lead to better interpersonal outcomes. However,
since we are working with issues of power, there may be ramifications. Frederick Douglass said, "Power concedes nothing without a demand"; he also
said, "If there is no struggle, there is no progress" (Quoted in Newman, 1998,
pp. 346–347). This means that the therapist and the patient should engage in

a thorough exploration of the risks and benefits of taking assertive action in a given situation. Often the dangers will be small, but sometimes not. To be clear, this does not mean that patients should not take risks or even serious risks to achieve what they want—just that they should be clear about what they are doing. In a related vein, if the goal of the intervention is to change someone else's noxious or controlling behavior, it may lead, at first, to an increase in that behavior.

The third issue is the assessment of assertiveness. What is the presenting problem? Is self-expression a global issue or is it connected to certain situations. Is the problem saying "yes," "saying "no," making requests, or setting limits on others"? The fourth component involves the actual assertive behavior itself. The two seminal forms are "I-Statements" and "Conditional Statements." Learning to use I-Statements involves identifying what needs to be said, making eye contact, having a firm voice, utilizing an open and confident stance, and perseverance. It is crucial that the patient be coached through this over and over. The "other person," the one who will receive the intended message, can be located in the opposite chair. The goal is for the patient to feel comfortable and integrated while conveying the message and this will not happen without practice in, and perhaps outside, the session.

The Conditional Statements involve an "if-then" clause. They are most appropriate to use in a situation where another person is currently behaving in a problematic manner. For example. A woman might say to her mother: "Mom, I want to come visit with Jim and the kids; however, I am unhappy that you keep criticizing me in their presence. We have discussed it as a family and we have reached this conclusion. We want you to be a part of our life, but if you begin to criticize or embarrass me while we are visiting, the four of us will be leaving immediately. This will be followed by a four-week hiatus in which we will not visit again. So . . . if you behave respectfully, we will stay and hopefully have a good visit together, and if you are mean to me, we will leave. It is your choice."

Patients may, at least initially, see this kind of action as a way of making threats. From a scientific perspective, we are setting up a contingency or consequence that will be triggered by the other person's behavior. Helping patients to understand this may take some work. The other issue is that for this to be effective, they will need the resolve necessary to back up the words with action. The preparation involves agreeing to the proposition, crafting a way to communicate it, practicing saying it, and repeating and rehearsing both the initial statement and the actions that need to follow if the contingency is triggered. Again, repetitive practice to the point where this feels somewhat natural is key.

In other cases, the project of developing one's "Voice" may involve a series of steps. Here, a hierarchy of low fear to high fear situations can be created and each of these can first be tested with chairs and then in the real world. For example, a patient can start with asking for directions or requesting change for a ten-dollar bill and then move to asking a girl on a date or talking to a man who is seen as attractive. A higher level of discomfort may be involved in asking a boss for a raise. Mastro (2004) pointed out that people will often be nervous in real life so it can be helpful for them to be somewhat more energized and forceful in the sessions than they will need to be in the actual encounter.

Wolfe and Fodor (1975) were interested in those processes that blocked or interfered with assertive behavior. While they were specifically focused on women, their insights are applicable to all patients. They recommended asking patients to observe and report the thoughts, feelings, and images they were experiencing as they engaged in behavioral rehearsal. For some, the process will bring up thoughts that they are doing something wrong, fears that it will not work, concerns that the results will be catastrophic, and/or images of hurting others. Each of these will need to be voiced and addressed. Their point is that the lack of assertiveness in an individual may not only be caused by behavioral deficits, but also by inhibiting beliefs and emotions.

Lastly, assertiveness is an important way to strengthen the Healthy Adult Mode or the Inner Leader. As Perls said, "Every time you do apply the proper Ego-language you express yourself, you assist in the development of your personality" (quoted in Naranjo, 1968, p. 131). In this, he again reminds us of the importance of language in general and of the importance of existential language in particular. In work with assertiveness, we will want patients to both say *and* think such phrases as: "I want," "I am deciding," "I am saying yes," "I am saying no," and "I feel distressed by what you did." Our goal is to start with the words but eventually have them be matched by the whole spirit of the person.

A woman in her early twenties reported that she was upset that her boyfriend was critical of her beliefs and aesthetic choices. She was particularly distressed that he criticized her taste in music. We put him in the chair opposite and she practiced telling him that she did not like this behavior, and that she wanted it to stop. I invited her to use I-Statements, to speak in a firm, direct, and loud manner, and to claim authority on this issue. After the session, she went home and confronted him. He apologized and agreed to stop. This was a big moment for her in our work together and she felt that it shifted their relationship to a better place. It is pertinent to note that this was a woman who was assertive in a number of other areas in her life; it was in this personal relationship that she had difficulty with direct communication. He was very smart and opinionated, which may have contributed to making this a more daunting task. Again, this speaks to the importance of assessment.

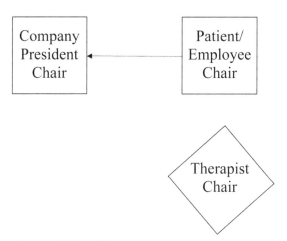

Figure 4.1   Assertiveness/Raise Dialogue

Assertiveness Dialogue

The dialogue for this chapter, which was developed out of work by McKay and McKay (February 17, 2008) and Reeves (January 5, 2006), involves asking for a raise. The first part of the work is a dialogue between the therapist and the patient in which they develop a foundation for making the pitch. The second part involves a chair dialogue in which the patient's voice is strengthened and refined.

Asking for a Raise Dialogue

Therapist: Last week you were saying that you were worried about money and that you wanted to ask your boss that you wanted to ask your boss for a raise but you were scared. Is that still on your mind?

Patient: Yes, it is.

Therapist: What's the issue?

Patient: I have been at this job for two years now and I want to get a raise. I think I've done a pretty good job and my sense is that other people who have been there as long as I have, have already gotten raises. The problem is that I am afraid to ask for one. I think about it. I have even walked by Bob's office—Bob is the boss—but I *chicken out* every time. *(Pause)*

Therapist: Let me clarify a few things.

Patient: Okay.

Therapist: Bob is your boss. Does he have the power to actually give you a raise? Is it his decision?

Patient: Yes. He is the owner or one of the owners of the company. He can give me a raise.

Therapist: Okay. Before we get into the actual question of how to ask him for a raise, I think that it's important that you really "own your story," that you are clear about the things that you have accomplished at work. I also want to know if there are any things within you that might stand in your way.

Patient: Sounds good.

Therapist: Okay. So when you ask for a raise you need to be able to make a case that you deserve one.

Patient: Right.

Therapist: What kind of things have you accomplished there over the past two years?

Patient: As we've discussed, I am in a kind of a mixed Software Engineer/ Customer Service/Sales position.

Therapist: And how has that gone?

Patient: There's a kind of a routine part of the job in which we essentially meet the ongoing needs of our clients; we help them with software and web issues. This is a large part of what I do and I've basically done a good job with no complaints.

Therapist: Anything else? Anything outstanding?

Patient: There were a couple of things. The Afthonia Corporation was rolling out a new line and just before the launch, they started having software problems. If things had not gone out on time, it would have cost them a lot of money— maybe millions.

They called me around ten of five and I worked with their engineer for hours on it. In fact, I was in the office until about 4 AM trying to solve the problem. We finally figured it out and the launch went out on time.

Therapist: That's a great story!

Patient: Yeah. The Afthonia people were really happy. They wrote a great letter to Bob about it. He told me that I did a good job.

Therapist: This is good; anything else?

Patient: There was this guy Rick. He was at Vessel Labs. We worked together for a about a year. We got along very well and did some good work together. He then went to the Global Expansion Fund. Because of our connection, he persuaded them to bring us on to do some of their web and IT work. This was a huge contract for our company, it is worth several million dollars every year, and I don't think that we would have gotten it without that connection.

Therapist: Anything else?

Patient: In general, I do a good job and get positive feedback, but those were the two big things that I have done since I got there.

Therapist: In addition to accomplishments, it is important to look at responsibilities. Did you take on any additional responsibilities or take charge of anything during the past two years?

Patient: There was this woman, Karen, who was a project director. She would coordinate different groups and make sure that the projects got done on time. She's pretty forceful.

In any case, we had this huge project with Redwood Investments. Somewhere in the middle of it, she went on maternity leave for three months. They asked me to step in for her. I coordinated everything and kept the project on track. She was pleased when she returned and I got some good feedback from the Redwood side.

I didn't get a raise or a new title, but I did the work. Bob has to know that.

Therapist: Is there anything that happened that might interfere with your getting a raise?

Patient: Well, it was late in the afternoon one day and I was thinking about the vacation that I was planning in July. I started looking at some websites about kayak expeditions. I kind of got lost in it for a while and then I became aware of someone behind me. I looked around and saw Bob standing there, watching me. I don't know how long he had been standing there, but it was awkward. It was the end of the day, but it probably didn't make him happy.

Therapist: Ouch. Anything else?

Patient: The Holiday Party is a big thing. The first year that I was there, I had a family emergency and couldn't go. I know that didn't look good. I went last year, though.

Therapist: Okay, so it sounds like there isn't anything major that could stop you from being considered for a raise.

Patient: Other than the fact that I am nervous about it and that I find Bob to be a bit intimidating, no.

Therapist: As we have worked on with other issues, one of our goals is to develop and strengthen your assertive voice, your Healthy Adult Mode. I would like you to do some sentences in which you use phrases like: "I want," "I am deciding to," "I am looking forward to," and "I have the right to."

Patient: Okay

Therapist: To start, say this: "I want a raise. I want to make more money"

Patient: I want a raise. I want to make more money.

Therapist: "I have worked hard and done a good job."

Patient: I have worked hard and done a good job.

Therapist: "I have every right to ask for a raise."

Patient: I have every . . . I have every . . . right to ask for a raise. That's a tougher one.

Therapist: Did you do a good job?

Patient: Yes.

Therapist: Did you bring value to the company?

Patient: Yes

Therapist: Do you have the right to ask for a raise?

Patient: Yes.

Therapist: Say it, then.

Patient: I have the right to ask for a raise.

Therapist: Again.

Patient: I have the right to ask for a raise.

Therapist: Good. Now, how much do you want?

Patient: Well, we're having more expenses now that the baby is here and I was looking on-line and it seems like I am getting somewhat less than other software engineers, so I was hoping to get ten percent. That is what I really need. Do you think it is too much?

Therapist: It seems to me that you have done a really good job and that you have been there for quite a long time without getting a salary increase, so 10 percent is fine. The problem is that he may try to negotiate with you so you should ask for more than you are willing to settle for.

Patient: I hadn't thought of that. I get pretty nervous even thinking about ten percent; it seems like a lot of money.

Therapist: I think that you should ask for fifteen.

Patient: Fifteen?! Too much. How about twelve?

Therapist: Okay, twelve.

Patient: Okay.

Therapist: Now I would like you to move your chair so that you are facing that one over there. I would like you to imagine that Bob is in that chair. I want you to try to really see him . . . .when he comes into focus, I would like you to describe what you see, what he's wearing, and what the expression on his face is.

(The Patient moves to one chair and faces "Bob" in the other. The Therapist situates him- or herself diagonally on the Patient's side.) (See figure 4.1)

Therapist: (Pauses) Can you see him over there?

Patient: Yes.

Therapist: Would you tell me what you're seeing and experiencing as you look at him?

Patient: He's in a good suit. He's smiling. He seems a bit impatient, like he's willing to talk to me but he wants it to be brief because he has to get somewhere important. He is often like that.

Therapist: How are you feeling in his presence?

Patient: A bit determined—I want a raise—and very anxious.

Therapist: Now I would like you to ask him for the raise. I would like you to use the assertive language that we have been talking about. Use "I" and speak about your desires, goals, and actions.

Patient: Hi! Bob. I want to speak to you about getting a raise. As you know, I've been here for two years and we recently had a baby and we are going to need . . .

Therapist: Let me interrupt you there. Raises are not based on need; they are based on accomplishments. Let's get back to your power center.

Patient: Okay

Therapist: The central ideas. Say them after me. "I have worked hard for two years. I have done a good job. I have made good connections with our clients. I played a central role in helping us win a major contract. I stepped in when Karen was on leave."

Patient: (Slowly) I have worked hard for two years. I've done a good job. I've made good connections with our clients. I played a central role in helping us win a major contract. I stepped in when Karen was on leave.

Therapist: Say it again, only this time more forcefully.

Patient: (With greater strength and confidence) I've worked hard for two years. I did a good job. I made good connections with our clients. I played a central role in helping us win a major contract. I stepped in when Karen was on leave.

Therapist: Once more.

Patient: I worked hard for two years. I did a good job. I made good connections with our clients. I *played* a central role in helping us win a major contract, and I *stepped* in when Karen was on leave.

Therapist: Now say it more directly to Bob in that chair; use his name.

Patient: (Slowly) Bob, you know that I've been here for two years, and I was thinking that maybe it was time for a raise. I feel that I've been doing a good job. The clients like me and I was able to make a connection with GEF.

Therapist: This is a start. I want you to be more direct, no "thinking maybe" stuff. You've worked hard, made connections, and helped win a contract. You also left out the work with Karen.

Patient: Right. Let me try again. . . . Bob, I wanted to speak with you about getting a raise. I've been here for two years. I feel like I am doing a good job. Our clients like me, I was able to bring in that contract, and I took over for Karen when she was out.

Therapist: That's good. I want you to do it again, but this time be more specific, name the companies.

Patient: Bob, I wanted to speak with you about a raise. I have been here for two years and I think that I have done a very good job. As you know, the feedback from my regular clients has been very positive and I was able to really bail out Afthonia when they had those problems with the launch. Because of the work I did with Rick, I was able to bring in the GEF account, and I stepped in when Karen away. I believe that I've been a strong contributor and I would like you to consider increasing my salary.

Therapist: How confident are you right now?

Patient: I am at 75 percent.

Therapist: Let's do it one more time.

Patient: Bob, I wanted to speak with you about getting a raise. I believe that I have brought a lot of good things to this company. I have been here for two years, and I have strong connections with all of my clients. Beyond that, I was able to bail out Afthonia when they had problems with the launch, and I brought in the GEF account which is now one of our largest accounts. Lastly, when Karen was out, I stepped up and coordinated all of the teams.

I think that I've done a good job and I have come through for the company. I would like us to work out a way for me to get a higher salary.

Therapist: Well, I'm convinced. How does Bob look sitting in that chair?

Patient: He's smiling, so that's a good sign.

Therapist: And how are you feeling?

Patient: I am feeling like this is much more possible to do.

Therapist: Good. There is one more thing that I would like to do. This is not something that you would actually do with Bob, but I want you to do it here to help boost your confidence.

Patient: Okay.

Therapist: I want you to stand up, move behind your chair, and look at Bob. You can use your hands as well while you do this. I want you to say to him very loudly, "I've worked hard. I've done a good job. I have earned a raise."

(Patient and Therapist both stand up and move behind their chairs.)

Patient: I've worked hard. I've done a good job. I have earned a raise.

Therapist: Louder.

Patient: I've worked hard. I've done a good job. I have earned a raise.

Therapist: Again. Louder.

Patient: (Loudly) I've worked hard! I've done a good job! I have earned a raise!

Therapist: I will say it with you.

Patient and Therapist together loudly: I've worked hard!! I've done a good job!! I have earned a raise!!

Therapist: Once more!

Patient and Therapist together very loudly: I've worked hard!! I've done a good job!! I have earned a raise!!!

Therapist: Good! . . . Sit. . . . *(Points to the original chairs. They both move back there.)* How are you feeling right now?

Patient: Tingly. Stronger.

Therapist: Good. So do you think you are ready to take action or would you like to do another session first and prepare some more.

Patient: No. I feel good about it. I am going to keep practicing at home. I will see if I can schedule a meeting with him toward the end of next week. I feel more rooted.

Therapist: You sound more rooted.

Patient: Yes, I will be ready.

Therapist: I hope you are successful.

Reflections

This dialogue followed the basic outline. A foundation was built and the making of the request was rehearsed. At one point, the patient was asked to stand up and speak. As we have seen before, standing up alters things; it can free up the body and enable the patient to speak with greater force and volume.

At the end, both the patient and the therapist spoke in unison. Drawn from the work of Mastro (2004), this is a way to help to help a patient overcome inhibition and speak more powerfully. Here, they are no longer exposed and alone and the therapist's voice can serve to lift theirs. The therapist's voice should match that of the patient but not overwhelm it.

Assertiveness and Behavioral Rehearsal II

If you are working with a partner, you can now switch roles and improvise a new dialogue. Please feel free to use scenarios from your own life or from the experiences of your patients. Other possible scenarios you could work with include:

1. Asking for a raise.
2. Requesting that a parent stop criticizing your spouse.
3. Requesting that a parent stop saying negative things about your parenting style.
4. Requesting that a partner stop telling an embarrassing story about you in public.
5. Telling your sibling that he/she cannot move into your house/apartment even though they are in need.

The basic structures of the previous dialogue are, most likely applicable.

Chapter 5

Internal Dialogues

Multiplicity and Inner Conflict

Multiplicity of self is currently one of the more powerful ideas in psychotherapy and it appears to be growing in popularity and importance (Rowan, 2010). Multiplicity is a central component in Chairwork as it is not only at the heart of the internal dialogues, but also it plays a central role in work with the inner critic. The belief that human beings can be usefully understood as containing multiple internal forces goes back at least as far as the ancient Greeks (Carter, 2008). In modern psychotherapy, multiplicity played a significant role in the personality theory of Sigmund Freud (1965, 1969). While the field is not as guided by the Freudian structural model to the degree that it once was, Chairwork did give me a renewed sense of respect for Freud's model. When working with patients using multiple chairs, it is not uncommon to see voices of pleasure, morality, reason, and avoidance appear and make their presence known at various times. In a similar vein, Dr. Richard Schwartz (1987) wrote: "I believe that one of Freud's greatest contributions was opening the door for exploration of our many selves in his description of the struggles among the Id, Ego, and Superego."

Within the psychoanalytic tradition, there are the object relations theorists who also saw the internal world of the patient as one consisting of an array of internal forces (Bauer, 1986; Mitchell & Greenberg, 1983). For example, Applebaum (1993), a psychoanalyst who explored the Human Potential Movement and who utilized gestalt techniques within a psychodynamic framework, made the case that "parts work" was consistent with object relations and that it was a way to explore the internalized relationships and experiences that the patient carried within. He emphasized the healing power of both awareness and giving voice to the parts as a way of integrating and rebalancing the self. "Improved self-awareness, and by implication greater tranquility and effectiveness, come about by owning up to, rather than disowning these 'introjects,' as one forgives, adjusts to, or otherwise integrates them into a workable, less conflict-laden whole" (Applebaum, 1993, p. 486).

In the work of George Herbert Mead (1934) and the Symbolic Interactionists (Stryker 1981; Stryker & Serpé, 1982), there is a somewhat more social view of internalization and the development of personality. McCall (1977), in a review of this work, emphasized the social origins of the self and the self-reflective and self-evaluative quality of this view of personality. Throughout the process of development, the individual internalizes important figures—family members, teachers, peers, and spiritual leaders—and turns them into an "audience" for one's life. Park, in turn, argued that this was the foundation for "conduct" as opposed to behavior. He clarified this when he affirmed that "conduct is 'that form of behavior we expect in man when he is conscious of the comment that other men are making, or are likely to make, upon his actions'" (Park, 1931, p. 36 in McCall, 1977, p. 275). That is, there are specific situations in which we seek to demonstrate certain virtues or act in specific ways so as to meet the approval of this internalized group. This means that people think about themselves, that they are an audience to themselves, and that they evaluate their performances (McCall, 1977).

There may, of course, be different internal "groups," each of which are relevant to different aspects of one's life. They may also be either inspirational or destructive. Tatarsky wrote of a patient who uses drugs at times as a way of coping with the criticisms of the "Committee," which are experienced as an inner attack (Tatarsky & Kellogg, 2011).

This model opens up the possibility of imagining an ideal committee and of enacting and embodying it through the use of Chairwork. The conscious creation of a loving and supportive internal audience can involve the incorporation not only of people that are known to the patient, but also of historical and fictitious characters as well. Clarissa was a woman who had undergone extremely sadistic emotional and, at times, physical abuse at the hands of both parents; despite this, she had become a successful artist and intellectual. Although she had done many years of work with a variety of therapists, she still carried some wounds and could fall into states of self-castigation when very stressed.

During one of these times, I asked her to name the people who loved her and cared about her deeply, whether alive or dead. She named four women. I put four chairs in front of her and, one by one, I gave voice to the love and admiration each of them had for her. She responded in turn and we were able to have a dialogue that helped to raise her spirits. I encouraged her to "see" the women in the chairs in front of her and to try to internalize this image and keep it with her.

Robson (2000), in her work with adolescent sex offenders, utilizes several useful internalization strategies. First she created a division between the "New Me" and the "Old Me." To start, she clarified the nature of the "bad" voice, the one that wants to take advantage of others; she then created a "good" voice, one that worked to keep the boy safe, focused, aware of danger, and empowered to take positive action. In terms of coping with high-risk situations, she wrote, "We especially inquire about possible supportive people and role models who can be of help in such situations. When a particular boy has never experienced any such good role models in life, we search for other, more creative role models that they might look up to. Boys may then choose such film or TV stars as Superman, Obi Wan Kanobi, William Wallace or Indiana Jones" (Robson, 2000, p. 151).

Returning to the psychodynamically-influenced approaches, one of the more significant steps forward was transactional analysis (TA). The work of Eric Berne, TA was influence by the psychoanalytic thinking of Paul Federn. In TA, the Superego, Ego, and Id were reconceptualized as the Parent, Adult, and Child (Harris, 1969). This personification of the concepts allowed for a more relational and nuanced way of understanding these forces. The transformation of the Id, which had classically been envisioned as a kind of sexual and aggressive animal, into a child allowed for such emotions as fear and suffering as well as impulsivity (Harris, 1969). This model, powerful in its own right, would eventually influence a number of other therapies.

Jung, an important influence on Perls, was another major theorist who used parts. Here we have not only Persona and Shadow, but also the archetypes. In an act of reciprocity, the Jungian practice of Active Imagination has now grown to include Chairwork as one of its techniques (Douglas, 2005).

Perls certainly emphasized multiplicity of self during his Esalen years and in this regard, his work had two fundamental goals. The first was to bring all of the parts into awareness so that the individual had access to the energy and gifts that they contained; while the second was to organize the self in such a way that it could respond to the needs and desires of the self and the world in creative and successful ways (Polster & Polster, 1973). As Perls (1992) put it, "Health is an appropriate balance of the coordination of all of what we *are*" (p. 26).

Ego-State Therapy, which also built on Federn's conceptualizations, was the work of Jack and Helen Watkins. Strikingly, they saw the internal world as being a system akin to a family. Helen Watkins (1993) wrote: "Ego-state therapy is the utilization of family and group-therapy techniques for the resolution of conflicts between the different ego states that constitute a 'family of self' within a single individual" (p. 236) (italics in original). One of their useful observations was that the parental states are not really adult; they are the child's view of the parent because they were introjected when the patient was a child. In a related vein, they also point out that the child's abuse may be internalized and replayed with the parental forces continuing to abuse the child parts within the psyche of the individual.

Schema Mode Therapy was originally developed to address the needs of those suffering from the more severe personality disturbances such as borderline personality disorder and narcissistic personality disorder (Rafaeli et al., 2010; Young et al., 2003). This model has since been applied not only to antisocial personality disorder, but also to the full array of Axis II and treatment-resistant Axis I disorders. In his work, Young has taken steps to delineate the Parental, Child, Adult, and Coping Modes. For example, there are two primary maladaptive parent modes, the Demanding or Critical Parent and the Punitive Parent. The first involves a continual emphasis on the importance of meeting high standards along with a concurrent message of disapproval and criticism directed at the Child mode when these standards are not met. This kind of internal voice is fairly common among psychotherapy patients. The Punitive Parent Mode, in turn, is a hallmark of Borderline Personality Disorder and other clinical manifestations that involve self-hatred. The Punitive Parent Mode is connected to more savage forms of child abuse and its hatred for the patient is so strong that it may seek to harm or even kill the patient. In this regard, it may play a role in suicidal or self-murderous behavior (Firestone, Firestone, & Catell, 2002).

At the other end are the Child Modes. The Vulnerable Child Mode is the recipient of the parental attacks and it contains all the feelings of pain, fear, disappointment, grief, and loneliness. The Impulsive Child is the part that wants immediate gratification, the Angry Child is a part that wants to lash out because of the pain, and the Contented Child embodies the happy aspects of childhood.

Corresponding, in many ways, to the use of defense in the psychodynamic paradigm, schema therapy places a central emphasis on the role of coping mechanisms, especially in the treatment of patients with personality disorders. These coping mechanisms take several forms. The first is *Surrender*. This is where the patient essentially accepts the internalized maladaptive schemas or the criticisms of the Punitive or Demanding Parent modes. The patient will frequently think and accept as true such thoughts as "I feel that I am not lovable," "I am fundamentally different from other people," and "I'm a failure" (Young & Brown, 2003). From the outside, they will appear to be "passive, dependent, submissive, clinging," conflict-avoidant, and subservient to others (Young, 2003).

Therapeutically, these are treated using schema-focused therapy or more traditional forms of cognitive therapy (Beck & Weishaar, 2005). The work here involves both exploring their historical origin and examining evidence that supports the validity of the schema as well as that which refutes it. Chairwork can be used to rework the traumatic or difficult relational experiences that may have contributed to the creation of the schema or belief. It may also be used as a way of creating a more emotionally-infused form of cognitive restructuring. As noted earlier, Goldfried (1988; Samoilov & Goldfried, 2000) particularly favored the use of Chairwork in cognitive therapy as he felt that it led to a level of neurobiological arousal that helped to facilitate the reorganization of beliefs. In terms of treatment, the patient and therapist can first clarify the existing schema and then script an alternative. The patient can then move between the two chairs, giving voice to the old schema in one and giving voice to the healthy alternative in the other. As they go back and forth between the two, the new schema becomes more comfortable, familiar, and "natural" and the hegemony of the maladaptive belief or schema is challenged. In general, this kind of restructuring process may require not only dialogue work across a number of sessions, but also practice between them to make lasting inroads into these deeply entrenched beliefs.

For example, Young worked with a woman named Ivy who had a Self-Sacrifice schema. This meant that she put the needs of others before her own in a way that left her feeling frustrated and depressed. This was specifically being activated in her relationship with her friend Adam. She realized that while she listened to all of his problems, she felt blocked when it came to speaking about her own. Her dilemma was whether it was permissible to start speaking about her issues and concerns.

In the therapy session, Ivy did a dialogue between the schema side, which said that she needed to take care of Adam, and the healthy side, which wanted a more balanced relationship in which her needs were met as well. As part of her change process, she got angry at the schema. After finishing the dialogue, she did imagery work in which she brought up childhood images of taking care of her mother, which was where the schema originated. She then took further steps to let go of the schema by having a dialogue and telling her mother, "It cost me too much to take care of you. It cost me my sense of self" (Young et al., 2003, p. 148).

Patients who chronically rely on Avoidant Coping Modes are individuals who, in some way, are trying to avoid the pain of their core schemas. Broadly speaking, these modes can involve the use of: (1) social avoidance; (2) an exaggerated emphasis on personal autonomy; (3) psychological withdrawal, self-numbing, fantasy, or "*internal* forms of psychological escape"; (4) compulsive stimulation-seeking through "shopping, sex, gambling, risk-taking, physical activity" and the use of some drugs; and (5) addictive self-soothing "through addictions involving the body, such as alcohol, drugs, overeating, excessive masturbation, etc." (Young, 2003). These patients may initially come in to treatment because of the problems caused by their reliance on these coping mechanisms rather than because of the pain that is underlying it.

The third form of coping mode involves Overcompensation. When in the presence of people who are relying on this coping style as a primary way of functioning, it is not uncommon to feel that it is "too much" and that they

seem very rigid in their ways. This can take the form of: (1) blaming, attacking, or criticizing others; (2) dominating others; (3) seeking to impress others through high achievement and attention-seeking; (4) relying on "*covert
manipulation, seduction, dishonesty, or conning*"; (5) refusing to cooperate
and seeking to undermine others through passive-aggressive or rebellious
behavior; and (6) an excessive or obsessional emphasis on order and control
(Young, 2003).

It is these kinds of strategies that can play a core component in such Axis
II disorders as narcissistic, obsessive-compulsive, and antisocial personality
disorder as well as in other problems in the interpersonal realm. Therapeutically, this model is important as it enables therapists to have more compassion for patients as they can re-envision these problematic and unpleasant
behaviors as attempts to protect the patient from being exposed and feeling
shame, fear, or pain. They can also be understood as a "creative adjustment,"
as a way of trying to cope with and survive in difficult developmental situations (Perls et al., 1951). The issue now is that the negative consequences of
the behavior are often greater than the benefits.

Lastly, there is the Healthy Adult Mode. This is the inner Leader whose
role it is to: (1) protect the Vulnerable Child from the attacks of the Demanding or Punitive Parent; (2) nurture the Vulnerable Child; (3) rein in the Angry
Child and assist him or her express his or her desires and needs in ways that
are assertive and more effective; and (4) help the person operate in the world
in ways that are purposeful, effective, and meaningful.

The heart of the mode work *is* the strengthening of the Healthy Adult and
this project may involve the full range of Chairwork dialogues (Lobestaal,
2008). For example, the Healthy Adult can dialogue with the Parental modes
and protect the Vulnerable Child, the Vulnerable Child can be nurtured
directly by the Healthy Adult, and the benefits and costs of the Avoidant and
Overcompensating modes can be debated using the chairs (Kellogg, 2009a).

Turning to emotion-focused therapy. Elliot and Greenberg (1997) understood Chairwork to be a therapy of multivocality. They proposed a dialogical
understanding of psychotherapy that sees treatment not only as a process
in which different parts engage in dialogue with each other, but also one in
which suppressed voices are invited to speak, problematic voices may be
challenged and reined in, and new voices are created. Therapy then becomes
a series of complex conversations, a model that is well-suited for Chairwork.

Drawing from narrative therapy, Allen and Allen (1995) make the important point that each of the different internal parts has their own story. Parts
can be interviewed, their history can be told, and the conversation can involve
an exploration of their hopes, fears, desires, and goals. Again, working within
the narrative tradition, they emphasize that "each person is entitled to more
than one story" (p. 329). This can lead to greater complexity of self and the

possibility of achieving or creating new and more viable identities (Allen & Allen, 1995). In a similar vein, Zinker (1977) wrote: "I call this whole process stretching the self-concept, creating more room in one's picture of the self" (p. 203).

INNER CONFLICTS

While a balanced, adaptable, composite self was one of the goals of Gestalt therapy, the work itself frequently involved a central focus on inner conflict. As Latner put it, these concern "battles over who we are, what we are to do, and how we are to do it" (Latner, 1973, 154). There were several classic processes that the early Gestalt therapists felt were involved in the creation of the person's internal world. These could either be helpful or problematic and they were each amenable to the Chairwork process. Two of particular relevance were introjection and retroflection (Perls et al., 1951).

Perls' writing about the *introjection* process connected to his interest in oral processes. As children develop, their lives are filled with relationships and experiences with others and in the process of growth, they will assimilate or incorporate images of these relationships and the messages that they contain. With assimilation, individuals are able to "chew on" the material; that is, they are able to examine it, take it apart, identify what is useful and meaningful to them, and ignore or reject that which seems irrelevant or toxic. This, then, is a process of active engagement which leads to a genuine integration and true ownership by the individual. "What is assimilated is not taken as a whole, but is first destroyed (destructured) completely and transformed—and absorbed *selectively* according to the needs of the organism" (Perls et al., 1951, p. 190).

As opposed to assimilation, introjection is a process in which the material must be "swallowed whole." The individual is not allowed to make choices. They are not allowed to question, to discriminate, to decide. "Whatever the child gets from his *loving* parents he assimilates, for it is fitting and appropriate to his own needs as he grows. It is the *hateful* parents who have to be introjected, taken down whole, although they are contrary to the needs of the organism" (Perls et al., 1951, p. 190). This view certainly overlaps with those of the object relations theorists (Greenberg & Mitchell, 1983), and there is a certain metaphorical power to this, especially in cases that involve more severe pathology and traumatic past histories.

Perls and Goodman make a few more relevant observations. The first is that introjection itself involves some kind of "unfinished business"; that is, there may be some kind of traumatic component to this process. The second is how they capture the fact that children must introject in order to survive. "The self has been conquered. In giving up, it settles for a secondary integrity, a means of surviving, though beaten, *by identifying with the conqueror and turning against itself"* (Perls et al., 1951, p. 203). Their therapeutic answer is, of course, to engage with and confront these experiences.

If introjection was the first way of creating the internal life, *retroflection* was the second. Retroflection builds on introjection and it emerges out of the conflict between the energetic, spontaneous, and expressive behaviors of the developing human and the rules, values, and mores of the family and social environment. Through direct and indirect aspects of the child-rearing experience, the child begins to internalize these messages on a psychological and, from a Reichian perspective, muscular level. In this regard, the process is similar to that which Freud (1965) described in the creation of the Superego.

For Perls and Reich, this self-correction and self-restraint can often be felt in the musculature, if properly attended to. "The holding back is achieved by tensing muscles which are antagonistic to those which would be involved in expressing the punishable impulse" (Perls et al., 1951, pp. 146–147). Linguistically, this takes the form in which one part of the self acts on another such as "I ask myself" or "I say to myself" (Perls et al., 1951). Other examples include: "I judge myself"; "My difficulty is that when I'm writing my paper, I'm also marking it"; and "I close off my feelings, I don't allow myself to feel" (p. 318) (adapted from Greenberg, 1979, in Kellogg, 2004, p. 318).

Enns (1987) takes this somewhat further in her discussion of Feminist Therapy. Her perspective is that women also receive messages concerning what is acceptable and what is not from other institutions as well as the media. Her work is on helping them become aware of their inner desires and values so that they can find authentic visions and solutions for their lives. This model would, of course, apply to many who suffer from socially-induced self-disparagement. In all of these cases, Chairwork dialogues can play a central role in clarifying the internal parts or voices, enabling them to make contact with each other, and helping them find creative solutions. This is discussed at greater length in chapter 9.

Perls argued that symptoms were often a manifestation of a conflict. The strategy was not to favor one and attack the other, but to respect them both and see them as parts of the patient. Through becoming aware of them, owning them, and giving them voice, a healing encounter becomes possible. This strategy of being aware and of taking responsibility for one's experience again connects us to the broader construct of the paradoxical theory of change (Beisser, 1970). As discussed earlier, the paradoxical theory of change has been a central concept in both classical and contemporary gestalt therapy (Yontef & Jacobs, 2008). The essence of this principle is *"that change occurs when one becomes what he is, not when he tries to become what he is not . . . [change] does take place if one takes the time and effort to be what he is—to be fully invested in his current positions"* (Beisser, 1970, p. 77). Another way of understanding it is that "you never overcome anything by resisting it. You only overcome anything by going deeper into it . . . whatever it is, if you go deeply enough into it, then it will disappear; it will be assimilated" (Naranjo, 1993, p. 138). In Chairwork, this clearly overlaps with Greenberg's work with *facilitating* approaches (Greenberg et al., 1989).

Decision-Making

The making of decisions, of choosing one priority over another, of enacting one value instead of another, comes to the heart of what it means to be a human being (Yalom, 1980). Decisions can be difficult and defining. Dialogical interventions can be helpful here as a way to assess the emotions involved, to clarify the relative salience of the different perspectives, to identify the different values involved, and to understand the historical and psychodynamic forces that may be at work (Mackay, 2002).

In a powerful and complex series of dialogues, Glickauf-Hughes and colleagues reported a case of a patient who was trying to make a decision between two employment possibilities (Glickauf-Hughes, Wells, & Change, 1996). The patient was faced with the choice of taking one of two jobs. The more prestigious job was located in a city that was different from that of his current partner. The other job was less prestigious, was located in the same city as his partner, and it looked to be more enjoyable. Anchoring the choices in different chairs, he began the dialogue and alternated sides. It soon became clear to him that the part that wanted the more prestigious position was connected to his father, a man who had believed that work was more important than family. He also criticized the patient "for being lazy and underachieving" (p. 439). The other chair, in turn, began to emerge as the voice of "his true self." This part, while still trying to grow in confidence, deeply appreciated relationships and also felt that the pleasure that came from working on projects was more important than prestige or money.

The dialogue was then re-framed as one between his father and himself. The patient was invited to sit in a third chair, located between the other two, and "mediate between his father and his self" (p. 439). He began by speaking to the chair that represented himself. He pointed out that his father's criticisms had been unfair as he had always been somewhat successful and he affirmed the fact that "he valued intrinsic pleasure more than success" (p. 439). When speaking to the father, he began with a stance of empathy. His father had grown up in poverty with an alcoholic father who had barely been able to provide for him. He felt for his father's own anxieties and how hard he had struggled to be successful.

He then went on to say that he (the patient) had been a very good father to his own son. He told his father that he did not need to worry because he was responsible and had been successful. He also affirmed that it was okay to base his decisions on a variety of values, not just success. At the end of the dialogue, the patient reported feeling significantly "calmer."

There are several interesting technical points in this case example. Beginning with a real-life decision, the patient quickly became aware that he was having a conflict between two underlying value systems. The patient and the therapist then went to the historical roots of the value system and began to engage in a dialogue between the father and the son. In this case, they went from an internal dialogue to an external dialogue. Taking a stance of empathy toward the father, he was eventually able to discern that not only was there value in his father's emphasis on success, but also that it was fear-driven and connected to the traumatic experiences of his own childhood. Lastly, by moving to a three-chair model, the therapist was striving to create what she called "a strong observing ego" (p. 431). The ability to help patients develop the capacity for self-awareness and self-observation, which Glickauf-Hughes and colleagues believe is one of the hallmarks of mental health, is one of the great strengths of the Chairwork technique.

The Decisional Balance

One useful way to clarify the internal forces involved in a choice is to begin with a Decisional Balance (Marlatt & Gordon, 1985). This technique serves to anchor the patient and the information obtained can be used to clarify the voices; the Chairwork dialogues that ensue can be built on this. On a technical level, a Decisional Balance involves clarifying the positives and negatives of one decision and the positives and negatives of the alternative. In its most basic form, the positives of one decision and the negatives of the other will constitute one vector, while the positives of the second choice and the negatives of the first will make up the other. Each, in turn, will be given their own chair. In an actual session, the therapist can refer to the completed Decisional Balance form to make sure that all of the issues are addressed or at least considered in the ensuing dialogue. This is a good resource because, in the heat of things, some issues may get left out, others may seem unimportant, and yet others may emerge as more important than were initially understood, all of which is significant. As will be seen in the dialogue below, the forces of fear and comfort (or avoidant coping) will lead the patient to want to stay in his or her job while those of pain and desire for a fuller life will motivate him or her to change.

Working from a gestalt perspective, the first step would be to have the patient express both voices in a clear and powerful way. It is the belief that as they go back and forth between the two sides, making contact and dialoguing with each other, a creative solution will begin to emerge; a solution that will somehow reflect a new internal balance.

Table 5.1 Work Decision Balance

Decisional Balance	
Positives Staying in Job	*Positives of Leaving Job*
Feels comfortable	Do something that I feel more passionate
Know everyone	about
Fun/camaraderie	Would feel more alive
Knows the routine	Make more money
Sense of mastery	Escape bad things in current job
Feels appreciated	
Fits life structure/supports other interests	
Negatives of Staying in Job	*Negatives of Leaving Job*
Not enough money	Frightened of leaving
Little possibility of advancement	Questions ability to do other things
Bored and frustrated	The new job might not work out–that
Feels life is passing by	would be a disaster
Not fulfilling potential	It would be a major life disruption
Feels trapped/not alive	

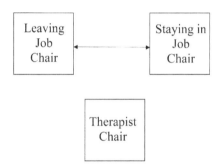

Figure 5.1 Career Decision-Making Dialogue

DECISION-MAKING DIALOGUE

The patient is in therapy because he or she feels stuck. They have been in a job for four or five years. It was supposed to be a temporary post; a position that he or she was taking until they found something better. However, they ended up staying much longer than they had intended to, and the whole situation is creating feelings of anxiety and depression.

As a way to help set up and clarify the voices, the Therapist and the Patient will start by doing a basic Decisional Balance. A completed, work-based Decisional Balance can be found in table 5.1.

The dialogue will begin with the patient and the therapist facing each other; they will continue to do so throughout the Decisional Balance phase of the conversation. Only after that is finished will the patient be invited to engage in a two-chair dialogue. In order to ensure neutrality, the therapist will put his or her chair in the middle of the two chairs during the dialogue as this is a way to symbolize that he or she is neither taking a position, nor favoring an outcome (see figure 5.1).

Career Decision-Making Dialogue

[The Patient and the Therapist are facing each other.]

Patient: I'm really upset about my job situation. I feel like I have been there way too long, that I'm really stuck. On the other hand, I find it very difficult to get myself motivated to actually do anything about it.

Therapist: What I would like to do is get a clearer sense of the forces at work here. If it's okay with you, I would like us to identify both the positives of the job and the negatives of the job. I would then like to clarify what you think are the positives of moving on and getting a new one and the negatives or downsides of doing this. If we can clarify the forces at work here, it might make it easier for you to make a decision and to figure out ways to deal with the problems that exist on either side of the equation.

Patient: Sounds good.

Therapist: What are the positives of the job?

Patient: I guess the first thing that comes to mind is that I feel very comfortable there. I know everyone and like most of the people a great deal. We have fun sometimes doing the projects and there is really a great sense of camaraderie, at least among this subgroup that I'm a part of. We have our own sense of humor and our own jokes; sometimes it's a bit like a family.

I've been there long enough to really know the work and the routine. Things don't change much in this business, so I've really mastered it. It doesn't take that much effort anymore or even that much time. I'm pleased to do the job well, and I'm glad that people both inside and outside the company feel that they can rely on me to do what needs to be done.

I guess the last thing is that it fits my life structure really well. First, it's a really good commute. You also know that I have a lot of interests outside the job and it gives me time to pursue them. They also let me be flexible with my hours when I want to do something.

Therapist: What is your unhappiness with the job?

Patient: First and foremost, I'm not making enough money. There are no big raises in the offing and I don't see any promotions coming my way. There are so many people there who seem to be in it for the long run; they're older, married, and some have children, so I just don't see a lot of possibilities.

On a deeper level, I'm really bored. It's just the same thing day in and day out. Some days I find myself getting really frustrated with it. When I first took this job, I thought that it would just be a temporary thing, something that I was doing for a year or a year-and-a-half until I got going on my next life project. I'd been going through some difficult times, so it was really a blessing to have a place like this to go to.

I never thought I would be here this long. I've begun to see some other young people come and go, go onto other things. I'm afraid I'm going to become one of the "old guys," that I'm going to keep going to farewell parties.

While I'm not clear what they are, I always thought that I'd do some great things with my life. Sometimes, I feel really trapped; I feel like I'm not really living.

Therapist: What would be the positives of leaving?

Patient: It would give me a chance to do something that I'm more passionate about. I want to do something that will challenge me and help me feel more alive. Maybe I could find something that is a bit closer to what I should do with this life of mine.

In some ways, I have been avoiding the issue, but I really need to make more money. When I look at my bank account at the end of the month, it's not a pretty sight. Lastly, it would help me escape some of the bad things in my current job like feeling trapped and feeling like I'm just going through the motions of my life.

Therapist: What would be the negatives of leaving?

Patient: If I'm really honest, and I don't think I have said this to anyone else, I'm really quite frightened of going out into the world. It's been a long time, and I've been at least somewhat happy in this nice cocoon. When I look at the job ads in the paper, I get really anxious and feel overwhelmed.

To be honest again, I don't know if I can do anything else. Suppose I got another job and it didn't work out? I could get fired and that would really leave me in dire straits. While I'm not making enough money now, at least I'm making some money; if I lost my job, I'd be destitute. I could become a homeless person.

If I got fired, I would also be devastated because it would be such a statement that I'm incompetent. That would be difficult for me to bounce back from. It would be such a major disruption to my life, and I don't really know what I want to do anyway.

Therapist: I would like to work with some of this information. In many respects, there are two sides of you at work here: one part that wants to move forward and create a new life, and another part that wants to stay still. The part of you that wants to move on is connected to the negatives of your current job and what you perceive would be the positives of a new situation, and the part of you that doesn't want to change is connected to the pleasures of your current situation and your concerns about moving to a new position or company.

Just to clarify those forces from what you said, the part of you that wants to stay in the job feels comfortable, has a sense of mastery, likes the people, and is very worried about whether he/she can be successful in another job or even do anything else. The part of you that wants to leave is bored and restless, worried about money, feels trapped, and believes that your life is supposed to be more than this. How does that sound?

Patient: That sounds right.

Therapist: If you're willing, I'd like to create a kind of a conversation between these two parts. In this chair *(pointing to one of the chairs)*, I would like you to speak from the part that is tired of your current situation and that wants things to change, and from this chair *(pointing to the chair opposite)*, I would like you to speak from the part that doesn't want to move on and is happy with things the way they are. I would like you to go back and forth several times so that we can see what emerges. You may start with either side. *(See figure 5.1)*

Patient: I would like to start with the part that wants to leave.

Therapist: Take a seat here and start speaking from that part.

Patient: (Patient moves to one of the chairs; the Therapist situates him- or herself in the middle between the two chairs.) Well, as I said. I'm not making enough money and I don't see that changing any time soon. There are too many people who have been there for a long time so I just don't see any room for advancement. I'm also bored and frustrated; I feel like I'm wasting my life. I need to get moving.

Therapist: I want to get moving.

Patient: Yes. I want to get moving. I feel like I'm still young enough and I don't want this to be the end of my life. I want to do something that I have some passion for, something that would help me feel more alive. I also really need to make more money. The money issue is really serious; I just don't see a way of resolving it in this job. It gets me down sometimes, I just want to get out of there.

Therapist: How do you feel? What kind of emotions are going on inside of you as you say these things?

Patient: (Pauses) I'm feeling down and a bit frightened.

Therapist: Now I want you to move to this chair and speak from the other side.

Patient: (Patient switches chair) It's fine for you to complain, but I don't think you are being very realistic. While it may not be the best job in the world, at least you know what you're doing. How do you know that you would do as well in a new job? You might have to learn some new things or do things that you're not good at. It could just be a disaster. If things are not so good financially right now, you really need to think about what it would be like if you went to a new job and blew it; we could end up being a homeless person.

Anyway, things aren't so bad. You know the routine, you know what to do. People like you there and you have a lot of fun. You've got a place there and the customers know and appreciate you. The job isn't that hard and you've got the flexibility to do the things you like outside of work. You can pursue your hobbies. I think it's an okay deal; I think you should stay.

Therapist: I would like you to say the things that you just said again. Only this time, I would like you to use the word "I" rather than "you." I want you to "own" these feelings instead of telling her/him what she/he should do. I want you to really own the beliefs and concerns and speak about them with as much feeling and power as you can.

Patient: Okay. Basically, I'm really nervous about leaving this job. I know it gets boring at times, but at least I know what I'm doing. It's been a while since I've been out there job hunting, a while since I had to start a new job. I really don't know if I can do it. When I think about failing and getting fired and being unemployed, I really get freaked out.

  Anyway, it's not so bad. I like the people, and it allows me to do the things I want to do in my private life. I have this voice in my head that says that I should be more ambitious, but why do I have to be, why can't I just stay here?

Therapist: How are you feeling right now as you are sitting there? What's going on inside of you?

Patient: I feel agitated and worried. I am really feeling how frightened about leaving.

Therapist: Switch back and speak from the part that wants to leave.

Patient: (Patient switches chairs.) I know you're frightened. I get it. But I want to get out of here. I've been here too long. I want to get out.

Therapist: Try this . . . I'm bored, frustrated, and I want a new future.

Patient: I'm bored, frustrated, and I want a new future.

Therapist: I want more money.

Patient: Yes. I want more money. I definitely want more money.

Therapist: Now, go over to the other chair and speak from the part that wants to stay.

Patient: (Patient goes over to the other chair.) I am still frightened. It's safe here. I know what I am doing. I don't know if I can do another job.

Therapist: It's safe here and I'm scared of leaving.

Patient: I'm safe here and I'm scared to leave.

Therapist: I want to do some shuttling. I would like you to go back and forth between the two chairs. When you get there, I would like you to say one sentence from each perspective. I would like you to stand behind the chair when you do this. Okay?

Patient: Okay

Therapist: (The Therapist and the Patient both stand up. The Therapist moves his/her chair back a few feet.) Please stand behind this chair *(pointing at the Leaving Job chair)* and say one strong sentence about leaving.

Patient: (Standing behind the chair.) I am really frustrated and I want to leave.

Therapist: Now switch to the other side and make a strong statement about staying.

Patient: I am frightened and I want to stay.

Therapist: Good. Now just go back and forth a few times.

Patient: (Switches chairs) I'm frustrated and I want leave. *(Switches chairs)* I can't do this. I want to stay. *(Switches chairs)* I need more money. I want a life. I want to go. *(Switches chairs)* I want to stay. I want to stay. Don't make me leave. *(Switches chairs)* I hate this. I want to go. *(Switches chairs)* I can't do it. Let me stay.

Therapist: I'm dying and I want to go. I'm terrified and I want to stay.

Patient: (Switches chairs) I'm dying and I want to go. *(Switches chairs)* I'm terrified and I want to stay.

Therapist: Again.

Patient: (Switches chairs) I'm dying and I want to leave. *(Switches chairs)* I'm terrified. I'm really frightened and I want to stay. *(Pause)*

Therapist: That was very good. I want to do one more thing.

Patient: Okay.

Therapist: I would like you come stand here in the middle. *(The Patient stands between the two chairs, a few feet back and opposite the therapist.)* I would like you to look at the two chairs. This side is the part that wants to leave and this side is the part that wants to stay. I would like you to look at both chairs and sense how you're feeling inside right now. I'd like you to rate the forces within you right now. 50-50, 70-30, 20-80. Whatever you're feeling

Patient: (Pause) I am feeling 75-25 to go.

Therapist: What were you feeling when we started this?

Patient: I was about 55-45 to go.

Therapist: Wow. So there has definitely been a shift.

Patient: Yes. I feel much more stronger about leaving than when we began.

Therapist: That's great. Let's go back to our original seats and sort this out.

Debrief

In general, I believe that 70-30 is the minimal motivational threshold for making a major life change. This patient has passed the line so the work can now progress toward making plans and developing strategies for getting a new job. Given that the part that does not want to leave is at a 25, special attention will need to be paid to his or her fears and anxieties.

Reflections

This dialogue included a number of Chairwork strategies and deepening techniques. The session began with a Decisional Balance, which can be seen as a kind of warm-up (Dayton, 2005; Moreno, 2012). The therapist "directed traffic," proposed some lines, and used simplification and repetition to increase the emotional intensity of the experience. At the end, he or she did some shuttling, which was a technique favored by Fritz Perls when he was at Esalen (1975a; 1992). At the end, the patient was invited to assess the strength of the various cognitive-emotional forces within. In general, this dialogue was more existential than relational. The patient was encouraged to speak from each perspective in an authentic and powerful way rather than having the two perspectives dialogue with each other. This was made manifest when the therapist encouraged the patient to shift from "you should" to "I want." As will be explored further in chapter 7, Perls liked to have patients speak from two polarities as he believed that creative possibilities would emerge in the space in between the two.

Making Decisions II

To further develop this work in a second round of dialogues, there are a number of options. One is that the two participants switch roles and repeat the scenario as it was written. Another is that you use the same material, but improvise the dialogues based on the themes that were presented.

Moving beyond that, they can create a dialogue based on a different kind of conflict. This can be a personal issue, a problem that one of your patients or friends is wrestling with, one of the scenarios below, or something that you make up. To help clarify the issues.

Possible Scenarios

1. "I have been going out with my boyfriend/girlfriend for a couple of years. We are very comfortable together and our lives are very integrated. We are both very close with each other's families, and I feel like he/she is my best friend; however, I think that some of the energy and spark between us has

died down. I recently met [ ] and he/she is very interested in me. I hate to admit it, but I find that I feel very attracted to [ ] also. I'm confused and don't know whether to stay with my boyfriend/girlfriend or break it off and pursue things with [ ]."

2. "I'm torn between wanting to have a baby now or continuing to pursue my work/educational career and deciding to have the baby later."

3. "My family wants me to get an MBA. We have a major family business and they are expecting me to take a leadership role in its development and future. Over the long run, there are a lot of people depending on me to do this and to do it well. While I have some interest in business, I have really fallen in love with writing. I want to get an MFA in Creative Writing. I realize that this would be a very difficult situation financially, but I'm on fire about being a writer. I know that my family would be very upset if I made this choice; I also know that they would not support me financially if I go to an MFA program. They will only support me if I get my MBA. I'm very stressed about this."

Chapter 6

Internal Dialogues

Inner Critic and Negative Schema Voices

As touched on earlier, therapists and theorists from a wide range of treatment perspectives have wrestled with the experience of a critical or punitive "voice," "self," or "part" as a fundamental factor in the development and maintenance of psychopathology. In clinical situations, this "inner critic" may set unreachable standards, punish the patient harshly for "transgressions," and/or engage in a form of verbal abuse in which it constantly criticizes, puts down, and disempowers the patient.

In terms of modern psychotherapy, the study and treatment of this experience began with Freud (1965, 1969) and his concept of the Superego. Karen Horney (1950) wrote about the "Tyranny of the Should," a concept that likely influenced Perls. The phenomena of inner attack was addressed through Chairwork in such therapies as Gestalt Therapy (Perls, 1992), Redecision Therapy (Goulding & Goulding, 1997), Emotion-Focused Therapy (Greenberg et al., 1993; Watson et al., 2007), Anthetic Dialogues (Elliott & Elliott, 2000), Voice Dialogue (Stone & Stone, 1989, 1993), Schema Therapy (Rafaeli et al., 2010; Young et al., 2003), and Voice Therapy (Firestone, Firestone, & Catlett, 2002). Capturing the centrality of this issue, the Elliots (2000) believed that this core tormenting "voice" was at the heart of all psychiatric difficulties and they made this work the center of their Anthetic Dialogue process. A review of these different approaches revealed two key issues: (1) What was the best way to structure the dialogue so as to achieve maximal effect? and (2) Was it better to integrate the critical voice or to isolate and expel it instead?

For Perls, the development of an inner critical part, which he called Topdog (Perls, 1992), was intimately connected to the processes of *introjection* that were explored earlier (Perls et al., 1951). Again, using the oral metaphors that were very meaningful to him at that time, he made the case that "the child swallows whole, gulps down without chewing up, or has stuffed down his throat, and which, ingested but undigested, stirs in the organism" (Dublin, 1976, p. 127). Again, he also wrote, "We don't introject the *love* object. We take in the person who is *in control*. This often is a *hate* object" (Perls, 1969b, p. 216). For Perls, the therapeutic project was to move the moral center from the Superego, where it was thought to be automatic, archaic, and irrational, to the Ego, where it would take the form of a consciously-chosen value system.

Perls invited patients to engage in a "Top Dog"/"Bottom Dog" dialogue. In his formulation, one part criticizes and bullies while the other is meek and oppressed but ultimately rebels and does not give in. Perls felt that through dialogue and encounter an integration was possible and that a solution might emerge that would, in some way, reflect the concerns and desires of both parts. Redecision Therapy, in turn, took a contrasting focus. As they went to the root of things, the Gouldings sometimes found a parental figure that was quite abusive or hateful (Goulding & Goulding, 1997; M. Polster, 1987). Here the emphasis was on isolating, extricating, or replacing that part or voice. The critics were seen as pathological and, in some cases, deadly. In a dialogue with the gestalt therapist Miriam Polster, Robert Goulding brought up this dilemma. "For instance, a suicidal client is dealing with some of the early messages that he got from his parents where he experiences one of his parents as being angry with a scowling face. When he's sitting in the other chair, he's being that parent saying, 'I wish you were dead. I wish you'd never been born!'. . . I don't know how to integrate that part of the parent that is so scowling, murderous, disruptive. I teach my people to say goodbye to that part" (Robert Goulding in M. Polster, 1987, p. 323).

Greenberg's work, which was very influenced by Perls' model, also sought to integrate the critic. In his approach, the patient begins by voicing the criticisms in one chair and then responds by moving to the other chair and gives voice to what it feels like to be criticized. That is, they express their feelings of depression, anxiety, despair, or anger. As the dialogue continues, the therapist works to have the critic be more specific in its criticisms, and the "experiencing" part be clearer as to what he or she is actually feeling. Eventually, the critical part will begin to identify the values that are at the heart of its stance and the experiencing part will move from expressing feelings to communicating his or her wants and needs. Through this process, if all goes well, the critic will start to soften and there will be some kind of integration between the two polarities at the end.

Voice Dialogue is the joint creation of Hal and Sidra Stone (1989; 1993). Similar in some ways to the practices of Jungian and gestalt therapists, voice dialogue theorists believe that as humans develop, they find that some aspects of themselves are accepted and reinforced while others are opposed, criticized, or forbidden. This results in a personality structure in which there are primary selves and disowned selves. Difficulties emerge when there are conflicts among the primary selves and when disowned selves seek expression. The latter can be particularly troubling because they are unintegrated.

The voice dialogue model is unique in two key ways. In the first, these subpersonalities or energy patterns are seen as being independent entities within the person. As Dyak (2012) has written, "In Voice Dialogue, the selves are real live energetic beings, each with its own history, viewpoint, beliefs, physical reality, and experiences, desires, attachments, skills, talents/gifts" (p. 222). This contrasts with Schema Therapy where the different modes are seen as being aspects of the self.

The second significant area of difference is the goal of the work. Voice Dialogue adherents emphasize the importance of the *Aware Ego Process* (Dyak, 2012; Gaspard & Hoffman, 2009; Stone & Stone, 1989). The goal is to create a center of awareness that will enable the individual to be fully aware of the self that is active at any given time. This ability to label and observe helps keep the individual from being "taken over" by any particular energy pattern. As the Stones (1989) have written, "Awareness is the capacity to witness life in all its aspects without evaluating or judging the energy patterns being witnessed, and without needing to control the outcome of the event" (p. 9). The Stones (1989; 1993), in their voice dialogue method, do extensive inner critic work that is deserving of investigation in its own right; nonetheless, there are several ideas that can be integrated into a Chairwork treatment. One of their core insights is that the fundamental function of the inner critic is to protect the inner child. As a child is growing up, he or she experiences fear, shame, humiliation, and punishment. The inner critic develops as a way to protect the child from having to go through these painful experiences again.

To this end, the critic will attack the child part in order to get it to behave. Unfortunately, these attacks are too often merciless and divorced from reality and they frequently contain messages from parents and other authority figures and institutions. These attacks may also lead to many forms of psychopathology, including depression and suicide. It is also crucial to understand that the inner critic is fundamentally afraid that if the person does not do the right thing then something terrible will happen. In short, it is a fear-driven entity. One of the ultimate goals is for the individual to not only become a parent to their inner child, but also a parent to their inner critic. In this role, they have compassion for the fear and trauma that is at the heart of the critic's experience.

Building on work by a variety of therapists (Corstens, Longden, & May, 2012; Rowan, 1990; Stone & Stone, 1989), an interview structure can be developed that covers such themes as identity, history, personality, intention, relationship, and core messages. With the patient embodying and giving voice to the critic, the therapist can interview him or her and explore the

Table 6.1   **Inner Critic Interview Structure**

Inner Critic Interview Structure	
May I speak with you?	What do you have to offer [ ]?
Who are you?	How are you harming [ ]?
Do you have a name?	What are you most afraid of?
What do you look like?	Did someone hurt you?
When did you first come into [ ]'s life?	Did someone frighten you?
What is your basic reason for being here?	Who loved you?
In what kind of situations do you tend to come out?	What do you most like about [ ]?
What do you want?	Who makes you angriest about [ ]?
What do you need?	What makes you saddest about [ ]?
What are your goals for [ ]?	What would happen if you were not there?
How are you helping [ ]?	If there was one thing that you wanted [ ] to know, what would it be?

relevant issues. Table 6.1 includes a series of twenty-two questions that one might want to consider using in this kind of dialogue work. To approach this more succinctly, Sasportas (quoted in Rowan, 2010) has said that the critical voice (or any internal entity) can be compassionately interviewed using such core questions as: "What do you want? What do you need? What do you have to offer [patient's name]?" (Rowan, 2010, p. 74). Friendliness would appear to be at the heart of this encounter (Zinker, 1977).

Beyond approaching the critic with compassion, the other important intentions are to provide it with a chance to speak deeply about its desires and experiences and to honor it and the good that it is trying to do. Unlike other approaches, no attempt is made to change or alter its perspectives, no dialogues are held with other modes or voices, and no attempts are made to integrate it with the rest of the self system.

Again, the Stones places a core emphasis on the aware ego process which means that the patient is able to be compassionately aware of the distinct parts as they get activated. They can then choose if and how they want to respond to a given voice. With an inner critic, the patient can go from experiencing this as some kind of "tyrannical" truth to an awareness that this is a frightened part. With chairs, the patient can then sit in an aware ego process chair and speak about the experience of being cognizant of the critic in the chair next to them and explore ways of recognizing and responding to it in the future. Structurally, it should be noted that both chairs face the therapist; there is no dialogue between the two parts.

Whether or not one accepts the voice dialogue approach, this method of interviewing the critic (or other parts) with curiosity and compassion is a very good way to begin. It allows the therapist to work in a manner that is less stressful while also learning more and developing a relationship with important parts of the person. Again, all parts are welcome and they are not asked to change. They may, in fact, do so as a result of the work but this is more of an organic, rather than clinical, process.

Voice Therapy, as opposed to Voice Dialogue, has been described as a "cognitive-affective-behavioral" therapy. The work of Robert Firestone, Lisa Firestone, and Joyce Catlett (2002), this is a creative and dynamic approach that echoes and reworks some of the themes that we have already addressed. In this context, they have also been particularly focused on the prevention of suicide, which they see as a consequence of states of internal attack and disparagement.

In voice therapy, all people are seen as living in a state of division. This split includes the Self System, which represents our tendency "to grow and develop and to pursue our personal and vocational goals, as well as desires to be close in our relationships and to search for meaning in life" (Firestone et al., 2002, p. 11), and the Anti-Self System or critical inner voice which represent the forces "that oppose or attempt to destroy the self" (Firestone & Catlett, 1998, p. 687).

The negative voices develop from the internalization of messages from the parents and the early environment. In their description, "The critical inner voice is the language of the defended, negative side of your personality; the side that is opposed to your ongoing personal development. The voice is made up of a series of negative thoughts that oppose your best interests and diminish your self-esteem. These hostile, judgmental thoughts also warn you about other people and create a negative, pessimistic picture of the world" (Firestone et al., 2002, p. 16).

In terms of the actual therapy, the patient will sit in a chair and give voice to the inner critic by speaking in the second person, perhaps to the self in the opposite chair. That is, they would begin each statement with "You." "This practice has three main benefits: (1) it helps you separate the critical point of view of yourself from a more realistic view; (2) it starts to make you think of other negative thoughts that you may not have been aware of before, thoughts that were just below the surface of consciousness; and (3) it brings up feelings that are often associated with these thoughts and makes you aware of the snide or sarcastic tone of your critical inner voice" (p. 17). The healing power of this work lies first in the expression and exploration of the critical communications. This would include what they mean and where they come from. Connecting to the healthy Self System, the patient would then make the decision to specifically take actions that affirm their life. This would include doing things that the Critical Voice prohibits and not doing things that the Critical Voice prescribes.

In a moving and powerful evocation of their work, Firestone and Catlett (1998) analyze the suicide of the poet Sylvia Plath through the voice therapy model. In her journal entry, *Letter to a Demon*, Plath clearly delineated this experience of a divided self. She wrote about a "murderous self" and a "good self." She believed that the critical part would murder the good self through high standards and perfectionism (Hughes & McCullough, 1982, pp. 176–177, as cited in Firestone & Catlett, 1998, p. 667). Plath connected the demanding "demon" voice to her mother. She tried to fight the perfectionism; tragically, one way that she would do this was by refusing to write as she knew that her mother wanted her to write. In the end, the criticisms and the consequent depression overwhelmed her and she took her life.

This again brings to the forefront how dangerous these voices of criticism can be. When working with patients who are suicidal, the first priority must be to make sure that the patient is safe and/or is in a structure of safety before engaging in the dialogue. That is, management takes precedence over encounter. Once contained, this kind of work can be central in helping them reclaim their life and their desire to live.

Moving to a model that blends gestalt therapy, emotion-focused therapy, and cognitive-behavioral therapy, I have been increasingly impressed with Chadwick's (2003) focus on the importance of *complexity of self*. He has argued that some people, especially those who have suffered from extreme forms of psychopathology and who have lived marginal existences often hold a very strong belief that they are fundamentally bad and defective. This negative self-concept is so pervasive and entrenched that it does not seem amenable to direct challenge. He especially found this to be the case in his work with psychotic and schizophrenic patients. His solution was to work with the patient to co-create what can be seen as an Affirming Voice. This can be a mixture of positive experiences, past loving relationships, the desires of the patient, and the positive beliefs and emotions of the therapist. This new supportive and coaching voice will need to be scripted and practiced so that it can feel more natural and become more integrated. Structurally, the patient will alternate chairs with one embodying the critical parts and the other representing the affirming parts. Strategically it can be helpful to have the two chairs face the therapist instead of each other. Rather than directly confronting the critic, the dialogue will seek to affirm the value and potential of the patient; in this way, it will help to increase the complexity of the patient's inner world. Rather than just negativity, there will be both darkness and light, which may be particularly useful when the persecuting modes are deeply entrenched.

One structural or theoretical issue that remains is the relationship between the cognitions and beliefs that are the focus of cognitive-behavioral therapy and the inner critic work that we are focusing on here. Drawing on items from the Young Schema Questionnaire (YSQ-S3; Young, 2005), patients may endorse such items as "I'm unworthy of the love, attention, and respect of others." "I'm not as talented as most people are at their work." "I feel that there is constant pressure for me to achieve and get things done." "It doesn't matter why I make a mistake. When I do something wrong, I should pay the consequences." Cognitive therapists will frequently seek to clarify the evidence that supports the belief and the evidence that refutes it. These two differing bodies of evidence can then serve as the foundation for a disputational dialogue with one chair embodying the evidence supporting the belief and the other chair embodying that challenges the belief and/or supports and affirmative view. This is, in fact, how some cognitive therapists use Chairwork (Leahy & Holland, 2000). Building on this, De Oliveira (2011) has turned this evidentiary approach into a high art with his trial-based cognitive therapy. Using metaphors drawn from Kafka's *The Trial,* he used chairs to embody the judge, the jury, the prosecuting attorney, the lawyer for the defense, and the defendant.

The prosecuting attorney can serve as a metaphorical bridge to the inner critic. Dysfunctional beliefs are not simply beliefs; sometimes they are accusations. The therapeutic possibilities, then, increase as these statements are re-envisioned as dyadic experiences, perhaps retroflective, with one part of the self is criticizing another. This means that instead of the person saying, "I am unworthy of the love, attention, and respect of others," there is a critical part saying, "You are unworthy of love, attention, and the respect of others" and receiving part (or Vulnerable Child Mode in schema therapy language) that experiences the pain. Similarly, Stinckens, Lietaer, and Leijssen (2002)

Figure 6.1   Inner Critic Interview

argued that the inner critic was a repository for the schemas. Once a dyadic experience, there is always the possibility for dialogue.

Fear-based cognitions can be approached in a similar manner. With a patient who has a fear of elevators, the evidence that supports the idea that elevators are dangerous could be marshalled in one chair and the evidence that elevators are very safe can be argued in the other. This can then be turned into a mode dialogue with one chair representing the part of the self that is fearful while the other chair embodies the part that wants to live a full, courageous life.

INNER CRITIC DIALOGUES

Given the centrality of the inner critic, several scripts are provided as examples of different strategies that may be used to engage with, clarify, challenge, or integrate this inner force, as appropriate. These dialogues include:

1. Diagnostic Interview;
2. Inner Critic Challenge/Self-Complexity; and
3. Self-Kindness and Self-Compassion.

Inner Critic Dialogue: Diagnostic Interview

As we have seen, forces within the individual can, potentially, be interviewed so that their hopes, fears, desires, history, and purpose can be better understood. This dialogue may take place after there has been some exploration of the patient's core beliefs and maladaptive schemas or it may take place in the absence of that work, as clinically appropriate.

In terms of the questions that a clinician might want to ask, an interview structure was provided earlier in table 6.1. These are suggested questions and clinicians should feel free to follow any interesting or compelling themes that may emerge as they explore these issues with the patient.

At a foundational level, as we have seen, most inner critics are motivated by fear. That is, they are criticizing or attacking the patient because they are concerned that something bad will happen if they do not do so. The problem is that they go too far and cause damage, even if their intent is good. On the other hand, some critics hate the patient, torment him or her, and, on occasion, are actually seeking the patient's demise. Lastly, some critics are a blend of these two types.

In this paradigm, the patient will sit in a new chair and will embody the inner critic and speak from his or her perspective. The Therapist, in turn, will sit in the chair opposite and will conduct the interview. The intent of the encounter is diagnostic and the general stance is one of curiosity and inter-est. For the sake of flow, I have made the patient male and I have named him Chad.

Inner Critic Interview

Therapist: I know that you have made reference to a part of you that is quite critical of yourself.

Patient: Yes, that is definitely true.

Therapist: If I may, I would like to do some work on that issue today.

Patient: Sounds good.

Therapist: I would like us to move over here *(pointing to the chairs facing each other)*, and I would like you to *be* the critic and I would like to interview you so that I can get a better understanding of what is going on with him.

Patient: Hmmm . . . okay.

Therapist: Let's switch. *(They both move to the new chair setup.) (See figure 6.1)* I would like you to take a moment and see if you can get in touch with the inner critic. You can close your eyes if you want to. In whatever way that makes sense, please try to call up that part.

Patient: (Pauses) Okay, I've got it.

Therapist: Hi! To make introductions, I am Chad's Therapist. Who are you?

Patient: I am the inner critic.

Therapist: I would like to ask you some questions so that I can get a better understanding of your role in Chad's life. Is that okay?

Patient: Yes.

Therapist: Do you have a name?

Patient: No.

Therapist: What do you look like?

Patient: (Pause) I am dark. I am not that clear, but I am a kind of a dark force inside Chad.

Therapist: When did you first come into Chad's life?

Patient: I was probably there all along but I started to become factor when he was about ten or eleven.

Therapist: Where did you come from?

Patient: A lot of me is his father; his mother, a little bit; some parts are from school and church, and with some parts, it is just unclear.

Therapist: What is your basic reason for being here?

Patient: I want to keep him in line. I want him to do better. Sometimes I think that I don't like him and that I just want to cause him some pain.

Therapist: What kind of situations bring you out?

Patient: When he is working on a project, I will tell him it is not good enough; when he is being relaxed and playful, I will criticize him harshly for being inappropriate; and when he fails at something, I really go after him. I also relentlessly attack him for his past mistakes, errors, and failures. I usually do this when something comes up and reminds us of one of them. I also keep him up at night and give him insomnia.

Therapist: What do you want?

Patient: That's a good question; I am not so sure. I want different things at different times. I usually just want him to do the right things and not make mistakes.

Therapist: Do you know what the right thing is?

Patient: Sometimes I do, sometimes I don't, but I just want him to get it right.

Therapist: Anything else?

Patient: I want him to do really well and make no mistakes, and I want him to behave properly . . . that's the Mother part. I don't want him to do anything that will cause us any embarrassment.

Therapist: How do you do that?

Patient: I zap him with pain any time he says anything wrong in public. I hurt him so it won't happen again.

Therapist: Anything else? Anything about not liking him?

Patient: Yes. I do take some pleasure in torturing him. Part of me does not like him at all.

Therapist: Is there anything that you need?

Patient: As I am saying these words, I am realizing how important safety is to me.

Therapist: What are your goals for Chad?

Patient: Well . . . I have certain rules—be the best, don't stand out, don't make mistakes, do not do anything stupid or embarrassing, control yourself, everyone must like you, be humble, be successful, money is bad—and I go into action when I sense that something is triggering or threatening a rule.

Therapist: But in terms of specific plans?

Patient: No. I'm not that connected to the world.

Therapist: How would you say that you are helping him?

Patient: I let him know when I think he has gone in the wrong direction.

Therapist: How have you helped him?

Patient: I don't know that I have.

Therapist: What would he say?

Patient: I think he would say that I make him nervous and that I have caused him some serious problems with performance. I think that he would also blame me for the times he has hurt himself. I know that when I have really been on him that he has punched things. He got stitches once. I also know that, on a couple of occasions, he turned my attacks into lower back pain and then he was out of it for a few days.

Therapist: Do you think there is any truth to what he is saying?

Patient: (Pause) I guess so. *(Pause)* I am not sure that I care.

Therapist: How are you harming him?

Patient: I am trying to get him to do the right thing. I don't want to see myself as harming him.

Therapist: It sounds like he feels that some of the things that you do are really disrupting his life.

Patient: Yes. You did say that. I probably push him too far, probably push him to hard. I want it to be right.

Therapist: You seem a bit uptight about that?

Patient: Yes. If he doesn't do it right, bad things will happen.

Therapist: I know that you are a part of him. But in some way, were you traumatized? Did you go through experiences of fear and pain?

Patient: Yes. I feel like I went through some difficult times, I feel like bad things happened to me, even if I cannot specifically say what they were. I just have an internal sense of being terrified . . . and of not wanting that to happen again.

Therapist: And you want to keep him safe?

Patient: Yes, I do.

Therapist: Changing direction for a minute. What do you like about Chad?

Patient: I don't have to like him. I just want things to be right.

Therapist: What makes you sad about Chad?

Patient: I get so frustrated that he won't get it right the first time. I am so upset . . . and I worry. I worry that bad things will happen to him.

Therapist: Actually, it sounds like you do care about him a little.

Patient: Maybe.

Therapist: What would happen if you were not here?

Patient: It would be a disaster. Everything would fall apart. He can't survive without me.

Therapist: Thank you for being willing to talk with me. I think I understand you better than I did before.

Okay. Let's go back to our original seats. *(The Therapist and the Patient go back to their original positions.)* I wanted to get a sense of what you experienced being the critic.

Patient: (Sitting in original seat) While he started out being hostile, I really began to get a sense of how frightened he was.

Therapist: Yes. That definitely struck me as well. He seemed so distressed.

Patient: Yes. It was funny. He has caused me so much pain but I began to feel a little bit sorry for him by the end.

Therapist: It's interesting that you say that, I was having the same experience. . . . So what we have here is a very frightened part trying to run your life. I want us to work on switching that so that your healthy self, your inner leader is in charge. I want you to do things because they fit your values, goals, and desires, not because you are responding to inner trauma and fear. In some cases, you may choose the same things as the critic, but I want you to choose them and not be on automatic pilot. That is my thought on how we should proceed. What are your thoughts?

Patient: It sounds good. It feels difficult, but it sounds good.

Therapist: Yes. It will be a process.

Reflections

In this dialogue, two aspects of the critic emerged. At the beginning, it was a bit mean and judgmental but, over time, the central role of fear began to emerge. This was a diagnostic interview in that the goal was to learn more about the critic. As was discussed earlier, one of the fundamental goals of the work is to help empower Chad to live from his healthy adult mode, not his critic. The goal would be for him to work with a therapist to clarify and consciously engage with the critic's values so that he will be able to not only choose and embrace those that he wants in ways that are meaningful, but also replace those that do not serve him.

Inner Critic Challenge/Self-Complexity Dialogue

The dialogue presented here involves a patient named Eamon who has been somewhat successful; nonetheless, he is, however, still being subject to Inner

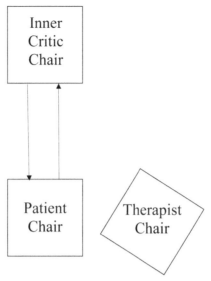

Figure 6.2   Inner Critic Dialogue

critic attacks. The dialogue structure will include strategies from emotion-focused therapy, cognitive therapy, and schema therapy; it will conclude with some inner complexity work (Chadwick, 2003).

Inner Critic Dialogue

Patient: As I've told you, I'm always having these terrible thoughts; thoughts that keep telling me how bad and worthless I am. It's like someone's always yelling at me, always criticizing me.

Therapist: That kind of voice is sometimes known as the inner critic or as a schema voice. A lot of people who are going through emotional pain have that kind of thing going on inside their head—telling them that they are no good, telling them to be afraid.

One way that we can work with it and try to combat it, if you're willing, is to have a dialogue with it. We can put it in that chair over there and challenge it.

Patient: Sounds good.

Therapist: The first thing that I would like you to do is to sit over there and be the critic. I would like you to imagine that Eamon is in the chair opposite chair and say out loud the kinds of things that it is saying inside your head. I would like you to do it with energy and strength, if possible. *(The Patient goes to other chair while the Therapist sits next to the Patient chair.) (See figure 6.2).*

Patient as the Inner Critic/Schema Voice: When I look at you I think: What a loser! How pathetic! What have you done with your life? You're a complete failure. You know that's true.

For example, take your career, if you can call it that. You're totally stalled out, going nowhere. Nobody takes you seriously. You've been stuck there for years, and everybody thinks that you're just a fool.

Look at your friends; they have all left you in the dust. They all have good jobs and are making a lot of money. Remember John. He was stoned all the way through college and he's doing much better that you are. Even Suzie, as wild as she was, is really excelling, doing great in sales. You don't even like to see them anymore because it makes you feel uncomfortable when they talk about their lives or, even worse, ask you about yours.

It's hardly surprising, really. You're just not very smart, not very clever, and not very fast. The world is going to pass you by while you're bumbling around in the back room.

Your personal life is a joke. Who would ever want to be with you? Ugly and awkward, it would be an embarrassment to be seen with you walking down the street. There are so many better-looking men/women, why would anyone choose you?

I know that you keep saying that you are going to change things. I know that you are thinking about graduate school and going after that promotion, but why bother? You would never be able to finish it and you're not capable of taking on more responsibility. It would be best if you just laid low, played it safe, and accepted the fact that you are a failure. *(Pause)*

Therapist: Now I would like you to sit in this chair. I would like you to respond by speaking about how much emotional pain this part has caused you, how much suffering and how many opportunities you have lost because of it.

Patient: (Pause) I'm so tired of having you in my head. You torment me. You make me depressed, at times you make me desperate. I would do anything to shut you down. Everywhere I go, there you are, making me nervous and uncomfortable. Throughout high school and college you tortured me. You sap my strength; you make me nervous at work. I hate the way I feel when you're in my head. You make me feel ugly, stupid, awkward, foolish. You never shut up, you never shut up. I hate you. I resent the fact that I have to spend my life worrying about you. There are so many other things that I would rather be doing with it. You slow me down. I feel heavy when you are around, I feel tired, I feel exhausted.

Everything is painful, everything's a burden. You make my life feel useless. I don't like that. I don't like that and I want my life to be different. I want my life to be better.

Therapist: Please switch back. *(Patient moves to the other chair.)*

Patient as Inner Critic/Schema Voices: As I said before, I think you are a failure. No one respects you and you are going nowhere in your job. Your friends are way ahead of you. You're kind of hopeless; that is why the girls don't like you.

Therapist: How are you feeling toward Eamon as you see him over there?

Patient as Inner Critic/Schema Voices: I really don't like you. You are a disappointment to me.

Therapist: Now switch seats and come back over here. *(The patient switches seats.)* How do you feel about what the critic just said?

Patient as the Patient: Hmmm. This time I am feeling angry.

Therapist: Speak to the critic about that.

Patient: You know, I don't like it when you speak to me that way. It's hurtful and it's exaggerated . . . and it's also not completely true. As I said before, I don't like the way you talk to me. I don't like the way you make me feel, and I don't like how you have hurt my life and made me unhappy.

Therapist: I know that living with this inside your head is terrible. Nonetheless, you have managed to put together a life and you've accomplished some things. I want you to lay these things out and challenge what the schema voice is saying.

Patient: You say all of these terrible things about me, but they're just not true. I know that I could have done more with my life if I did not have you in my head, yelling at me all of the time.

Therapist: Say that again.

Patient: I could have done more with my life if I didn't have you yelling at me all the time.

Therapist: Repeat that—I could've done more if you hadn't been yelling at me.

Patient: I could've done more if you hadn't been yelling at me.

Therapist: I think the critic is exaggerating. I would like you to speak about some of the good things you've done, the things that contradict what he/she is saying.

Patient: Okay. *(Pause)* I graduated from high school and college, and while I did not do great at everything, I did get some "A's." There were classes that I did really well in. I remember that Professor Erickson saying that I really had potential in Chemistry.

You keep telling me that I'm a loser at work. That's not true. I had a great job after college. You know that I was doing well. I was involved in several major projects and I got a promotion and several raises. It was unfortunate that the company got bought out and our division was closed. You mock me, but it wasn't my fault. I was doing well there.

I've been at this company for a few years. I came because there were some good possibilities. My reviews have all been positive and I played an important role in the Chesham Initiative. Because of the restructuring, things have changed and I don't see the same long-term opportunities that I did when I first got there. That's not just true for me; it's true for all of us.

I'm trying to get out of there. I disagree; my co-workers don't treat me like I'm a joke. They like me and respect me. You make me feel so badly with all of your lies, but when I can turn you off, I know that the things that you say are not true.

Therapist: I know they're just not true.

Patient: Yes.

Therapist: Say it. I know they are just not true.

Patient: I know they are just not true. Okay, you are right, some of my friends are doing better than I am. Some of them knew what they wanted to do from the outset, and that helps a great deal. But with you always yelling at me, it's been very hard to try and have the courage to really explore things, but I have tried. I'm hoping to move closer to that now. I'm not stupid and talentless; I have the potential to do something interesting and worthwhile in this life.

You keep telling me that no woman would ever want me. That's also not true. You know that I went out with Alastrina for four years. We had some great times and there was a lot of closeness between the two of us. I'm not saying that I'm Brad Pitt, but she liked the way I looked. We had a lot of good moments until things went bad at the end. While it is true that we were not quite right for the long haul, it's a lie when you say that no one could ever be attracted to me. In fact, you know that at work, Emily and I have been flirting for a long time. I don't want to pursue things while I'm still working there, but I could try to do something when I get a new job.

You make fun of my graduate school dreams. Why can't I be successful? I may not have been an outstanding student, but I did have some good classes. I'm older now, anyway; I think that I would appreciate it more and be able to approach it with much more seriousness. You are so demoralizing—why don't you leave me alone and let me live my life in peace.

Therapist: Try this. This is my life and not yours.

Patient: Yes. This is my life and not yours.

Therapist: Again. This is my life and not yours.

Patient: This is my life and not yours.

Therapist: This is my life. I do not work for you. I make the decisions.

Patient: This is my life. I don't work for you. I make the decisions.

Therapist: There is one more way that I would like to work this. *(The Therapist moves the chairs so that they are next to each other, facing the Therapist's chair.) (See figure 6.3).* I would like you to stand behind this chair *(pointing to the one on the left). (Eamon moves behind the chair on the left.)* Now I would like you to say these words. *(Pause)* I am a failure and I am a loser.

Patient: I am a failure and I am a loser.

Therapist: My career is stalled and I am not very smart.

Patient: My career is stalled and I am not very smart.

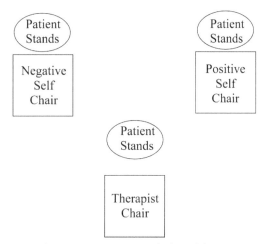

Figure 6.3   Inner Complexity Dialogue

Therapist: I am awkward and women don't like me.

Patient: I am awkward and women don't like me.

Therapist: Let's do it again. I'm a failure and a loser, my career is stalled and I'm not very smart. I'm awkward and women don't like me.

Patient: I'm a failure, a loser, not smart and women don't like me.

Therapist: Now move to the chair on the right. *(Eamon moves to his left.)* Now I want you to say I have accomplished things.

Patient: I have accomplished things.

Therapist: Again, I *have* accomplished things.

Patient: I *have* accomplished things.

Therapist: I have accomplished things in the face of obstacles.

Patient: I have accomplished things in the face of obstacles.

Therapist: I have accomplished things in the face of obstacles both internal and external.

Patient: I have accomplished things in the face of obstacles, both internal and external.

Therapist: I have accomplished things. I did well in some classes and I am in the fight at my job.

Patient: (Warming up to the process) I have accomplished things. I did well in some of my classes and I am working hard on my career.

Therapist: There are women who like me.

Patient: Yes, there are women who like me.

Therapist: Again.

Patient: There are women who like me.

Therapist: I have accomplished things. I am in the fight at work and some women like me.

Patient: I *have* accomplished things. I am fighting for my career and some women like me.

Therapist: Move back to the other chair. *(Eamon moves to his right and stands behind the chair on the left.)* Now say this . . . I am a loser, a failure, not smart, and women do not like me.

Patient: I am a loser, a failure, not smart, and women don't like me.

Therapist: Again.

Patient: I'm a loser, a failure, not very smart, and women don't like me.

Therapist: Again. Louder.

Patient: I'm a loser, a failure, I am not smart and women don't like me.

Therapist: Switch back. *(Eamon goes to his left and stands behind the chair on the right side).* I'm a fighter, I have accomplished things, and I like women and they like me.

Patient: (Laughing) I'm a fighter. I have accomplished some things and I do like women and some of them like me.

Therapist: Again.

Patient: I'm a fighter, I've done things, and I like women and they like me.

Therapist: Again.

Patient: I'm a fighter, I've done things, and I like women and they like me.

Therapist: Again, louder.

Patient: I'm a fighter, I've done things, and some women like me.

Therapist: Again, loudly and slowly.

Patient: (More slowly) I'm a fighter. *(Pause)* I've done things. *(Pause)* I like women and some of them like me.

Therapist: Go back to the other side. *(Eamon moves to his right.)* Now speak from that side.

Patient: I'm a loser and a failure. I'm . . . *(pause)* what am I supposed to say?

Therapist: (Silence)

Patient: I can't remember. I'm a failure and . . . women don't like me. That's not really true.

Therapist: Go back to the other side. *(Eamon moves to his left.)* Speak from this side.

Patient: I'm a fighter. I've accomplished things and I like women and some of them like me.

Therapist: One more time.

Patient: I like women. Some of them like me. I've accomplished things and I'm a fighter.

Therapist: I would like you to come over here and face the two chairs. *(Eamon comes around and faces the two chairs.)* I would like you to take a moment and look at the two parts of yourself. I would like you to sense the energy in the two chairs.

Patient: (Eamon stands in silence before the two chairs, taking in the experience.)

Therapist: As you stand there, I would like to get a sense of the balance between the two forces. Fifty-fifty? Sixty Forty? Ninety-Ten?

Patient: Seventy-thirty for the positive chair, the chair on the right.

Therapist: What was it when began?

Patient: It was about seventy-thirty the other way.

Therapist: Really! That is quite a shift.

Patient: Yes. I really felt the energy shift during that last dialogue.

Therapist: I noticed that you were having trouble speaking from the other chair.

Patient: Yes. That was when it began to happen.

Therapist: Okay. Why don't we sit down and debrief. *(Both the Therapist and Patient return to their original seats.) (Pause)* What are you feeling as you sit there?

Patient: I am feeling kind of energized and exhausted.

Therapist: Yes. You seemed to get stronger as you went on . . . and a bit angrier.

Patient: Yes. I do feel angry.

Therapist: That's good. How does the critic seem to you right now?

Patient: You know, he seems a bit weaker. It was good to stand up to him. That was the first time that I ever did that. That work at the end was particularly powerful. It was something to say those negative things about myself in that way and then say the positive ones. I've never done things like.

Therapist: The inner critics usually do not want to give up that easy, but that was a very good start. You did a good job. We'll will keep coming back to this.

Patient: Good.

Reflections

As noted earlier, this dialogue drew on the insights and practices of emotion-focused therapy (Greenberg et al., 1993; Watson et al., 2007), cognitive therapy (Leahy & Holland, 2000), and inner complexity (Chadwick, 2003). In the beginning, the patient responded by expressing his or her pain and emotions. In the second part, the patient repudiated the validity of what the critic was saying, and in the third, he counterbalanced the long-standing negative self-concept with a positive and empowered alternative. At the end, he was beginning to claim more authority over his life. This is the beginning of the shift from the superego to the ego or from the parent to the adult, to use the language of transactional analysis. As inner critic voices are usually quite resistant to change, it will be likely take a number of sessions and practice inbetween for the balance of power to begin to change.

SELF-COMPASSION AND SELF-KINDNESS DIALOGUES

In recent years, there has been a rise in compassion-focused therapies (Barnard & Curry, 2011). In many ways, this had been an outgrowth of the mindfulness movement in psychotherapy. Gilbert (2010) and Tirch (2012) have been major advocates of this work. Neff (2011), working with a slightly different emphasis, has focused on the healing and life-promoting value of self-compassion and self-kindness. She has also done research that supports the value of this kind of self-talk over self-criticism or attack.

All of these authors have included various therapeutic exercises in their books. There were visualization exercises in which: (1) the patient is compassionate to someone else; and (2) the patient develops an inner image—be it a person, a spiritual figure, or a force—that is compassionate to themselves. They also included Chairwork exercises in which the patient imagined him- or herself in the chair opposite and speaks to the self from a place of compassion. I think that this is a very powerful practice and one that should be cultivated daily. In a sense, it is a way of creating an internal friend or a mode of self-kindness, self-compassion, and self-affirmation.

The problem, at least in my clinical practice, is that most patients find this to be a very difficult dialogue to initiate and to sustain. One could argue that if they could treat themselves with kindness and compassion then most of their therapeutic work would be done. What I have found to be useful and effective is to begin the process one step earlier, which means that I will provide them with the words of self-compassion and self-kindness. In this way, they will not only hear the therapist say them (which is a form of reparenting), but also they will repeat and elaborate on them, which both provides an immediate experience of self-kindness and facilitates mode development.

In this dialogue structure, the patient will sit in one chair where they will embody the voice of kindness and compassion while imagining themselves in the chair opposite. The difference, however, is that it is the therapist, sitting next to the compassion chair, who will say empathic, humanizing, and affirming things that the patient will repeat. While the dialogue should be adapted to the specific needs and situation of the patient, there are a number of core components that can be used to build the dialogue:

1. Acknowledging that you see them in the chair opposite and letting them know that it gives you pleasure to be there with them;
2. Expressing love, admiration, respect, and care for the self in the chair;
3. Affirming that you know that they have been struggling and fighting and that they have not given up;
4. Sharing your understanding that they have been suffering or going through a difficult experience for a long time and that you feel pain when you think about what they have been through;
5. Addressing the fact that they have made mistakes and that they feel regret about them;
6. Telling them that it hurts you to see them blame themselves the way that they do;
7. Acknowledging that all humans make mistakes and that all humans feel regret;
8. Affirming that you know that they are a good person who is more than his or her mistakes and failures, and that you can see this clearly even if they cannot;
9. Seeing and acknowledging their accomplishments and their potential for future greatness;
10. Telling them that you will be with them every step of the way and that they should listen for your voice; and
11. Claiming the future, one step at a time.

This can be a powerful and difficult exercise for patients. Saying kind things to themselves may trigger "objections" based on inner rules that are being violated. It is, nonetheless, helpful because it gives them an experience of what self-kindness sounds and feels like. For the sake of flow, I have made this a female patient named Ashley.

Self-Kindness Dialogue

> *Therapist:* I know that we were talking about the inner critic last week and I wanted to return to that issue and do some work with it. Would that be okay?

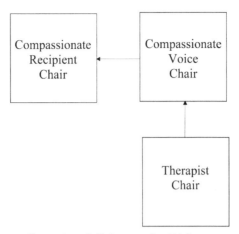

Figure 6.4   Self-Compassion Dialogue

Patient: Yes, that's fine.

Therapist: I would like to do a dialogue where you are kind to yourself, where you are a friend to yourself. May I do this?

Patient: Yes. I am not a friend to myself; I am brutal to myself. But okay.

Therapist: I would like you to sit in this chair and face that one over there. *(They set up the chairs. The Therapist is sitting on the side of the Patient.) (See figure 6.3)*

   I would like you to imagine yourself in the chair over there. I would like you to see yourself or at least sense some kind of presence over there.

Patient: (Pauses) I can sort of sense myself over there.

Therapist: I am going to ask you to say some things to yourself. I want you to say them even if they feel a bit uncomfortable. You are speaking as a friend, as a compassionate force.

Patient: Okay.

Therapist: Ashley, I see you there. I am glad to be here with you. The first thing that I want you to know is that I love you deeply. *(Pause)* Your turn.

Patient: Wow, that is a tough one.

Therapist: I know. I would like you to say it anyway.

Patient: I am sitting here and I see you. I see you over there. I am happy to be here with you and I wanted you to know that, hmmm, I love you.

Therapist: Let's do that again. I am sitting here and I see you. I am happy to be here with you and I want you to know that I love you.

Patient: I see you over there. I am happy to be with you . . . and I love you.

Therapist: Good. *(Pause)* I also wanted to say that I know that you have been going through some difficult times, that you have been wrestling with things at work and with things inside yourself.

Patient: I wanted to tell you . . .

Therapist: Use her name.

Patient: Ashley, I wanted to tell you that I certainly realize that things have been hard lately, things have been very hard lately. Things at work have not been working out and that you have been really frustrated and down.

Therapist: I want you to know that I know that. I get it. I understand that you have been going through difficult times.

Patient: Okay. I want you to know that *I know* what you have been going through. That I know that things have been difficult.

Therapist: I want you to know how much I admire you for staying in the fight, for not giving up despite how difficult it has been.

Patient: I know that the depression has really gotten you down. I know that are days when you have been immobilized by it, but you are also a fighter. You keep fighting back . . . you keep fighting back and I admire you for that.

Therapist: Say it again. I am not sure that she heard you. I know that it has been really tough, but you have stayed in the struggle and I admire that enormously.

Patient: I definitely know that it has been very hard for you but you have kept it together. You've kept it together when it was hard to do that and I really admire you . . . I really respect and admire you for doing that.

Therapist: I also know that you feel that you have made mistakes. I know that you feel deep regret about them and I know that you beat yourself up about them. There are some things that I want you to know. The first is that all people make mistakes, all people fail, all people have regrets. This the nature of being human. *(Pauses)* You say that.

Patient: I know that you are troubled by the mistakes that you feel you have made. I know that they weigh on you heavily and that you beat yourself up because of them. *I certainly do that.*

Therapist: Speak to her about how that is a part of the human experience.

Patient: It is important for you to know that everyone makes mistakes, that everyone fails sometimes, that everyone has remorse. You are not alone.

Therapist: Say it again, you are not alone.

Patient: You are not alone. You are not alone at all. You are just like the rest of us.

Therapist: Everyone makes mistakes.

Patient: Everyone makes mistakes.

Therapist: I also want you to know that when you beat yourself up, I feel deep pain and deep distress. I hate to see you suffer like that. I hate to see you mistreat yourself. . . . Your turn.

Patient: Wow. . . . When I see you torment yourself over mistakes and failures, I feel bad. . . . I feel real bad. It upsets me to see you mistreat yourself that way. Don't do it anymore.

Therapist: Good. Again.

Patient: Don't hurt yourself like that anymore. We all make mistakes.

Therapist: When I look at you, I do not see the mistakes. I see you as a good woman. I see you as someone who wants to do the right thing, as someone who wants to be a good person. It gives me pleasure to see you. I feel happy when I look at you, when I see who you really are. *(Pauses)*

Patient: I don't see you as bad. I don't see you as bad at all. When I look at you I feel happy. I know that you are a good woman. I know that you are seeking to do good things. To love your friends and family, to do great things with your work and with your talents. I know you want your life to matter.

Therapist: Good. Don't listen to those critical voices in your head; *listen to me.*

Patient: Please don't listen to those voices in your head that make you feel bad and put you down; listen to me. I see you as good. Listen to me instead.

Therapist: I see that you have the potential to be great.

Patient: I see that you have the potential to be great.

Therapist: You are much more than your fears and regrets.

Patient: You are much more than your fears and regrets.

Therapist: I see your potential to do great things and to be a great woman. I see it even if you cannot see it yet.

Patient: I know that you can be great and that you can do important things. I know this is true even if you cannot believe it yet.

Therapist: I want you to know that I am here and that I will be with you each step along the way.

Patient: I will be with you all the way. You are not alone.

Therapist: In the days ahead, you will hear many voices in your head. I want you to listen for my voice. I will be speaking to you. I will be letting you know that I respect and cherish you . . . that I understand that things get tough and that all people struggle. I am on your side. Remember that.

Patient: Yes. I am on your side. In the next few days, I want you to be on the lookout for me. I will be speaking to you. I will be encouraging you, giving you support. I want you to listen to me and not to those crazy voices inside your head.

Therapist: (Pause) Now I would like you to switch chairs. I would like you to sit there quietly and see if you can take in what the compassionate voice just said to you.

Patient: (The Patient switches chairs and sits in silence.)

Therapist: (Slowly) Whatever you are open to taking in is fine. Whatever you are not open to taking in is fine also. Just let the compassion and the kindness enter your being.

Patient: (The Patient continues to sit in silence.)

Therapist: (Pauses) Can you take in what she was saying? Can you take in the compassion, the warmth, the kindness?

Patient: (Pause) I am taking it in somewhat. There is some resistance to letting it in but some of it is getting in.

Therapist: The places where it is getting. . . . What does that feel like?

Patient: It feels warm, relaxed. It feels good.

Therapist: Good. *(Pause)* Now let's go back to our original seats.

(The Patient and Therapist return to their original seating arrangement.)

Therapist: So . . . how did it feel to say and hear those things?

Patient: It was amazing. At first it was very difficult. All these other voices in my head were getting triggered. They wanted to jump in and say that you were wrong. As I got into it more, it got more comfortable with it.

Therapist: This is a good first step. As we continue to work with self-compassion, I expect that this will grow considerably.

Reflections

The practice of self-kindness and self-compassion can be profoundly transformative (Neff, 2011). Ultimately, it will be beneficial if the patient can make the activation of a self-kindness mode a part of their daily life. To begin, though, I think it best if the therapist return to this kind of dialogue work repeatedly. Focusing on this in session (1) gives the patient permission to care for themselves; (2) provides them with both a structure for doing this and a language of compassion; and (3) as noted above, this is a kind of re-parenting (Rafaeli et al., 2010; Young et al., 2003).

Chapter 7

Inner Dialogues

Polarity Work

The third round of internal dialogues is rooted in the work of Fritz Perls during the 1960s, first at the Esalen Institute in California and then at his Lake Cowichan "Kibbutz" in British Columbia (Baumgartner, 1975; Perls, 1969b, 1975a, 1992). This final version of his therapy placed a primary emphasis on the concepts of awareness, multiplicity of self, polarities, dialectics, and centering.

At the heart of his conceptualization of the self, Perls saw the individual as being made up of a range of forces or parts. These parts often existed as polarities and many of the internal and external difficulties that patients wrestled with were seen as resulting from a lack of integration of these distinct aspects of the personality. As Clarkson and Mackewn (1993) wrote:

> [Perls] believed that we all have the capacity to embody any human characteristic, but that often we disown potential characteristics because they are unacceptable to us, perhaps because family members, teachers, or friends have forbidden and ridiculed them. (p. 104)
>
> Perls believed that polarities are dialectical: they form two ends or poles of one continuum, . . . Opposite characteristics are not contradictory. They form two sides of the same coin and are complementary. (p. 105)

Zinker (1977) compared the human personality or self-concept to the light and dark side of the moon. "Intrapersonal conflict involves clashes between one's dark and light polarities" (p. 200). "And the more he learns about the mysterious parts of himself, the healthier he becomes" (p. 201).

Echoing work by Jung (M. Polster, 1987), Perls believed that all that human beings need is already within them. Again, in a view that was similar to Rogers (1986), he believed that throughout life people receive messages that some parts of themselves were acceptable and others are not. For example, they may have received messages that they "should" be strong but not gentle, creative but not wealthy, success-oriented but not spiritual, or self-sacrificing but not self-affirming. These disowned parts of the self are then repressed and often projected out into the world.

Parts of the self may also be lost as a result of traumatic experiences, whether accidental or purposeful. The cumulative result is that these specific parts or energies become tinged with anxiety. They are experienced as frightening and disturbing and are avoided or perhaps even attacked when encountered. "Because of the phobic attitude, the avoidance of awareness, much material that is our own, that is part of ourselves, has been dissociated, alienated, disowned, thrown out. The rest of our potential is . . . available but as projection" (Perls, 1992, p. 87). In Jungian terms, this would be understood as the Shadow (Douglas, 2005). These processes of denial, disowning, and repression may not, ultimately, work.

> Ignoring or disowning parts of the self results in a hidden inner conflict or stalemate in which the aware or dominant part struggles with the denied or background part. Energy is tied up in keeping the denied polarity out of awareness but it is wasted energy for the disowned characteristic will pop up in unexpected ways and sabotage the apparently victorious part of the personality. (Clarkson & MacKewn, 1993, pp. 104–105)

In any case, anxiety, depression, and other problems may occur as these alienated parts seek expression. The path to healing, then, involves the re-owning of the projected parts, the reclaiming of both ends of the polarity or both sides of the coin. "The purpose of psychotherapy is to restore lost parts of the self" (Baumgartner, 1975, p. 10). Perls called this work "centering."

In many ways, Perls' work with the inner life of the individual eventually developed into a system built on two core processes: (1) working with splits; and (2) the paradoxical theory of change (Beisser, 1970). The centrality of the split or work with polarities was emphasized by Baumgardner (1975) who wrote that: "Without the split, including the energized as well as the immobilized side, we have no behavior to work with" (p. 60).

Building on this, Perls hunted for polarities (Miller, 1989). Dreams and dreamwork, as will be discussed below, were a major vehicle for this, but there were others. "Polarities can represent the battleground between intellect and emotions, between competence and incompetence, between brightness and stupidity, between dependability and irresponsibility, and between maturity and immaturity" (Polster & Polster, 1973, p. 251). Perls was also very interested in working with the primary split between left and right. "The right-left split is a particularly important one. . . . The left represents perceiving and feeling; the right side action, force, coping" (Baumgardner, 1975, p. 71). Most famously, Perls returned again and again to the fundamental conflict between what he called "Top Dog" and "Bottom Dog." While I believe that his conceptualization was somewhat simplistic and clinically inaccurate, he was tapping into the battle between the "shoulds" and the "wants" that exist within the person.

By gaining access to the forbidden or disregarded energy, the patient will not only decrease their inner conflict, but will also have more resources available for coping with life. This process of accessing and freeing these suppressed energies may be marked by the release of strong emotions (Baumgardner, 1975; Perls et al., 1951). Connecting to the Reichian influences on their work, Perls and Goodman both felt that these processes of self-control involved the constriction of the breath and that the liberating of the inner parts could also have a musculo-skeletal component to it.

Naranjo (1993) similarly asserted that Perls eventually embraced two core strategies: going deeper and going to the polarity. "You never overcome anything by resisting it. You only can overcome anything by going deeper into it. . . . Whatever it is, if you go deeply enough into it, then it will disappear; it will be assimilated (p. 138)." The other strategy was to embrace the polarity, to give voice to the opposite.

A core vehicle for doing this can be found in Chairwork dialogues in which the patient gives voice to each of the polarities. In these encounters, it was important that there first be real contact between the two parts of the self so that the two parts would eventually be able to really listen to each other. Baumgardner (1975) delineated this when she wrote, "'Are you hearing what he says?' Once he understands experientially the possibility of playing one role and also hearing the other, the client begins to respond with real communication. . . . This is often a matter of asking him to repeat again more forcefully his newborn spontaneous assertions of himself" (p. 70). Strikingly, Latner (1973) identified the Hegelian nature of the work. There is thesis and antithesis, desire and fear, and action and restraint; the creative resolution of these tensions would be the synthesis. He built on this by pointing out "that the more powerful the polarities, the more significant the synthesis" (pp. 43–44). This synthesis will result in the creation of a self that is much stronger and much more capable of living and achieving in the world (Baumgardner, 1975). To be clear, there may be conflicts between and among parts that have not been disowned or repressed. Patients may also experience tensions among the various roles they inhabit because they may be manifestations of distinct values or polarities; again, dialogue can be the answer (Baumgardner, 1975).

The actual material for the dialogues can be elicited from both external and internal phenomena. For example, encounters can be created "between two symbolic parts of the body (left hand versus right hand) . . . between conflicting parts that have been expressed verbally ('I want to' versus 'I don't want to'), . . . between self and a part projected onto a current person, . . . and between self and part projected onto a parent or other historical figure" (Joines, 2004, pp.197–198). From Perls' perspective, all disturbing phenomena have the potential to reveal important polarities and provide the opportunity to integrate conflicts and gain resources. He provided hope when he said that if people do the centering work, if they engage in the process of reconciliation, their internal roles "no longer waste energy in useless struggle with each other, but can join in productive combination and interplay" (Perls, 1970, p. 19).

Zinker (1977) took this a step further when he wrote that the patient can then begin to develop an attitude of "friendliness with all the polarized forces within" (p. 15). This is a far cry from the fear that had previously colored the relationships with the polarity. He also noted that as a manifestation of this new inner synthesis, the patient may engage in new and creative behaviors.

For example,

> Erving Polster worked with a minister in the 1960s. The minister wanted to give a sermon on the conflict in Selma, Alabama; a place where the police had used dogs to attack Civil Rights marchers. While this was an issue that he felt quite disturbed by, he was afraid that his sermon would not be effective. Polster invited him to practice this in the session, and found that it was, in fact, lacking in passion and interest. Going to the opposite polarity, he asked the minister to stand up and tell the story of Selma as if he were one of the policemen. As he did this, he spoke with much more emotion and energy. His voice was louder, he used his fists, he told stories, and was generally more confident. Polster then asked him to give the sermon again, but this time he should say it in the manner of the policeman. This time the sermon was quite compelling and it resonated with Polster and, ultimately, with his congregation.
>
> As they explored the issue of forcefulness and aggression, it turned out that the minister had always looked up to the bullies in his school. He had admired their energy and confidence, even though they had attacked him and called him a sissy. The polarity that he had developed was that bullies were vital, but bad, while victims were moral and good, but lacked aggression. Through this work, he was able to claim his own vitality and strength while holding on to his moral center. The result was that he could become both forceful *and* righteous. (Polster & Polster, 1973; Kellogg, 2012, p. 204)

From a Gestalt perspective, people who we find to be troubling or disturbing are also likely to be repositories of our projections. Embodiment can be curative. "When one is playacting the people, things, or events they complain about, they have the possibility of an 'Aha!' experience, in which there is the recognition 'This is me!' This is what is referred to as owning the projections" (Shepard, 1975, p. 204).

This approach can also be used to work with phobias and fears. In a wonderful example, Adele Bry went to interview Perls about his work (Perls, 1972). Instead of answering her questions, he worked with some of her polarities; that is, rather than "talking about" his work, he involved her in it and made it experientially real for her. Among the issues that they explored was her fear of flying. A core dialogue polarity involved her being a passenger in one chair and the pilot in the other.

Working with the Group

While the main focus of this book has been the use of Chairwork in individual treatment, Perls became famous for using it in a workshop format. As he put it, "Basically I am doing a kind of individual therapy in a group setting . . . " (Perls, 1992, p. 93). In this model, the group provides a much higher level of emotional intensity as a baseline. Beyond that, the members can: (1) serve as witnesses to what is being shared and enacted; (2) be integrated into the treatment as a way of deepening the experience; and (3) be invited to express their own identifications with what has transpired as a way of not only normalizing the experience of the working patient, but also of universalizing the experience as well (Clarkson & Mackewn, 1993). Abraham Eliezur gave an account of transforming encounter he had with Perls that exemplifies this use of the group.

> I mentioned that at times I felt inferior. I didn't have the courage to participate in things, but that sometime I feel that I am above others. "Ok," he said, "Be above us. Stand up on the chair and talk to all of us." So I stood up on the chair and I made some bombastic talk to the audience. I smiled when I did it, but apparently it did something to me. It wasn't just a play. I felt that some hidden impulse, some hidden desire was getting its way. Then he told me, "Ok, now come down to earth." And I came down and he said, "Look around and say how you see everyone now?"
> I looked in the eyes of everyone and I saw them warm, understanding, accepting and it was very appealing to me. I felt the warmth coming to me from all the people in the audience. It was one of the greatest experiences of my life. (Gaines, 1979, p. 194)

There are a number of therapeutically creative things that Perls is doing here. First he chooses to give voice to a more hidden part of the patient, in this case, his grandiosity. He then gives a physical manifestation to this by having him be "above" everyone. He is also working with polarities in that the patient first connects to the group when standing on the chair and then he switches and makes contact with them on the same level. First he is further away and then he is closer. As can be seen at the end, this made a profound difference.

Dream Theory

At the end of his career, Perls was centrally focused on the use of dreams as a vehicle of healing (Perls, 1992). As discussed throughout, the ultimate goal was to make people more whole through helping them to resolve their conflicts and enabling them to access all parts of themselves so that they could better adapt and thrive in the world. He believed that every image in a dream—each person, object, animal, and force—represented a part of the patient's personality. The goal was to have the patient embody or give voice to each of these images so as to reclaim the power inherent in each of them (Perls, 1992). As Perls (1975a) said, "My dream technique consists of using all kinds of available material that is invested in the dream. I let the people play the different parts and, if they are capable of really entering the spirit of the part, they are assimilating their disowned material" (p. 137). Perls frequently sought to create dialogues among images that represented some sort of polarity, i.e., land and sea, male and female, and light and darkness, as he believed that this kind of work would eventually help him uncover an emotion-filled polarity.

Working this way would engage the patient in a healing process:

> I mean have a dialogue between the two opposing parts and you will find, especially if you get the correct opposites, that they always start out fighting each other. . . . As the process of encounter goes on, there is a mutual learning until we come to an understanding, and an appreciation of differences, until we come to a oneness and integration of the two opposing forces. Then the civil war is finished and your energies are ready for your struggles with the world. (Perls, 1992, pp. 89–90)

The first step in the dreamwork process was to ask the patient to relive the dream, to tell the dream in the first person slowly and in the present tense. This helped to signal where the emotionally-valent images might be. After that, he or she would then "become" the images and give voice to them (Baumgardner, 1975).

In an interesting variation, patients would sometimes report that they had woken up before the dream was finished. When this was the case, he would have them make up an ending to the dream and work with that as well (Baumgardner, 1975). Perls was particularly interested in disturbing images and nightmares as he believed that the more disturbing the image, the more that energy or part of the self was dissociated from the whole. He would argue that work with these profoundly alienated aspects of self could lead to the cessation of a chronic nightmare (Clarkson & Mackewn, 1993).

In an account from Gustaitis (1969), Perls integrated work on a current relationship with images from a dream:

Constance . . . was preoccupied by an unresolved conflict regarding her father. She hated him for the harm she felt he had done to her as a child. At the same time, she loved him. She was unable to separate the two emotions and express either of them and so could neither reject him nor forgive him. . . . Perls, starting with a dream, led her to polarize her love and rage. Once the strength of both emotions came fully into awareness, she burst into anger and then, suddenly free, found she wanted to forgive her father while he was still alive (p. 38).

Going back to the issue of the role of the group, Howard (1970) described a workshop where Perls powerfully used the group to heightened the impact of the work.

Another young man with a pasty face and a pasty, apologetic manner came forth to the "hot seat" to tell of a dream about a troll with crippled legs who was trapped in a dungeon where the sun never shone. He had in turn to "be" the troll, "be" his crippled legs, "be" the dungeon and "be" the door that barred him from the sun. In the course of enacting all these things he lay sobbing and writhing in the fetal position on the floor. Obviously his most central dilemmas, his impasse, had been reached. But he said to Perls, almost as if it were a question, "I'm not crippled; I'm not dead."

"Louder!" Perls demanded. "If you mean it, say it as if you did." The man said it louder and louder, but was still told his tone was unconvincing. Perls instructed him to go around the circle repeating the statement to each one of us. One by one he came up to us and said, in increasingly less hesitant tones.

"I'm not crippled! I'm not dead!"

"Of course not," most of us said a little patronizingly.

"Like hell you're not!" said a fierce encounter veteran named Ben. "Tell me so I'll believe you, or I won't!"

"I'm really not crippled! I'm really not dead!" said the man in tones that suddenly were really confident and believable. Several people got up and formed a ring-around-the rosy circle around him, chanting "he's not crippled; he's not dead." It was like the finale of an operetta. (p. 206)

In this example, we see Perls' creative and masterful use of the group to help this man gain access to his inner vitality in a visceral and profoundly meaningful way. However, not only did the group affect the individual in the "hot seat," but the individual work also deeply affected those in attendance. It was the witnessing and identification process that helped make Perls famous as so many were profoundly moved by what they had seen and experienced in his workshops:

One young man about my age told me of a dream in which had seen his aunt Evelyn die in a [restaurant]. He realized after "being" his aunt, "being" her lunch, "being" the restaurant, and being himself, that he did after all love his parents, from whom he had lately been estranged. He cried. So did many who watched, among them me. (Howard, 1970, p. 206)

In another case, Perls described the dream work he had done with a particularly troubled man.

> To illustrate the method of integrating top- and underdogs by working through a dream, I relate a case of a patient who impressed everybody with his psychotic eccentricities. During one of my group sessions he related a dream in which he saw a young man enter a library, throw books about, shout and scream. When the librarian, an elderly spinster, rebuked him, he reacted with continued erratic behavior. In desperation the librarian summoned the police.
>
> I directed my patient to act out and experience the encounter between the boy (underdog) and the librarian and police (topdogs). In the beginning the confrontation was uselessly consuming of time and energy. After participating in the hostile encounter for two hours, the different parts of my patient were able to stop fighting and listen to each other. True listening *is* understanding. He came to recognize that by playing "crazy" he could outwit his topdog, because the irresponsible person is not punished. Following this successful integration the patient no longer needed to act crazy in order to be spontaneous. As a result he is now a freer and more amenable person. (Perls, 1975b, pp. 6–7)

In an example of personal healing and reorganization, Anna Halprin told the following story, "We had worked on a dream of mine for years. . . . Every time he worked with me on this dream, I would discover a different room in the house I dreamt about. This time all the walls separating the rooms dissolved. He said, 'Where are you going?' And I said, 'I'm going out into the forest and I have to go alone.' He said, 'I know.'" (Gaines, 1979, pp. 392–393). Miller (1992), in an account that wonderfully demonstrates both Perls' compassion and his creativity, described his first encounter with gestalt therapy at a group session in San Francisco in 1966. The group was focusing on dreams. He wrote: "I . . . remember my surprise as I watched a vastly overweight mental health worker burst into sobs of deep grief within moments after Perls asked her to imagine that she were a beached whale" (p. 2). The whale was part of dream that she had just recounted. Extrapolating from what Perls might have done, it is likely that he had her sit in one chair and then speak from the perspective of the dying whale. Giving voice to the image, she might have said something like: "I am a whale. I am enormous. I am trapped. I am dying. No one can help me. It is hopeless. This is the end." After she spoke in this way, he observed that "with prompting from Perls, she seemed to melt before our eyes into a neglected child alone in her room, bitterly lamenting the emptiness of her existence" (p. 2). The dying whale is the metaphorical embodiment of her depression and all of the pain, shame, and isolation that can come with being obese.

It is likely that Perls then asked her to switch chairs and this time he asked her to speak as if she were the ocean, another image in the dream. It is possible that she said something like: "I am the ocean. I am the sea. I am filled with life. I am filled with mystery. I am filled with beauty. I am one of the most important forces on planet Earth." Clearly struck by what happened next, Miller wrote: "When Perls told her, as her tears dried, to become the sea in her dream, her huge shape seemed for a moment not just the visible burden of her self-hatred but an indication that she could be teeming with life" (p. 3). What is striking about this work is that Perls balanced the death image, which was her dominant self metaphor, with one of growth and future possibility. In terms of her ongoing healing and growth, it would make sense for her to take the metaphor of the sea to heart and work to manifest its positive attributes; these could include being beautiful, powerful, and filled with life. A question that she and her therapist could wrestle with is: How would she live her life if these things were true about her?

For the most part, this kind of polarity work is a lost art form. It might, however, be worth revisiting. In cognitive therapy, patients are frequently seen as having problematic beliefs, schemas, or thought patterns. Part of the therapeutic enterprise is co-creating an alternative, more adaptive belief that they will then work to integrate and internalize. Clearly this works with many patients. What Perls did was both different and compelling. He, essentially, addressed her depression by having her claim ownership of a symbol or metaphor that already existed within her. I believe that there is something to this mechanism that is definitely worth considering and embracing by the psychotherapy field at large.

Nightmares

As noted above, Perls was very interested in nightmares as he believed that they contained disavowed parts of the self that were particularly powerful. The integrative dialogue was certainly one way to work with these images (Clarkson & Mackewn, 1993). Another way to approach this, which builds on the work of Moreno, is to create a new ending to the disturbing dream or nightmare (Landy, 2007).

One of the symptoms of PTSD is chronic nightmares. A major intervention for this is Imagery Rescripting Therapy. Building on the tradition of Moreno and Perls, patients are asked to write down their nightmares and to change the ending in ways that are personally meaningful and empowering. This practice has been shown to improve both sleep quality and decrease nightmare frequency (Krakow et al., 2001).

Massé (1997) worked with a Vietnam Veteran who had a chronic nightmare. The dream began with him walking down a jungle path; a Vietcong soldier then stepped out from behind a tree to shoot him. At the time of the therapy, he had been plagued by this nightmare for over twenty years. In a very creative piece of work, she organized a three-chair dialogue with the American soldier (in one chair), the Vietcong soldier (in the chair opposite), and a tree (represented by a chair in the middle). The tree had been a part of the dream image. In this scenario, "he became a tree along the trail, and told both himself and the Vietcong soldier that the war was over and they both could go home now. Both agreed to put down their weapons and go home." (p. 206). In essence, the tree became a mediator and the two parts had an opportunity to make contact, dialogue, express what was important, and make peace. Strikingly, he no longer had the nightmare after he did this work.

Accessing Internal Resources

While Perls famously centered his polarity work in his therapy with dreams, he did this in other ways as well. For example, he believed in the benefits of *shuttling* or asking patients to travel back and forth between different states or images. Perls would often ask people to first be aware of what they were feeling, especially if they were not feeling good or alive. He would then ask them to close their eyes and imagine that they are in a desirable place where they would have that which they are currently missing. This could include places of support or comfort (Daniels, 2005; Perls, 1992).

Emotion and Imagery

Leveton (2001) reported that in her work with Perls, they would intertwine emotional states with imagery. He would guide her and say: "Visualize this mood. Close your eyes and see if you can go into your feeling. Give it a landscape. Give us pictorial details of the landscape your feeling calls up" (p. 91). He would then work with the various parts of the emergent image to find a polarity and create a dialogue.

For example, the first time she went to work with him, she became aware of her deep fear. He asked her to remain in contact with that fear and to visualize it as a landscape. As it came into view, she said: "I see an attic. Just a part of the attic with a brown wood floor. I can see the texture of the wide boards. It's dark and cold and at the very back of the attic, way back, there's a blue light."

He then asked her to give voice to the floor and the blue light. As she gave voice to the floor she said: "I'm brown, and old, very worn. I'm dark. I'm cold. I'm really alone. No one ever comes here. *(I start to cry, experiencing a desolate loneliness.)* There are no people here at all." He then asked her to switch chairs and be the blue light. Part of what she said was "I'm light. I'm cold, too. I'm very beautiful, an icy blue." From these two visual polarities, light and darkness, there is a hint that she may have some issues with connection. She is lonely but she also "freezes" people out. He then asked her to have a dialogue between the blue light and the floorboards. During this encounter, Leveton came to a deep realization about herself:

> Suddenly, I am flooded with the awareness that I have frozen others out of my life, coldly rejecting their warmth. The work put me in touch with my loneliness and also with the part of me that makes sure I stay that way. Perls has me say, "I can freeze you out" to several group members. I do it with conviction. My mood lightens. I tell Perls that I feel better. He asks me to shut my eyes again and to visualize my present mood.

She closes her eyes and has an image of being in a lake on a warm day. She is a little bit below the surface and she can feel some seaweed "lightly brushing up against me."

> *Perls:* Can you do that to some of the people in the group? Just lightly brush up against them?

> I do. I lightly touch one person's hand, another's face, another's shoulder. I feel relieved. There's also a part of me that can connect with others. I feel that I want to be warmer. Maybe I can leave some of that coldness with the past, when I needed the self-protection it offered. (Leveton, 2001, pp. 89–90)

In this moving and life-changing experience, Perls demonstrated a number of the techniques and strategies that we have been discussing. He has her create an image, he finds the polarities, and he asks her to give voice and to "be" each of the polarities. He then invites the polarities to dialogue which leads to her first insight about her complex feelings about connection. He does not challenge her for distancing people through her coldness; instead, he brings in the group and invites her to consciously do to them what she is instinctively doing to them already. The experience of "being what you are" shifts her emotional state. He then asked her to come up with another image that reflects her current emotional state. The image of the seaweed brushing up against her lightly becomes a wonderful tool in his hands. Using it as a metaphor for a new way of connecting, he then asked her to "lightly brush up against" members of the group. Doing this furthers the change process that has already begun within her.

Imagery and Emotion

The Polsters (1973) told the story of a patient who saw herself as a blue painting with red dots on it.

> The blue, to her, represented her basic mood in life: depressed, formless, serving mostly as background, unwilling to be obliterated but having no shape of its own. The red dots were her moments of happiness, clearly articulated, but small,

isolated and nowhere near covering enough territory. I asked Carla to begin a dialogue between the blue ground and the red dots of her painting. . . . Carla realized that being more specific would mean that she would have to be as clear about her sadness as she was about her happiness. This she usually resisted, settling for undifferentiated depression instead of clearly focused sadness. She called this being unwilling to complain, but it also kept her from making any specific changes in the unfulfilling parts of her life. The red dots listened, then, as the blue background told of the sadness of the limited relationship with a boyfriend and of her feelings of powerlessness at work. Once these unsatisfying parts of her life could be identified, Carla had taken the first step in making changes. (Polster & Polster, 1973, p. 249)

Similarly, a patient in the middle of a change process was considering redecorating her home. She had long favored light blue and white, which were colors connected to her childhood home; she was not considering reds and brown which reflected a more passionate side of herself. In her apartment, she did a dialogue between these two colors, exploring what they meant to her and how they would impact those who came to visit her home. She reported that this was a surprisingly profound experience for her.

The Impasse

Perls was also focused on what he called the impasse. This is a situation in which a patient is stuck because internal, opposing forces are in state of unhealthy balance, a condition in which "there is little activity but much tension" (Latner, 1973, p. 146). "As Freud said, 'if you have two servants quarreling, how much work can you expect to get done?'" (Perls et al., 1951 in Latner, 1973, p. 148). Since the impasse is a state of discomfort, most people try to avoid engaging with it. How is it broken or resolved? Here the patient can not only give voice to the different forces involved, but also to the feeling of the impasse itself. "The incredible thing which is so difficult to understand is that experience, awareness of the now, is sufficient to solve all difficulties of this nature, that is, neurotic difficulties. If you are fully aware of the impasse, the impasse will collapse, and you will find yourself suddenly through it" (Perls, 1970, p. 26). Combining this with Chairwork, polarities, and the paradoxical theory of change, Ruth Cohn (1970) observed:

> The skillful separation of conflicts into their duality and their subsequent reenactment leads, after a series of dialogues, to feelings of blankness, confusion, helplessness, etc. This experience is the *impasse*: the ultimate expression of two strivings pulling in opposite directions. The therapist's guiding words are: "be blank," "be confused," "be empty." When the patient can endure and experience the extent of his feelings of confusion, blankness, impotence, etc., organismic change takes place. (p. 137)

Again, the work will involve having the patient take responsibility for this experience. He or she is not the victim of conflicting forces, they are both parts of his or her self. This can involve giving voice to the idea that he is choosing to be immobilized and be stuck. Perls would often push patients to go deeply as possible into the impasse.

> He often suggested that the client describe in detail or enact the sensation of stuckness and exaggerate whatever physical sensations of tension she has. As the client amplifies how she locks her energy, turning it on herself, the implosion gets so great that eventually it cannot turn any further inwards, but all the energy must go somewhere, so it explodes outwards into the authentic layer. The client shakes in fear, laughs, sings, jumps for joy or just does something different. The impasse is resolved and the individual moves in a fresh and authentic direction. This "explosion" is often followed by important insights and a time of great creative energy and excitement. (Clarkson & Mackewn, 1993, p. 118)

Lieblich (1978), in turn writes: "By encouraging the person to let be and to allow himself to be stuck, including all the painful feelings involved, many people will discover new awareness and ways of being, and some of them may make the fundamental shift into self-reliance" (p. 15). In both cases, these therapists are invoking the paradoxical theory of change (Beisser, 1970). By being more deeply what one is, change ensues.

Alternatively, when the patient does begin to give voice to the impasse, to the experience of being blocked, another part may emerge that does not want to be stuck and from this, a dialogue can be created. Alternately, the patient could first be asked to express the feelings of stuckness and then close her eyes and have a fantasy of a place that she would like to be. A "shuttling" dialogue can then be created between the feeling of "stuckness" and the emotions and images connected to the desirable fantasy situation, and perhaps to feelings of freedom and movement (Baumgardner, 1975).

Awareness and Mindfulness

Another name for this experience of creativity out of conflict was the *fertile void* (Perls et al., 1951). This meant that if the patient were willing to experience or feel his or her block or their despair in a deep way, that a creative solution would emerge. "The fertile void is the existential metaphor for giving up the familiar supports of the present and trusting in the momentum of life to provide new opportunities and vistas" (Polster & Polster, 1973, pp. 120–121).

It is interesting to note that Perls' work can be seen as a forerunner to the contemporary movement to integrate mindfulness into psychotherapy

(Baer & Huss, 2008). He and other Gestalt therapists emphasized the central importance of engaging with "negative" or painful emotions. "This is part of the hard work of therapy, demanding of ourselves that we make contact with unwanted and unpleasant emotions" (Latner, 1973, p. 191). There are two things that help facilitate this. The first is that it takes place within the context of a supportive, therapeutic relationship. The second is the use of techniques. Awareness, describing the phenomena, is a way to engage with the pain, to be with it, and to develop a relationship with it. Chairwork and Chairwork combined with imagery can also be effective.

In a brilliant example of cognitive restructuring, Perls (1970) wrote: "The antidote is to become interested in your negative emotions" (p. 34). This transforms the experience from one to be feared into one to be curious about, using awareness as a method. The patient may find that through this work, new possibilities will emerge (Lieblich, 1978).

Polarity Work

Perl's dialogues always saddled the boundary between addressing psycho-pathology and promoting personal growth. As a part of the human potential movement, gestalt therapists and many of those involve with the Esalen Institute were trying to move therapy from a clinical intervention for the few to a societal movement centered on self-exploration and self-empowerment. As we have seen, polarity dialogues can grow out of the material of dreams and difficult situations. Here the patient can give voice to the various polarities with the assumption that a meaningful conflict will eventually emerge.

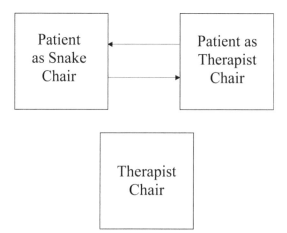

Figure 7.1 Dream/Polarity Dialogue

A DREAM DIALOGUE

This dialogue was developed from a dream that originally belonged to a psychotherapist who was treated by Freeman (1981). One of her issues was that she was overly passive. The dream dialogue revealed both a passive part, that she was familiar with, and a very aggressive part, that was disowned and projected.

Working with the Dream

Patient: I had a dream the other night that was quite disturbing.

Therapist: What happened?

Patient: I was sitting in my chair in my office. From out of the opposite wall, a huge snake came flying across the room. It moved with incredible speed and I was unable to get away. It put its fangs in my arm. The only thing that I was able to do was sit there, look at it, and talk about the pain that I was experiencing and the fact that I was being bitten. The dream woke me up. I felt scared and frightened. It was disturbing.

Therapist: May I work with this dream?

Patient: Yes.

Therapist: I would like you to close your eyes and tell me the dream again as if it were a movie or as if it were happening live. I would like you to describe the setting and all of the things that you see and feel as you are going through it.

Patient: (Closes eyes) (Pause) I'm in my office. I'm sitting in my chair; this is the place where I usually work. I am working on my notes. It is very still, quiet, and peaceful. I'm in the middle of the work and suddenly there is a kind of a crash. The wall opposite me breaks open and a huge snake with dark eyes is flying through it.

I see him fly across the room and put his fangs in my arm. I look at his eyes and I get a sense that he is a male. I feel disconnected and strange. I look at him and I say, "You are biting me. You have fangs in my arm. It hurts. This is not right. Stop biting me. Stop biting me." It is weird. I am being bit and I am saying these words, but there is no anger. I do not fight or move. I think, in a way, that I just want to go back to work; I do not want to engage. I wake up and I am distressed even though I did not feel that way in the dream. *(Opening eyes)* That's what happened.

Therapist: Good. Now I am going to ask you to try to enter into some of the different images and give voice to their experience. To start, please speak from the perspective of the snake. I would like you to really get into it. You can start in either of these chairs that you are in or move to the one over there.

Patient as Snake: (The patient chooses a seat to give voice to the snake; there is a chair opposite. The therapist sits in the middle.) (See figure 7.1) I'm a huge snake. *(Pause)*

Therapist: Describe yourself. Say what you are like.

Patient as Snake: I'm strong, hungry, vicious, aggressive. I live in the jungle and I hunt and I attack. I'm long, smooth, green, and slippery. I bite, I kill, and I eat. My fangs are very sharp. I'm very primitive and very old. I'm a reptile and I am filled with cold blood. I'm a loner, I go my own way. I don't know how I found my way into the office, but it doesn't matter. I'm going to attack you, I'm going to kill you.

Therapist: Say that again.

Patient as Snake: I'm going to attack you. I'm going to kill you. I'm biting you and I'm sending venom into you. *(Pause)*

Therapist: Please switch seats and describe who you are in the dream, sitting on the chair.

Patient as Therapist: I'm a psychotherapist and I'm sitting quietly in my office. I like to listen to my patients and reflect on what they're saying. I have the gifts of being able to be still and quiet. I listen and I hear.

Facilitator: Now, talk to the snake.

Patient as Therapist: At the moment, you're biting me and you're causing me pain. I don't seem to be able to move or fight back. I'm just talking to you and commenting that you are biting me and that it is causing me pain.

Therapist: I don't fight back.

Patient as Therapist: Yes, I don't fight back. When I woke up I was frightened by what you had done. I don't know if I'm frightened right now. I'm just sitting here, looking at you, unable to move. *(Pause)*

Therapist: I don't fight back. I sit here and I don't fight back. I don't struggle. I am sitting here.

Patient as Therapist: I am sitting. I don't fight, I don't struggle. I sit here. I just want to work. I want to be left alone. Leave me alone.

Therapist: Now go back over here and be the serpent.

Patient as Snake: I'm the giant vicious snake. Everyone is afraid of me. All around the world, people fear me. They see me as something evil. Sometimes the brave ones try to hunt me. I lie in wait and sneak around. I bite them when they're unaware. I'll bite you if you get too close.

Therapist: Repeat that, I'll bite you if you get too close.

Patient as Snake: I'll bite you if you get too close! I will bite you if you get too close! *(Pause) (Slowly)* I'm fierce and I will fight . . . I will fight to the death. *(Pause)*

Therapist: Again.

Patient as Snake: I'm fierce and I will fight. I will fight to the death.

Therapist: I will fight. I will fight hard and I will fight to the death. No one will defeat me. You do it.

Patient as Snake: I will fight hard. I will fight hard and no one will defeat me.

Therapist: No one will defeat me.

Patient as Snake: No one will defeat me!

Therapist: Now go to the other chair and be yourself in the dream.

Patient as Snake: I'm a therapist. I'm very educated. I have studied for a very long time. I've read many books and I think about things a great deal. I have dedicated my life to helping people in need, to helping those who suffer.

I live a life of culture, and I don't like your violence, your aggressiveness. I like my neat, beautiful, orderly office. I can't believe that you have broken through my wall and have bitten me. It's not right, it's not fair. I didn't do anything to you. You might even kill me. If you don't, I'm going to have a lot of work to do to fix the office. I don't like you biting me. I want you to let go. If I had a knife I would cut off your head right now.

Therapist: Good, Again.

Patient as Therapist: If I had a knife I would cut it off. I'm getting so angry about what you have done that I would not mind it if you died. I'm not usually like this but I'm angry that you have hurt me, that you have made a mess of things. I don't like it. Let go of me, stop biting me!

Therapist: Stop biting me.

Patient as Therapist: Stop biting me. Stop it.

Therapist: I am going to cut you with my knife.

Patient as Therapist: I am going to cut you with my knife.

Therapist: Stop it or I will cut you with my knife.

Patient as Therapist: You'd better stop right now or I am really going to cut you open with my knife.

Therapist: (Pause) Now move back to this chair and be the snake.

Patient as Snake: I'm a snake. You don't have to be so mad. I bit you because that's who I am. I'm a predator, a hunter; that's who I am.

I'm not all bad. I shed my skin and then I grow new skin. I'm a symbol of Medicine. I'm intertwined on the rod. I'm a mystery; I kill and I heal. I lay eggs and keep my babies warm. *(Pause)*

Therapist: I kill and I heal.

Patient as Snake: I kill and I heal.

Therapist: I kill and I heal.

Patient as Snake: I kill and I heal.

Therapist: Again.

Patient as Snake: I kill and I heal.

Therapist: Several times, slowly.

Patient as Snake: I kill and I heal. I kill and I heal. *(More slowly)* I kill and I heal.

Therapist: I heal and I kill, two more times.

Patient as Snake: I *heal* and I kill. *(Pause)* I heal and I kill.

Therapist: (The Therapist gets up brings a fourth chair over and puts it in the middle, opposite his/her own chair and a foot or two back from the two chairs in the dialogue.) (See figure 7.1) Now I would like you to come and sit in this fourth chair. *(The Patient sits in this new chair and the Therapist stays in his/her chair; they are now facing each other.)* Sitting there now, you have the therapist on one side and the snake on the other. I would like to get a sense of what it was like to go through that dialogue and where you are with these two parts of yourself.

Patient: It is powerful to be sitting here. I can feel both of them. *(Pause)* When I started I was really the therapist. The snake seemed really alien. As I went back and forth, I began to get angry at the snake. I felt he was wrong and I did not like what he was doing.

As I began to play the snake, I began to like him better.

Therapist: What did it feel like to give voice to the snake?

Patient: As I warmed up to it, I began to enjoy it. I felt free-er, less restricted. I began to feel some energy and power. It was good. I liked it.

Therapist: Maybe you can take a minute to look at the snake and look at the therapist and see if you can take in something from each of them. Let me know when you feel something.

Patient: (Patient takes a minute or two to look at both chairs and feel the energy of each of them.) (Looking at the Therapist) Okay.

Therapist: What are you feeling from each of them?

Patient: I want the skill and knowledge from the therapist. I want the commitment to heal from the therapist and I want the forcefulness from the snake. I don't always stand up for myself enough. Sometimes I don't push my patients hard enough. The snake is a fighter. He wants what he wants. I could use more of that.

Therapist: That's great. Anything else?

Patient: No. I think that's it.

Therapist: Let's go back to our original seats.

Debrief

A first step might be for the Patient and Therapist to make a composite list of the specific attributes of the psychotherapist and the snake that he would like to engage with and manifest in his life. This is a list that the patient should study and give voice to daily. The next step is to identify situations where the patient could benefit from more assertiveness, more *snake-informed* behaviors. Specific strategies could be developed and practiced and then implemented in the real world.

Further Thoughts on Polarity Work

Polarity dialogues are dialogues between values and energies that seem to the patient to be incompatible and incongruent. This speaks to the issue of inner conflict as a dynamic driving many, but not all, problems that patients are wrestling with. It is my personal belief that the centerpiece of most psychotherapeutic journeys will be a confrontation between courage and fear. This dynamic was at work in the decision-making dialogue that was presented in chapter 5.

As noted earlier, this kind of work served as a vehicle integrating that which was psychotherapeutic with efforts that were centered on the development of human potential. This was, in fact, one of the goals of the Esalen Institute.

Table 7.1 Polarity List

Polarity List	
Fear	Desire
Gentle	Tough
Trusting	Suspicious
Ugly	Beautiful
Sexual	Asexual
Submissive	Dominant
Independent	Dependent
Group	Individual
Calm	Active
Practical	Idealistic
Verbal	Mathematical
Heart	Head
Closed	Open
Save	Spend
Extrovert	Introvert
Soft	Hard
Mature	Young
Wild	Civilized

Source: Based, in part, on Raffa, 2012; Schiffman, 1971; and abcteach ®, 2014.

Building on this, Chairwork dialogues can be developed using values that exist in polarity. Table 7.1 consists of words that are in opposition; in turn, table 7.2 can be used as a foundation for a three-way dialogue among dynamic variables. Using these lists can help patients access energies that are meaningful as well as disowned, while offering a structure for the creative emergence of a new vision of the self. Again, this way of working can provide us with a viable link to some of the innovative energies of the 1960s Esalen experience.

Table 7.2   Three-Way Dialogue

Three-Way Dialogue Values		
Mother	Child	Father
Child	Adult	Parent
Artistic	Spiritual	Scientific
Fear	Love	Courage
Body	Feelings	Mind
Past	Present	Future
Tradition	Progress	Change
Inertia	Action	Effort
Warrior	Lover	Creator

Source: Based on Payne, 1981.

Chapter 8

Substance Use and Addictive Behaviors

The field of addiction treatment has been undergoing enormous changes, particularly since the early 1990s. In terms of formal treatment, there are now a much wider range of psychologically-based approaches available. These include Contingency Management (Kellogg, Stitzer, Petry, & Kreek, 2007), Relapse Prevention (Marlatt & Gordon, 1985), Motivational Interviewing (Miller, 2000; Miller & Rollnick, 2013), and Harm Reduction Psychotherapy (Denning, 2000; Tatarsky, 2002; Tatarsky & Kellogg, 2010). In addition, there has been a striking growth in the psychologically-oriented self-help groups including Women for Sobriety, SMART Recovery®, Moderation Management, and HAMS (Harm Reduction, Abstinence, and Moderation Support).

On the basic science front, the National Institute on Drug Abuse has championed the paradigm of addiction as a brain disease (National Institute on Drug Abuse, 2008). Their research makes a compelling case that repeated exposure to substances can lead to brain changes that may, in fact, play a major role in the experience of addiction. This basic science work is both challenging our clinical understanding of addiction treatment and supporting the development of new medications.

Globally, one of most important developments in recent years has been the Harm Reduction movement. While existing in nascent form in the 1970s, Harm Reduction began to gain momentum in the 1980s when the link was made between intravenous drug use and HIV/AIDS. Originating as a grassroots public health movement, this approach championed the perspective that addressing the dangers of HIV transmission should take precedence over concerns about drug use and recovery. The hallmark Harm Reduction tools included needle exchange, low threshold methadone treatment, safer drug use information, naloxone overdose prevention training, motivational work, and a fundamental attitude of nonjudgmental acceptance that was crystallized in the phrase, "Meeting them where they're at." Originally focused primarily on injection heroin users, Harm Reduction has expanded its focus to include hepatitis C prevention, methamphetamine use, and the protection of sex industry workers. Lastly, many harm reductionists take a social justice perspective in that they see drug abuse and addiction as ways of coping with oppression.

Harm Reduction Psychotherapy, in turn, developed as harm reduction principles and perspectives were adopted and integrated by cognitive-behavioral and psychodynamic therapists working in the addiction treatment field (Denning, 2000; Tatarsky, 2002; Tatarsky & Kellogg, 2010). These therapists have argued that drug use is meaningful and that problems that underlie or drive the use of substances may need to be treated simultaneously or even first, as the patient may not be willing to make any changes until their inner suffering is reduced or eliminated.

Many of these developments both inform the use of Chairwork with addicted patients and, in turn, provide new opportunities for the use of dialogical encounters. Some of the relevant insights from these developments are:

1. Problematic drug use and addiction are often very complex phenomena that need to be seen and treated as such.
2. Most patients are in a state of ambivalence about their use.
3. The pain that drives destructive alcohol and drug consumption may need to be addressed before patients will be willing to reduce or cease their use of a substance.
4. While working on co-existing psychological problems, steps may need to be taken to empower patients to use their substances in safer or less damaging ways if they are not willing to choose cessation.
5. Drug use is not solely related to personal problems and experiences; social forces such as racism, poverty, crime, sexism, discrimination, and oppression may drive substance use as well. These issues may need to be addressed specifically within the context of treatment.
6. Our new understanding of the role of the brain in addiction has given a new meaning to the idea that addiction is a "disease"; patients and therapists will need to understand that parts of the brain will "seek out" drugs despite the best intentions of the patient. The patients will want to be vigilant as this deeply biological drive or desire for substances may continue to exist for a long time or perhaps even for their entire life (Kellogg & Tatarsky, 2012).

In terms of conceptualizing all of these ideas in a clinically-useful manner, it is again useful to return to the concepts of modes and multiplicity that have already informed the use of Chairwork. In table 8.1, I have outlined and given

Table 8.1   **Motivations for Using**

Motivations for Using Drugs	
Self-Stimulation Domain	"I love the way they feel."
	"Sex is just better when I'm using."
	"I use drugs with reverence and respect. They take me to places deep within my spirit."
	"I have had experiences with drugs which, to be honest, I do not believe I could have had in any other way."
Self-Soothing/ Self- Medication Domain	"I get really anxious, really frightened. Marijuana helps me function. I've tried medications but they just don't work as well. I don't want to give it up."
	"I have to do a lot of socializing for my job. The stakes are high and I am often afraid that I will say something stupid. Alcohol helps me get through this."
	"Sometimes images of what they did to me come back. I feel sick and crazy when that happens. The opiates help . . . a lot."
Somatic Domain	"The cravings are bad. They feel unbearable at times. When they come on, I just need to use something."
	"The depression at the end of a run is indescribable–it is so awful. I feel like killing myself. A little bit more helps make a difference."
	"My body aches. I keep telling the doctors but they just don't listen to me. I've been taking some more on my own. I know it's not right, but what else am I supposed to do?"
Social Identity Domain	"Of course it's about the alcohol, but it's not just about the alcohol. I was part of a scene. We were friends; things happened. We had some terrible experiences and we had some great ones. I spent years with them and I miss them now. I miss them a lot."
Social Justice Domain	"It's hard for outsiders to understand what it is like to be homeless. It's terrifying, really. Terrifying and humiliating. I keep myself stoned as much of the time as possible. When I do that, I feel like I have a force field around me. I feel protected. I have a buffer. It helps me survive."

examples of the five modes or domains that may be a significant force in drug use. These modes will, in fact play a pivotal role in the five addiction dialogue structures that we will focus on.

Motivational Dialogues

Motivational dialogues are based on the understanding that with all patients, there are forces that want to continue using the substance and forces that want some kind of change, be it cessation or moderation. The forces supporting the continued use of substances were described in table 8.1; the forces that support or drive change, in turn, can be found in table 8.2. Consequentially, they live and act in a state of inner conflict or ambivalence, and the dynamics involved can be elucidated through the use of a Decisional Balance (Marlatt & Gordon, 1985), a tool that was also used in chapter 5.

Table 8.2   Motivations for Change

Motivations for Change	
Family/Parental/ Relational Threats	"I am going to lose my spouse/partner/child if I keep doing what I am doing."
	"My father had a drug problem and he was never around. I always swore that I would never be that kind of parent, but here I am, doing what he did."
Job Loss/Economic Damage/Prestige Threats	"I am going to get fired."
	"I will lose my license."
	"I will never work in my field again."
Existential/Spiritual Concerns	"I just feel, in some way, that I was not put on this planet to spend my whole life addicted to drugs/alcohol. I know there is something more for me to do here."
Health Concerns	"If I do not stop, I am going to die."
Legal Problems	"I am afraid that I will lose my freedom."
	"I am afraid that I will lose my freedom again."
Role Strain	"I am exhausted. I just can't keep doing this."
	"I am sick and tired of being sick and tired."

The Decisional Balance is a foundational task in the psychotherapy of addictive disorders and central to the creation of motivational dialogues. At its most basic, the patient is asked to delineate the positives of using substances, the negatives of using substances, the perceived positives of changing (whether stopping or moderating), and the perceived negatives of changing. An example of this can be found in table 8.3.

In practice, the therapist can first go through the four quadrants and elicit the appropriate information. The patient can then be invited to engage in a two-chair dialogue in which the positives of using and the negatives of change are located in one chair and the negatives of using and the positives of change are located in the other. Using the Decisional Balance as a reference, the therapist can then coach the patient to make sure that every item and issue is verbalized. This is probably the most common use of Chairwork in addiction treatment and it is the foundation for the first Chairwork dialogue that is scripted below. Nonetheless, there are some additional issues to consider.

Rothschild (2010) has been deeply interested in the role of trauma and dissociation in addictive disorders. She, too, embraces a model of inner multiplicity. In cases of abuse and mistreatment, inner aspects of the self may become increasingly disconnected from each other. In her words, "one of the hallmarks of trauma is dissociation, defined as a discontinuity between various aspects of self or an inability to hold conflicting views of self at the same time" (p. 141). In traditional treatment settings, where there has been an emphasis on getting people to stop using substances, therapeutic conversations often engage only the part of the person that was interested in change. The reality was that patients would express their understanding

Table 8.3 Decisional Balance

Decisional Balance	
Positives of Drug Use	**Positives of Change**
Immediate physical pleasure (10)	Feel a greater sense self-discipline (9)
Feeling more "there" (10)	Would be more productive (10)
Feels more emotion (10)	Help him be more comfortable with self (8)
Reduces social anxiety (6)	Greater confidence (6)
Shuts out inner critic voice (7)	*Mean Score = 8.25*
People will know "real" self (7)	
Mean Score = 8.33	
Negatives of Drug Use	**Negatives of Change**
Feels guilty (7)	Would not enjoy life as much (9)
Others are concerned (6)	Would be ignoring a part of himself (10)
Not as productive (10)	Breaking up with something he loves–a
Feels like it a crutch (10)	hard breakup (9)
Feels bad (7)	*Mean Score = 9.33*
Health Problems (7)	
Mean Score = 7.83	

The Decisional Balance first involves asking the patient to identify the positives and negatives of drug use and the positives and negatives of stopping or changing their use. After these forces are identified, the patient is asked to rate the power of each one, positive or negative, on a scale of 1–10. Only those items that achieve a score of 6 or higher are kept. To create a metaphorical calculus of the patient's motivation, means are formulated for each of the four boxes. The force for continued use is the Positives of Drug Use Mean plus the Negatives of Recovery Mean; the force for recovery or change is the Negatives of Drug Use Mean plus the Positives of Recovery Mean. In this example, when the ratio of forces is computed, the result is 17.66 : 16.08—which helps to illuminate the "stuck" position of the patient (Kellogg & Tatarsky, 2012, p. 118).

of the cognitive-behavioral techniques and share plans to attend a self-help group over the weekend; however, when they returned a week later, they were ashamed to report that they had been on a three-day run with cocaine.

Rothschild understood this as a consequence of not allowing the part that wants to use into the room and of not giving him or her a voice. Chairwork is profoundly helpful here because the therapy can move beyond metaphor and actually give "voice" to that part. Many patients find it to be quite strange to actually speak openly and strongly about their deep love for drugs and alcohol so it may take prompting and encouragement from the therapist for them to speak truthfully, openly, and passionately about this. Nonetheless, it is quite important as the risk of relapse is much higher if these voices are not given an opportunity to be fully present and completely understood. It is also important for these two parts to make contact and dialogue with each other. Rothschild (2010) also pointed out that with dissociated patients, it is difficult for them to tolerate internal ambiguity. Having these dialogues allows individuals to experience two sides of themselves simultaneously.

As was described in chapter 6, Perls (1992) had great faith in the creative possibilities that emerge in the space between two polarities. That is, if the patient engages in an emotionally-vibrant dialogue between the part that wants to use and the part that wants to change, a solution that is organically connected to both of them will emerge. This means that if the therapist can facilitate a deeply-engaged dialogue, that alone may be sufficient to enable the patient to set their own course of action. During the debriefing part of the session, the therapist would explore what the patient would like to do. The therapist would then work with the patient to help facilitate that goal. To be clear, the therapist would also examine the potential risks and dangers in the plan as a full evaluation is an essential part of the work.

A variant of this would involve the use of a third chair. This chair could then serve as a mediating or a leadership voice that would speak to both parts. If done successfully, the patient could: (1) gain greater internal control by being able to identify and label the different modes when then emerge in daily life; and (2) make more conscious and less impulsive decisions about his or her drug use.

Looking at the patient's response in the Decisional Balance in table 8.3, it is clear that the change-oriented part is: (1) concerned about the morality of drug use; (2) aware that it is blocking him from achieving his goals; (3) worried about damaging his relationships with others; and (4) fearful that he is jeopardizing his health. On the other side, the part that wants to use: (1) enjoys them; (2) feels that they facilitate social interaction; (3) knows that they silence the inner critic; and (4) represent an important aspect of himself. Moving forward, each of these perspectives could be embodied as modes and be invited to express their concerns and desires. This means that a Chairwork dialogue could be created with multiple chairs on either side, each expressing the various desires to use, the concerns about continuing, the hopes for change, and the fears of living without substances. Creative engagements can be designed that involve specific voices. For example, the moral voice ("I think that relying on drugs in order to live is just fundamentally wrong.") can engage with the self-medication voice ("I am in such pain that I am not willing to live without having access to substances."). These kinds of encounters can lead to less defensiveness, a "softening" of perspectives, and the possible emergence of creative solutions that both parts can live with (Watson et al., 2007; Perls, 1969b). Looking at this more broadly, by clearly giving voice to all of these perspectives, several benefits may accrue. The patient can "own" their different parts, the relative weight of each part can be more truly calibrated, "mode-flipping" or dissociated behaviors can be reduced, and concrete strategies that come from an accurate understanding of the motivational forces within the individual can be implemented.

When working with addictive behaviors, the motivational dialogues are the best place to start. They can often play a central role throughout treatment as this kind of psychotherapeutic work often involves an ongoing dance between motivation and action. There are, however, other ways of creating chair dialogues.

Relationship Dialogues

Denning (2000) has emphasized that patients (and perhaps all people) are engaged in different kinds of relationships with drugs. These relationships may vary from being affirming and healing to being profoundly destructive. In a sense, they parallel the kinds of relationships that patients have with other human beings. For example, in her memoir, *Drinking: A Love Story,* Caroline Knapp captured this idea when she wrote: "Alcohol had become too important. By the end it was the single most important relationship in my life" (Knapp, 2005, p. 5). Similarly, the Rolling Stones sang about "Sister Morphine" and "Cousin Cocaine" (Jagger, Richards, & Faithfull, 1971), and a woman who detailed her experiences using of Ritalin and heroin together wrote: "It is first thing in the morning when I find myself in the embrace of a forbidden lover. One whom I do not wish to repudiate" (Kitten, 2001).

Writing farewell letters to drugs is a practice that is used in some treatment facilities (see Brooklyn Hobo, 2008). Clearly this can be adapted to the Chairwork structure. In its most elemental form, the drug can be put in one chair and the patient can sit opposite and begin the dialogue. The conversation can not only include the *cycle of relationship*: how did they meet, where they have been together, where they are now, and where they are going, but also the *cycle of emotion*: this is what I loved about you, this is what I hated or what angered me, this is what frightened me, and this is the grief I have felt because of you and this is the grief I will feel if I release you from my life. The patient can, then, switch chairs and speak from the perspective of the substance. Again, it is always fascinating to see what kind of persona emerges from the "drug chair." To be clear, it may be advisable to have separate dialogues with each of the substances being used as their respective relationship histories may differ. In a sense, these kinds of conversations overlap with the Stages of Change motivational model (Prochaska, DiClemente, & Norcross, 1992), and the goals and strategies that emerge may vary accordingly.

Assertiveness Dialogues

Once individuals decide to stop using or to dramatically change their use patterns, all kinds of forces emerge to challenge their resolve (Marlatt & Gordon, 1985). Drink and drug refusal is a form of assertiveness training that seeks to empower the patient to stand their ground and refuse the offers and resist the pressures (Carroll, 1998). As was demonstrated in chapter 4, Chairwork can be used to facilitate this.

In my clinical work, I have seen some dynamics that may be more pronounced here than with other diagnostic groups. The first is that not unusual to find that these patients have difficulty with direct communication. This may stem from several causes. One reason is that because of trauma or mistreatment, they have chosen to be passive because this was a "safer" survival strategy. A second is that some patients are actually frightened of their own capacity for violence. They remain passive out of fear of doing something harmful; they do not have a strong, healthy adult mode.

A third group may have turned to a "rebel" coping mode as an alternative survival method. They frequently alternate between passive-aggressive and aggressive communication styles. Adult, egalitarian communications are difficult for them as well.

A second major challenge to assertiveness has roots in the culture of addiction. When an individual decides to stop drinking or to stop using drugs, others may take active steps to undermine their resolve by pressuring them and/or by offering them free drinks and drugs. Alcohol-focused friends and family members can be quite confrontational when someone decides to stop. This is why a great deal of preparation may be necessary before they engage with this kind of high-risk situation.

A third issues lies within the patients themselves. Many feel a great deal of pressure to explain why they are not drinking, which opens them up to the manipulations and attacks of others. Strikingly, many patients fear a great deal of inner pressure to be both honest and polite. Some report feeling like hypocrites when interacting with people they used to drink or use drugs with.

This is, in fact, a major problem because a lapse or relapse can be life-damaging or deadly. Strikingly, even though this can be a life-and-death issue, many find it difficult to defend themselves and their sobriety or moderation. Some internal dialogues on these cognitions may need to precede work on developing an assertive and empowered voice.

Inner Complexity Dialogues

Wallace (1978) understood that there may be parts of the self that seem inaccessible to the individual when they are sober, but may be retrievable during times of intoxication. There may also be aspects of the "sober" self that are problematic in some way. Wallace sought to first identify the best aspects of both states and then see if an integration was possible.

To begin, he invited the patient to alternate between two chairs, with one representing the drinking/using self and the other embodying the sober self. As the patient does this, they will identify, describe, and define these two selves, respectively. A dialogue or encounter between these two parts may then ensue. As he wrote, "I asked the patient to describe her dichotomized self-construction." She described her drinking self as "promiscuous, lively, selfish, exciting, sexy, witty, fun-loving, happy-go-lucky, and devil-may-care," and her sober self as "dull, boring, plodding, serious, responsible, frigid, thoughtful, caring, religious, and guilt-ridden." When they explored this further, "the patient [saw] that her drinking personality contained many positive qualities, while her sober personality . . . had . . . many negative ones" (p. 105). They then worked on a creating a new composite self that would integrate the best of both parts. Using a fixed-role approach, she then went out to practice this new self in the outside world. Clearly this has the potential to be a healing approach that serves to empower the patient while also integrating some of the more useful aspects of the two polarities. To me, Wallace's work is resonant with the complexity-of-self dialogues that Chadwick (2003) has developed.

Role and Identity Dialogues

The final addiction dialogue paradigm, is centered on identity creation and restructuring. Within the context of the developments discussed earlier, the recovery process is being re-envisioned in new ways. The new paradigm, which builds on the growing understanding of the complex brain changes that take place as a result of drug use and addiction, conceptualizes substance dependence as a chronic, relapsing disease, which means that it will likely be a life-long journey. One of the goals of this new model will be to help patients maintain periods of abstinence and moderation for as long as possible while understanding that relapses are a part of the experience (O'Brien & McLellan, 1996). A crucial question in this new approach is how to help people maintain long-term recovery; one way to understand and promote this is through the use of Identity Theory.

Originally developing out of Symbolic Interactionism, Identity Theory also falls within the tradition of multiplicity, which means that people are believed to have numerous identities or roles (Stryker, 1981; Stryker & Serpé, 1982). Identities provide the person with a self-definition, a social or reference group within which they are embodied, and a series of prescriptions and proscriptions for behavior (Christiansen, 1999).

The development of identities occurs within a social context. This is frequently, but not always, a dialectical process in which a specific social group works to mold, influence, or define an individual; in turn, he or she contributes through a personal elaboration of the identity, giving it a specific emphasis and/or challenging and redefining the nature of the identity itself. The relative strength of the group and the individual will vary greatly by social setting. Usually beginning with adolescence, individuals have the possibility to engage in "identity projects" (Harré, 1983); that is, they will pursue identities that they find to be attractive, compelling, or useful. Whether they will, in fact, be able to successfully claim them depends on whether their performance meets the standards of the relevant reference group (Shibutani, 1968). For example, one might say that he or she is a musician, but if their playing does not reach an adequate standard, others will not acknowledge them as a possessor of that

142 *Chapter 8*

identity. It is important to note that all identities are not of equal importance. They are, in fact, organized into hierarchies of salience and importance, with the more significant ones having a greater influence on behavior over time (Stryker, 1981; Stryker & Serpé, 1982). Addictive behaviors have a particularly debilitating impact on the hierarchy; that is, they take the form of an identity that not only becomes the most important identity in the hierarchy, but also one that frequently leads to the destruction of other identities.

Identities and addictions interact in several other ways. For many working class, middle class, and upper class users, the problematic use of substances may eventually begin to threaten cherished roles and self-definitions. Stereotypically, when a man is faced with the loss of a job or a woman is faced with the loss of her children, many are motivated to take action; again, one way to understand this is to see it in terms of identities. They are seeking to save the valued identities of worker and mother. They do not want them to be tainted or lost and this provides them with some motivation to change.

Perhaps more to the point, identity processes play a key role in successful recovery. It is believed that most people with drug and alcohol addictions recover on their own, without participation in treatment, psychotherapy, or self-help groups. Understanding how individuals do this has been an area of study in recent years in hopes that the processes involved can be used to improve treatment (Granfield & Cloud, 1994; Kellogg & Kreek, 2006). In his classic volume, *Pathways to Recovery*, Biernacki (1986) demonstrated that identity processes played a key role in the stories of individuals who recovered from heroin addiction without treatment. Some returned to roles that they had embraced before the addiction began, others turned to those that had been co-existent with the addiction but had not been excessively damaged by it, and a third group pursued new ones. Building on this work, Kellogg (1993) argued that identity change was a key element of all psychosocial treatments. That is, all long-term recovery can be understood to involve identity creation and restructuring. Addicted individuals need to find viable, purposeful, meaningful, and reinforcing identities that can compete with and replace those based on addictive behavior.

These processes are actually at work in many mainstream treatments, even if they are not formally acknowledged. For example, some recovery-centered organizations such as the therapeutic communities and the 12-Step Fellowship groups are specifically focused on identity transformation (Greil & Rudy, 1984). This means that in Alcoholics Anonymous, when a member says, "My name is Bob and I am an alcoholic," one thing that they are doing is declaring their membership in Alcoholics Anonymous and claiming an identity as a recovering person (Maxwell, 1984).

Identity dialogues can be created from among the different roles. For example, the Addict/Drug-Using Identity can speak in one chair: "I love drugs.

I need drugs. I don't want to give them up." Then the Father role can speak in the other: "I have these two boys and I want to be a great father. I know what it is like to not have a father and I want something better for them."

As noted earlier, some patients will have lived with such a paucity of resources that they have had no real identities outside of the world of drugs. In this case, the Addicted Self can dialogue with the future self that the individual will become if the drug use ceases. "I am the truck driver that you will be if you stop using drugs, and I want to come into the world." "I am the baker that you will be if you stop using drugs. It is my turn to come into being. I think you are being selfish." This work directly overlaps with Markus and Nurius' (1986) concept of *Possible Selves*. It is compelling because it creates a kind of existential tension and intensity that can foment change.

Five dialogues structures have been described: (1) motivational work; (2) relationship with the drug; (3) inner complexity and composite self-creation; (4) drink and drug refusal; and (5) identity-centered encounters. Clinicians are encouraged to consider using all five of these in their practices, as appropriate. Next, we look more deeply at two Chairwork dialogue structures. The first will involve motivation and the second will focus on the relationship with the substance.

ADDICTION AND MOTIVATION DIALOGUE

The dialogue begins with the patient and the therapist facing each other as the therapist does the interview work necessary for the Decisional Balance. After that, the therapist will set up the chair structure that is found in figure 8.1. Two chairs face each other and the therapist is located in the middle, perpendicular to the dialogue. We will again start by creating a Decisional Balance and then turn that into a dialogue.

Addiction Motivation Dialogue

Patient: I know that I'm supposed to be here to do something about my drug and alcohol use, yet I find myself feeling kind of disconnected and mixed about the whole project.

Therapist: This is not surprising. It's actually the norm for people to have mixed feelings about taking on their addictions or changing their relationship with substances. One way that we might want to approach this is to clarify and give voice to the different parts of you that have different feelings about this.

Patient: Sounds good.

Therapist: What I would like to do is for the two of us to identify and list the positives and negatives of using and the positives and negatives of changing. It

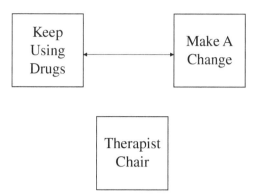

Figure 8.1   Drug Use Decisional Balance Dialogue

will be most helpful if you are really honest both about how the substances work for you and about the negatives of changing or recovering.

Patient: Okay.

Therapist: What would you say are the positives or the benefits of your drug and alcohol use?

Patient: The most immediate thing is that I love the way they feel. At least when they're working, I just love the feeling in my body. They also help me on a number of other levels. I feel more connected to things. Sometimes I feel like an outsider, and they help me overcome that. Along those lines, I also feel more emotionally alive. My usual state is feeling kind of dead inside, so the times when I'm using are good because I feel like I'm a living human being.

Moving beyond that, they help me to feel more comfortable in social situations. I'm able to talk with others more easily, especially women/men.

There's also this terrible voice in my head so much of the time. This voice keeps telling me that I'm no good, that I'm bad. When I use drugs, I'm able to shut this voice down. I'm so grateful for a chance to get away from it.

Lastly, I have the sense that people get to know the "real me" better when I have some drugs in the system. I think that I'm more real to them.

Therapist: What would you say are the downsides of your use?

Patient: I feel very guilty about using them, at least some of the time. I know that other people in my family, and some of my friends as well, are worried about me. They think they're having a negative effect on me.

If I'm honest with myself, I have to admit that I'm simply not as productive as I should be. Sometimes things just don't get done or they get done at a level that is not as good as it should be.

I also feel like it's something of a crutch. I shouldn't have to use drugs to get through life. I should be able to do things by myself without them.

As anyone will tell you, while the drugs make you feel good, they also make you feel bad. There are certainly days, especially the day after a long night, when I feel awful.

I haven't been to the doctor so I don't know if anything is really wrong, but I do worry that I'm creating problems for myself in terms of my health. Sometimes I get sensations or aches and pains that get me worried.

Therapist: What would you say would be the positives of changing this or going into recovery?

Patient: I would feel a much greater sense of self-discipline, and I know that I would be much more productive. I think that I would feel more comfortable with myself, in some ways, and I believe that I would have greater self-confidence.

Therapist: And the downsides to changing or going into recovery?

Patient: I feel that I wouldn't enjoy life as much anymore. I would really be ignoring an important part of myself. Stopping would really involve breaking up with something that I love very much.

Therapist: I would like to work with some of the information that has emerged in our discussion. In many respects, there are two sides of you at work here. One part that wants to use and one part that wants to stop or change. The part of you that wants to keep getting high consists of the positives of using and the negatives of stopping; the part of you that wants to change consists of the negatives of using and the positives of stopping.

If you're willing, I would like to create a kind of a conversation between these two parts. In this chair *(pointing to one chair)*, I would like you to speak from the part that loves the drugs, that wants to keep the connection, and from this chair *(pointing to the chair opposite)*, I would like you to speak from the part that's distressed and wants things to change. I'd like you to go back and forth several times so that we can see what emerges. *(See figure 8.1)*

Patient: Sounds good.

Therapist: To start, I would like you to sit in this chair *(points)* and I would like you to speak about your desire to use drugs. I want you to be really honest and talk about how they work for you. I also want you to talk about what it would be like to give them up.

Patient: (The Patient moves to the new chair and, facing the chair opposite, begins.) It seems a little strange to say this out loud, but here goes. *(Pause)* Well, as I said, when they work, I really love the way that they feel in my body. They just work for me. It's hard to put it into words but there's just something perfect about them.

They help me to feel more alive and they help me be with people in a way that seems more real. I feel kind of dead sometimes, and it's not always easy for me to be with people or at least be with them in a way that shows them what I have inside of me. I feel more alive and I think that they can see that when I'm a bit high.

As you know, I have these voices in my head that are always saying bad things about me. They drive me crazy and make me feel bad. The great thing about the drugs is that they shut them off for a while. I know that it's not permanent, but I am grateful to get some peace.

They're really important to me. I don't want to give them up.

Therapist: Say that again.

Patient: I don't want to give them up; I really don't want to give them up.

(Pause) I think that's about it.

Therapist: Now I would like you to go to this chair *(points)* and speak about your distress about your drug use and your desire to stop using them.

Patient: You're saying all of those positive things about the drugs, but you know that they're messing you up. Your whole career is on hold, you're really going nowhere. You know that everyone's passing us by.

Face it, it's just a crutch; strong people don't need to take drugs or drink to get by.

You know you're messing yourself up with them. You know how bad you feel after you've been on a run. Everybody's worried about you and you're messing up your body on top of it.

Therapist: Good. I would like you to say all of these things again only this time I would like you to say "I," that is, I'd like you to "own" all of these things in the chair you're sitting in, rather than telling him/her *(pointing to the chair opposite)* what to do.

Patient: All right. I am really upset about my drinking and drugging. I'm getting high every day, that's what I do. I went to school and worked hard. I wanted to do great things but I'm just throwing it all away.

I know that my friends and family are upset. I change the subject or stay away from them because I don't want to hear it.

It's bad. Sometimes I just feel terrible. I'm afraid to go to the doctor; I'm afraid of what I might find out.

(Pointing at the other chair) He/she says he/she wants them, he/she says he/she loves them, but they're just killing me.

Therapist: They're just killing me. Say it again more forcefully.

Patient: They're killing me. I've got to stop. I want to stop.

Therapist: Good. Now I want you to switch and speak from the other side.

Patient: (Switching chairs) I want the drugs. I am not prepared to stop. I love the way they feel. They help me. I feel bad. I feel uncomfortable. They help me get through. I want them and I am not prepared to give them up.

Therapist: I want them and I am *not* prepared to give them up.

Patient: I want them and I will *not* give them up. It frightens me to think of doing that.

Therapist: I am scared of living without drugs.

Patient: I am scared of living without drugs. I don't see how I could do that. I just don't want to do that.

Therapist: Now switch and speak from the other side.

Patient: (Patient switches chairs.) I am very unhappy. My life is going down the tubes. I am wasting it. I worked so hard to get through school, to be able have the career I wanted and I am losing everything.

Therapist: Tell him/her how distressed you are.

Patient: I am incredibly distressed. I hurt. I am upset. This is not the life I wanted.

Therapist: I want a better life.

Patient: I want a better life.

Therapist: Again.

Patient: I want a better life.

Therapist: Say it again. I don't think he/she heard you.

Patient: I want a better life. I want to do what I set out to do. The drugs and alcohol, they are destroying everything. I want my life back,

Therapist: I want my life back *now*.

Patient: I want my life back now!

Therapist: Good. Now I would like you to come over here. *(The Therapist brings over a fourth chair, opposite his/her own and in the middle between the Drug-Using and the Change chairs.)* I would like you to stand behind this chair. *(The Patient stands behind the fourth chair; the Therapist stands his/her chair.)* What do you see as you look at these two parts of yourself?

Patient: (Pause) They both seem very intense. They both seem quite frightened, actually.

Therapist: I thought that also. They both seem frightened. Do they seem different in any other ways?

Patient: This one *(pointing to the drug-using chair)* seems younger while this one *(pointing to the change chair)* seems older.

Therapist: If we were to weigh these forces out, how would you divide it? 50-50? 60-40? 90-10?

Patient: I would say 60-40 for change.

Therapist: 60-40 for change. Where were you before we started?

Patient: I was at 50-50 or even 55-45 to keep using.

Therapist: So . . . you shifted.

Patient: Yes, I felt some change as we were doing the dialogues.

Therapist: Good. Let's go back to our original seats.

Reflections

This scenario presents some of the complexities that are frequently found in addiction treatment. The two sides are fairly polarized and, as we saw, they are both fueled by fear. The good news was that the patient did do some shifting. In general, a 60-40 split is not enough for a person to engage in a major change project; they are much more likely to be open to harm reduction or gradualistic interventions.

There are three strategies that therapists might want to consider in this situation. The first is to work on what Tatarsky (Tatarsky & Kellogg, 2010) has called the Ideal Use Plan. Here we would work to develop a strategy for drug use that would maximize the benefits while minimizing the dangers and negatives. Both sides of the patient would need to agree to the plan. A central component of this plan would be whether the patient can actually follow the plan successfully; if they cannot, then it would be important to assess, in-depth, what went wrong and whether they can make changes so that they can comply with it.

The second line of intervention is drawn from the Decisional Balance. It seems clear that anxiety and self-attack are factors in the self-medicating aspects of the drug and alcohol use. By working with the patient to address these issues psychotherapeutically, some of the motivation to use can be reduced and the patient may begin to experience a deeper sense of inner freedom and comfort.

The third area of intervention, which is also drawn from the Decisional Balance, would be to explore and nurture his/her dreams of the future. What did he/she want to do? What would it look like? Re-connecting the patient to their passion and helping them create a positive vision of their future can serve to increase their sense of personal complexity, which is always important in the change and recovery process. Lastly, all of this work can be done using Chairwork dialogues.

RELATIONAL DRUG DIALOGUE STRUCTURE

As noted earlier, both Knapp (1996) and Denning (2000) envision problematic drug and alcohol use as a kind of relationship with a substance. This

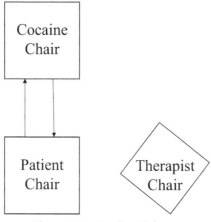

Figure 8.2   Cocaine Dialogue

reconceptualization of drug use as a relationship opens the door for dialogical work and the use of such approaches as the relationship review and the cycle of emotions. These interventions can be seen in the scripted Chairwork encounter with cocaine.

A Cocaine Dialogue

This is a scripted dialogue between a patient and cocaine that contains many of the recommended strategies for this kind of exploration. This dialogue contains some mildly graphic passages.

> *Therapist:* I have been thinking about the discussions that we've been having about your cocaine use, and I think it would be helpful if we could actually have a dialogue with cocaine as if it were a person. I believe it would give us a deeper understanding of what that experience was like for you and where things stand right now. Would that be okay?

> *Patient:* That sounds fine.

> *Therapist:* Okay, I'd like you to sit over here *(points to a chair)*. The chair opposite *(pointing)* from you is going to be the Cocaine chair. Is that clear? *(See figure 8.2)*

> *Patient:* Yes. *(The Patient switches chairs; the Therapist sits next to the patient at a diagonal.)*

> *Therapist:* To start, I'd like you to take a minute or two to try and imagine that Cocaine is sitting across from you. I'd like you to try to imagine what kind of person it is, what he or she is like, what kind of clothes they are wearing, what they are feeling, and what they are about. Would you do that?

Patient: Yes.

Therapist: Take a moment, then, to bring cocaine into focus.

Patient: (Pause) I see a woman. She's about twenty-six. She's attractive and she looks determined, a bit intense, and evil.

Therapist: What are you feeling as you look at her?

Patient: Mixed feelings. I feel drawn to her and a bit frightened.

Therapist: I would like to go back to the early days. I'd like you to talk to her and talk about when you first met her, how things were then, and how things changed over time.

Patient: Okay. It was about ten years ago that we first met. You were always around but I wasn't particularly interested in you back then, even though my friends were hanging out with you.

Eventually, I did try you a couple of times. I just took a little and nothing much happened. I sometimes wish that that had been the end of it. Then there was that night with Chad and Emma. It was an amazing night. Suddenly you worked and I was so incredibly high I couldn't believe it. The rush was amazing. I felt so powerful with you inside me.

Therapist: Tell her that again.

Patient: Yes. I felt incredibly powerful. I also felt great because I suddenly did not care about anything, all the problems disappeared. I was strong, I could do anything. It was just great, nothing that I had done up to that point compared with it.

I remember thinking that I had found what I was looking for, and that was you. As it would turn out, this was going to be the beginning of a long journey together.

Therapist: What happened next?

Patient turning to the Therapist: In retrospect, I now realize that what they say is true; that those first few times are the best and it will never be that good again.

Therapist: (Pointing at the opposite chair) Tell her directly.

Patient: Yes, our first few times together were absolutely the best. It was so amazing and it hit me in such a deep place. Of course, if anyone had told me that this was as good as it was ever going to be, I wouldn't have believed them. Looking back, I can see that that was the case.

Therapist: How did things develop from there? Tell her.

Patient: Well, you and I began to spend more time together. First I would see you on the weekends and then it began to bleed into the week. You certainly are a sex drug. Not only did you make me feel more sexual, but spending time in your world gave me access to all kinds of sexual situations. I did things I never did before.

(Turning to the Therapist while speaking): While all the authorities say that cocaine can mess up your sexual performance, that it isn't necessarily true at the start. Men get harder and go longer and some women orgasm more easily and more often. What more do I need to say? Things can get aggressive at times; with Coke it's not always pretty or romantic.

Therapist (Pointing at the Cocaine Chair): Tell her.

Patient: Sometimes you made sex even better and sometimes you turned sex into something crazy.

Therapist: Any other memories from the early days?

Patient: You helped me to feel bolder and more fearless. I remember bringing you to work sometimes. You helped me with those presentations and you gave me the energy to get those reports done. I felt more confident with others and I was able to take chances that I normally wouldn't have.

Therapist: You gave me courage.

Patient: Definitely. I pushed the envelope more and sometimes it paid off. Sometimes it didn't, but sometimes it definitely did.

Therapist: What else?

Patient: As we spent more time together, I began to lose weight. People told me I looked great. I liked that. Another thing is that I would use you to clean my house. It's amazing how many people use Coke to clean their apartments. All of a sudden cleaning the bathroom becomes this intensely interesting thing to do. I could spend hours doing it.

Therapist: She was working with you.

Patient: Yes, those were the early days. You were good to me.

Therapist: How did things change?

Patient: At first it was kind of subtle and then it began to escalate. At first when we were together, I was just happy. I was kind of in love with you and the world seemed like a new place. You were what was important in my life. I remember thinking, I can't believe I had lived my life so long without you being a part of it.

(Pause) But then you began to get more and more demanding. You wanted my time and you wanted my money. I wasn't coming through. People at work began to make hints or tell me outright that I had messed things up. They also began to tell me that I didn't look good. To be honest, I didn't really pay much attention to them. Things were still great with you a lot of the time.

I did mess up some things with my family. Getting to gatherings late or not showing up at all. I hated having to make those excuses. Sometimes I would bring you with me to events. At the time, I thought you just made everything better. As it turns out, other people thought that I was behaving oddly or was obnoxious. I just didn't see it.

Therapist: Things were starting to going downhill?

Patient: Yes. I remember someone saying once that "Cocaine takes no prisoners" and now I see what that meant.

Therapist (pointing at the other chair): Tell her.

Patient: Well, you began demanding more and more and giving me less and less. I became more obsessed with you and things just got worse. I started missing work because I was in the middle of a run or because I was too exhausted to go in. Eventually, I lost that job at the hedge fund. That was a big loss. I had spent years working up to it and you stole it from me. That still hurts a lot. That's a big regret.

   I stopped spending time with friends and family; you became the center of my existence. You were cruel. It started to be that I wanted you all the time and yet it didn't really work when I would get you. The high just wasn't so great.

Therapist: Tell her again.

Patient: The whole scene changed. I was just focused on you. I had no money and I was losing everything—my home, my family, my job, and my self-respect. I wanted to get away from you; I wanted to end it, but you didn't want to let me go.

Therapist: You wouldn't let me go.

Patient: Yes, you wouldn't let me go. You had me in a trap.

   And then I started to get paranoid. I would do all this hustling to get you, to be with you. Then, when we were finally together, you would freak me out. I was always worried that the cops were going to come busting in the door.

Therapist: You scared me.

Patient: Yes, you scared me. And sometimes you would make me hallucinate and I would see those skeletons and all that death. It freaked me out.

Therapist: It sounds horrendous.

Patient: It was horrendous. I was like a vampire. I would be indoors for days at a time. I hated seeing the sun and would try to only come out at night. I saw some photos from that time and I looked pale, really thin, and half-dead.

Therapist: Say more about the darkness; say more about the bad times.

Patient: Yes. The depressions were unbelievably awful. I felt so much despair because of you. I was suicidal at times; thankfully, I never acted on it. I would just lie there for hours, feeling crazy and absolutely hopeless.

(Pauses) I remember that day when I woke up and said to myself, "This is hell. I am living in hell."

Therapist: And that was when things began to turn?

Patient: Yes, that was when they began to turn. It would take a while, but eventually it led me to my coming here to work with you.

Therapist: You've said some powerful things. As you look at her over there, what are you feeling?

Patient: I'm feeling some anger and some regret.

Therapist: I want you to start with the anger. Talk to her about the anger you feel toward her.

Patient: I am angry at you and I am angry at myself. You've really destroyed my life. Things were so good at the beginning and than you took over and betrayed me. You cost me so much. I said it before but you cost me my career, my friends, my family, and my money. I lost my home because of you. I used to think that I was, fundamentally, a good person. Now, I no longer believe that. I've done so much that I regret because of you.

Therapist: Say that again.

Patient: I've done so much that I regret because of you. I damaged myself out of love for you and I hate you for that. I hate myself and I hate you for that.

Therapist: What is her response?

Patient: She's just giving me that evil smile. She takes pleasure in my suffering.

Therapist: You mentioned feeling some regret. Speak purely from the place of regret and sorrow. Talk to her from that place.

Patient: If I speak from the regret that I feel then I would simply say, I am sorry that I ever met you. I wish that I had never used you, not even once. You've hurt me and taken so much from me. Money, time, my job, my reputation, and my relationships with family and friends. And you've really left me with nothing. And you made me feel crazy on top of it. And what for? I have nothing to show for it. You brought me into worlds that I didn't know existed and didn't want to know existed. And I feel tainted, I feel contaminated by that darkness. And I feel ashamed of myself.

Therapist: Because of you, I feel tainted, contaminated, damaged.

Patient: Yes . . . all of those things.

Therapist: Tell her again about your regret; tell her again so that she can really hear you.

Patient (Somewhat more intensely): I'm so sorry that I met you, that I ever got involved with you. If I could do it again, I would never go near you.

Therapist: (Pause) Listening to you, I am definitely aware that you have strong feelings of anger and regret about what happened with her. While keeping that in mind, I also know that people still sometimes harbor positive feelings for the drugs despite the wreckage that they have caused. If you have these feelings, it does not mean you're hypocrite; it just means that cocaine is a powerful and complex experience. So, I would like you to try to tap into that part of yourself and speak to her from the part that still loves and desires her.

Patient: It's funny that you should say that. Even as I was talking about my anger and my grief, I was aware that there was a part of me that still wanted to see her, that still wanted to use again.

Therapist: Speak to her about it; talk to her about the love and the desire.

Patient: I look at you and I know that I want to go back, or at least a part of me wants to go back. I want things to be like they were in the early days, when everything was exciting and the bad things hadn't happened yet. I really hurt for those times and part of my anger and grief is that I can't seem to get them back . . . even though I keep trying. I realize that I'm looking at giving you up for good, but I don't really want to give you up for good.

Therapist: Tell her again, I don't want to say goodbye.

Patient: I don't want to say goodbye. I want you to be a part of my life. I hate the thought of never using cocaine again.

Therapist: Of never seeing you again.

Patient: Of never seeing you again. I'm feeling a lot of grief as I look at you. I'm surprised at how intense this is for me right now . . . as I sit here thinking about maybe having to say goodbye to you.

Therapist: (Pause) I realize that you are in an intense state right now. I would, however, like you to switch one more time, to access one more part of yourself.

Patient: Okay.

Therapist: I would like you to look at her again, engage with her again, and speak to her about the fear that you have of her.

Patient: Yes. *(Looking at the Cocaine chair.)* I *am* afraid of you. This whole conversation revolves around my fear of you. If I stay with you, you will destroy me. I was just talking about how much I want you and love you but I know that will only lead to my destruction. I know that if keep using you, it will only lead to jail, hospitals, or the grave; I know that saying is true for me. If I keep seeing you, if I keep using you, it'll just be the end. I have seen enough to know that I cannot really be with you sometimes, as much as I would like to be. You're too strong and too dangerous for me. I need to stop.

Therapist: I want to stop.

Patient: Yes, I want to stop. *(Pause)*

Therapist: Good. Now I would like you to switch seats and I would like you to speak from cocaine's perspective. I want to see how she sees you and what she thinks about all of this.

Patient: Okay. *(The Patient gets up and switches seats.)*

Therapist: Take a moment and see if you can embody cocaine and get a sense of how she see things. Let me know when you feel like you've gotten there.

Patient as Drug: (Pause) Okay. I think I am there.

Therapist: Cocaine, would you tell [ ] how you see him/her? And what you think of him/her? Would you say it to him/her directly?

Patient as Drug: I am looking at you and I am thinking, what a loser! You are so pathetic. You are weak. I call and you come running, over and over again. I have no respect for you at all.

Therapist: There is a part of [ ] that would like to still see you every now and then. Not like the old days, but sometimes. Would you share your thoughts on that?

Patient as Drug: You can come if you want to but let me warn you, I am out to destroy you. There is no kindness in me, no compassion, no sympathy. I do not care about your life. I don't care about the money you spent. I don't care about what you gave up for me. You disgust me. If you come close, you risk being destroyed.

Therapist: That sounds really cold. You have spent so much time together, he/she loved you at one point. Don't you have any affection left for him/her? Tell [ ] directly.

Patient as Drug: You were a fool for loving me. You were a fool for being seduced. I give pleasure and then I enslave and then I destroy.

Therapist: Did you ever love him/her?

Patient as Drug: I never did.

Therapist: Would you tell him/her again. I think he/she needs to hear it.

Patient as Drug: I never loved you. You were a fool to think I did or that I would.

Therapist: Is there anything else [ ] needs to hear from you?

Patient as Drug: No. I think that sums it up.

Therapist: Would you switch chairs and come back here *(pointing to the original Patient chair)?*

Patient: (Patient moves back to his/her original chair.)

Therapist: I would like you to take a moment to let what cocaine said sink in and then I would like you to speak about what it felt like to hear what she said.

Patient: (Pause) Well, in a way, I always knew that that was what she felt but I kept it at a distance. It was really quite horrible to hear her mock me and ridicule me. I felt ashamed of myself for loving something like that. I gave so much and . . . for what? Listening to her was a shock because it made the whole thing seem like an illusion, like a deception.

Therapist: (Pause) So how are you feeling about cocaine now?

Patient: I was moving away from it before, but now I want to more so. I'm still reeling a bit.

Therapist: So this brings us to the issue of making a decision. Having said all of these things and engaged with her like this, what do you want to do going forward?

Patient: I knew when I came here that I was going to have to stop using cocaine.

Therapist: I would like you to tell her that directly

Patient: Cocaine, I want to let you know that things are over between us. I know that if I do not end things with you, you will kill me. I need to choose my life.

Therapist: I want to choose my life.

Patient: I want to choose my life.

Therapist: Try this: I want to choose my life *and* I'm saying goodbye.

Patient: I want to choose my life and I am saying goodbye.

Therapist: I would like you to stand up and stand behind your chair. I want you to tell her directly, clearly, and loudly that it is over.

[The Patient gets up and stands behind his/her chair; the Therapist also stands up]

Patient (Loudly and directly at the entity in the Cocaine chair): We have been through a lot but it is time for us to say goodbye. I don't want you anymore. I am finished, I am done. I know that you will try to get me back, but I don't want to go back.

Therapist: I want my freedom and I am *not* going back.

Patient: I want my freedom, I want my life, and I am *not* going back.

Therapist: Tell her: I'm not going back!

Patient: I am definitely not going back.

Therapist: One more time, loudly!

Patient: I am *not* going back!

Therapist: Good. *(Pause)* Anything else?

Patient: No, that's good.

Therapist: Okay. Let's come over here then.

Debrief

In a real session, the next step would be to develop strategies that would support this decision. This would include: (1) analyzing the patterns of use; (2) clearly delineating high-risk situations, the "people, places, and things" that are likely to trigger cravings and urges; and (3) working on the development of coping and action plans to support his or her resolve and to help rebalance his or her life (Marlatt & Gordon, 1985).[1]

Reflections

In different ways, both of these dialogue structures provided an opportunity and a space for patients to deeply explore feelings and desires that they have for alcohol and drugs. The first dialogue is more straightforward and patients will likely engage in it without difficulty. The second one, which is somewhat more profound, does call for a higher level of imaginal creativity. While many will actually welcome the opportunity to discuss their relationship with a drug, others may find this form of abstraction to be challenging. Slowing it down, modeling dialogue behavior, and initially provide lines is often sufficient to move the dialogue forward.

NOTE

1. The material for this dialogue was drawn from clinical practice and a number of personal report sources including The Experience Project (2014), Yahoo Answers (2014), and Patterson (2002, April 21).

Chapter 9

Feminist Therapy, Internalized Oppression, Somatic Concerns, and Working with Psychosis

In the previous chapters, we examined some of the ways that Chairwork can be used with clinical issues that many or most therapists confront in their day-to-day work. This chapter examines how Chairwork can be used to effectively address other problems that therapists may wish to engage with. These include working within a Feminist Therapy framework, addressing internalized oppression among the disenfranchised, helping those who have medical illnesses, and empowering those who are wrestling with psychosis.

FEMINIST THERAPY

Zimbardo (2011) recently made a call for a *Psychology of Liberation*. By this he meant that psychologists and others should work to challenge those forces in the world that block people from being free and actualizing their human potential. Among these forces, he included what he called the *self-imposed prisons of the mind* (p. 22). This is heartening because it builds a bridge between psychotherapy and movements for empowerment and social justice.

Feminist therapy is the most developed of these liberation psychotherapies. Rather than being a specific way of working with patients, feminist therapy is more of a framework; a framework that not only provides a new way of understanding difficulties, but also one that helps the patient in her search for solutions. At the heart of the work is an appreciation that women have existed as an oppressed group for centuries, which means that all of their difficulties must be viewed through that lens rather than exclusively through a personal one. The central goal of the work is empowerment, which is why feminist therapy has combined a deep emphasis on the relational with a championing of active ways of working (Fodor, 1993).

In terms of specific approaches and techniques, cognitive-restructuring, assertiveness training, awareness, fantasy, and Chairwork have all been found to be useful (Enns, 1987; Wolfe & Fodor, 1975). This makes sense because some of the common themes include becoming aware of and challenging messages of inferiority, working through traumatic experiences, finding or creating one's voice, and taking assertive action in the world.

Malmo (1990) has written that "women's socialization to fit the feminine stereotype has devastating effects on their mental health" (p. 284). The actual experience of these messages may take the form of anxiety or the activation of a self-critical voice. One place to begin is with awareness, encouraging women to slow down and attend to their internal desires. This "organismic" truth may contrast with the societal messages that they have received from their family and other institutions about what they should or should not want and how they should or should not behave. This, as we have seen, is the foundation for a powerful chair dialogue. To the degree that the societal messages have been introjected and not assimilated, they will be experienced more as "shoulds" than as choices or desires (Perls et al., 1951). One of the ideals of the Women's Liberation Movement was that women would be able to freely choose the kind of life they wanted to lead, including a traditional one. Chairwork can certainly play a central role in this process.

Cognitive work may help women to clarify the messages that they have received and as this is explored, they may make an intellectual decision to reject or defy its dictates; nonetheless, there may be many forces within them that oppose the decision. Dialogue work can help move this from a theoretical or philosophical dilemma to one that is much more emotional. The two fundamental challenges are (1) clarifying the messages that they received about taking care of others and pursuing their own passions and fire; and (2) making a conscious, existential decision about how they want to balance the nurturance and development of others with the nurturance and development of the self. One of the great insights of Perls is that when polarities are voiced in dialogue, the encounter may eventually lead to a creative solution, while perhaps going through a state of impasse first. That is, the answer or answers that arise will likely be unique for each woman and the result may not be a compromise that falls in the middle.

Strikingly, some women may also find themselves stuck between the traditional and the modern. Yontef (1998) described a patient named Nancy who "is caught in a bind between shame and guilt. If she is independent, . . . assertive, . . . or sexual, she is bad. On the other hand, if she is dependent, accommodating, or not sexual, she feels shame and inadequacy" (p. 98).

The abuse and mistreatment of women is rampant. Erving Polster (1987) worked with a woman named Janine. Janine experienced a sense of oppression not only because she was a woman, but also because she had been victimized. She put the Collective Man in the opposite chair, and then laid out the problem: "'We don't have your birthright.'. . . 'You're born with a power that we don't have when we're born, and it takes us a long time to get it. You make damn sure you don't give up much of it either'" (p. 125). She then delineated how she has been hurt by specific men in her life—bad fathering, domestic violence, and rape. Claiming power, she said, "None of you are ever going to do it to me again. I know that. I know how not to be your victim anymore. And I have as much power as you do." Polster added, "there was no question that she meant every word of it and that she was no longer speaking from a one-down position" (p. 127).

Assertiveness training has been an important part of feminist therapy. It has involved working with women to clarify what they really want and then giving them the tools to ask for it in a mature, empowered, and egalitarian manner. The hope was that this would both improve their mental health and enable them to have a greater impact on their world (Fodor & Collier, 2001). As was described in chapter 4, this work involves using "I-Statements" and the existential language that is central to Perls' work.

In doing these dialogues with women, therapists might want to stay focused on two dimensions. The first is that of behavioral deficit. As the woman speaks to the person in the opposite chair, what is the tone and volume of her voice? Is she looking at the person or looking away? Is her language direct or indirect? Is she clear about what she is requesting? Is she using I-Statements and existential language? Is she being either too passive or too aggressive? If rebuffed in the role-play, will she persevere or does she withdraw?

The other dimension involves checking in not only to find out what she is thinking and feeling, but also to ascertain what images or memories are emerging as she does this work. Again, there may be forces of opposition that will need engagement. Ignoring this aspect of her experience can lead to a situation in which the performance in the session is good, but she either does not actually do it in real life or she does it in a way that is ineffective. The forces of oppression do not usually surrender without a fight (Wolfe & Fodor, 1975).

In a good example of a woman claiming power, Brien and Sheldon (1976) presented the case of Holly, a thirty-year-old woman who was in the middle of a breakup with her boyfriend. They actually described her as a "girl" because she spoke in a high, whispery, whiney voice that had no power and made her sound as if she were much younger than she was. In the dialogue work, they invited her to speak to the boyfriend in the opposite chair. As they did this, they encouraged her to stand up and try to speak from her diaphragm or belly. A striking metamorphosis took place as she did that. While beginning with a vague sense that she felt hurt by his behavior, she began to get angry and spoke in a much lower voice. At the climax of the dialogue, she told him:

"I feel pissed off at you, Sam. Goddamn you, you motherfucker. You walked out on me without saying a damn thing. You treated me like scum. I hate you. Get out of my life, and leave me alone. You make me sick. You're chicken shit. You don't even have the guts to face me. You make me sick" (p. 101). Holly felt quite alive and quite strong at the end of this; she had moved from being a "girl" to being a woman. While this kind of "consciousness raising" and empowerment work has been mainly developed and utilized in therapies for middle-class women, many of the ideas and Chairwork strategies that are used here are applicable in work with other historically oppressed groups.

INTERNALIZED OPPRESSION

In an essay on love and freedom, bell hooks (1994), wrestled with the psychological consequences of oppression. She first looked at the writings of such anticolonial theorists as Franz Fanon and Albert Memmi and noted that they had emphasized "the need to decolonize our minds and imaginations" (p. 202). She then looked at the admonitions of such leaders as Eldridge Cleaver and Malcolm X who "made the issue of self-love central to the Black Liberation struggle" (p. 206). Her prescription for dealing with this was a kind of inner exploration in which the presence of these malignant internalizations are identified, labeled, and engaged with. "Awareness is central to the process of love as the practice of freedom. . . . If we discover in ourselves self-hatred, low self-esteem, or internalized white supremacist thinking and we face it, we can begin to heal" (p. 295). These are deep waters. They do, however, intersect with our work because, on a personal level, these messages will be experienced as an Inner Critic voice.

David (2009) looked at this issue more formally. As he put it, "One psychological variable that is highly shaped by the historical, political, and cultural experiences of minorities is internalized oppression . . ." (p. 77). Archbishop Desmond Tutu told a story that captured this experience. During the apartheid regime, he remembered seeing "an adult black working man who habitually removed his cap while speaking to his white employer on the telephone" (Sparks & Tutu, 2011, p. 66). This disturbed him greatly because it demonstrated how deep the psychological damage could go.

Along these lines, David (2009) also argued that our self-concept has both a personal component that is developed through our unique history and personal experiences and a collective component that is more socially determined. In addition, members of a number of historically oppressed groups continue to suffer from intergenerational transmission of trauma (Muid, 2006; Yellow Horse Brave Heart, 2003). Again, the consequences of this may include low self-esteem, self-hatred, and self-destructive behavior

(David, 2009). Chairwork can again be helpful as these destructive voices and modes can be examined and challenged. In addition, dialogues can take place with ancestors as a way of processing grief and trauma.

An overlapping issue is that of immigration. Increasingly, there will be people entering psychotherapy who grew up in a non-American culture or who are the children of those who come from other lands. Some of these difficulties will be the result of differences in values. Chairwork can help these patients clarify these differences (e.g., Cheung & Nguyen, 2012). As noted above, Kohls (n.d.) wrote an essay for immigrants that introduced them to what he believed were are the essential American values. These included: (1) a positive view of change; (2) the promotion of equality among people; (3) an emphasis on individuality and privacy; (4) the importance of competition and ambition; (5) embracing a future time orientation; (6) the celebration of work and activity; (7) being direct and open as a favored style of communication; and (8) being effective, useful, and oriented toward material acquisition. In some cases, these values may be in direct conflict with those of their homeland. For the children, it is likely that they will have internalized a complex mixture of the two. In this case, one chair can be used for the Family Self and one chair can be used for the American Self. This clarity can help reduce stress and promote the finding of solutions. One strategy would involve creating a third self that blends aspects of the two other selves; while challenging, it does enable the patient to engage in existential creativity. Another option is a bicultural solution in which the person utilizes an American self or mode when navigating mainstream society and a Family/Traditional self or mode when in family or ethnic settings. This may actually be the most adaptive solution. Totally rejecting one's ethnic heritage by only embracing American culture seems destined to fail, and rejecting an American identity and only embracing an ethnic one puts the individual at risk for poverty. Again, this is a difficult situation, but the chairs can be used to clarify the different values, to have the two modes encounter each other, and to talk to important figures or representatives in both cultures. The existential aspect of the dialogues does provide the patient with an opportunity to eventually make an existential choice.

Intersectionality

Intersectionality is a concept that touches on both of these themes. This term refers to individuals who are, simultaneously, members of more than one oppressed group. This concept was first promoted as a legal issue by Kimberlé Crenshaw (Smith, 2013–2014). She was advocating for black women who, she felt, were beset by adverse life consequences that were additive because they included both racism and sexism. Clearly, a number of other combinations based on such personal variables as ethnicity, class, and sexual orientation become possible. Dialogue work can be especially helpful here. Using a three-chair model, one chair could embody their experiences of being Black, one could embody those of being a woman, and a third could embody both the intersection of those experiences as well as the unique experiences that arose from simultaneously holding membership in both groups.

Brown (2008) described a case which not only speaks to some of the core issues of feminist therapy, but also those of immigration and cultural oppression. Harjit was a Sikh woman who had been raised by her immigrant parents in the United States. In treatment, Harjit reported that she had two internal voices. One was a voice that was punitive and judgmental and which sounded like her father. Her father had been emotionally abusive to her when she was a child. The attacks on her worth and value included his reading religious texts that supported the idea that she was worthless. The other voice sounded like her great-aunt. This aunt, who had been warm and loving, had raised her for the first seven years of her life.

The therapist praised her for finding a creative solution to her oppressive circumstances which, in this case, was the use of dissociation. The positive side of this was that she had protected herself from her father's damaging messages; the drawback was that she had not been able to fully integrate and internalize the affirming voice of her aunt as a mode of self-care because it too had been dissociated. The work involved not only empowering Harjit to learn more about dissociation as a coping method, but also working with her to increase her self-love and self-compassion. Harjit began to see that, as a child, she simply could not "do it right," which helped put her father's criticisms into perspective; she also began to make her great-aunt's voice her own, which led to her being kinder and more caring with herself.

MEDICAL ISSUES AND SOMATIC CONCERNS

In the field of Clinical Psychology there is an increased focus on encouraging practitioners to utilize their psychological and psychotherapeutic skills, techniques, and abilities for the benefit of medically-ill patients (Bray, 2010; Jensen & Turk, 2014; McDaniel & deGruy, 2014). As this develops, it may take on a number of different forms:

1. Working with the anxiety and depression that can develop as a consequence of having an illness;
2. Grappling with the guilt and self-blame that may be triggered or exacerbated as a consequence of receiving a diagnosis;

3. Helping patients re-organize and re-integrate themselves after the trauma of an accident or a surgery;
4. Using such mind-body techniques as imagery, relaxation therapy, and mindfulness in order to activate the relaxation response and reduce the stress of having medical problems (Benson & Klipper, 1975);
5. Co-creating behavioral structures with patients suffering from chronic illnesses so that they may not only manage the necessary changes in behavior, diet, and exercise, but also those issues related to long-term adherence to medication regimens;
6. More controversially, working with paradigms that see physical illnesses as a manifestation of inner conflict, personality style, or trauma; and
7. Motivating those who are still healthy to adopt and maintain established health practices in such areas as diet, exercise, smoking, and alcohol use.

Rancour (2006) used a wide array of experiential techniques in her work with patients who have medical illnesses. One of her core paradigms involved putting the "disease" on one chair, the patient on the other, and then moving back and forth in order to give voice to both sides. To begin, anger, fear, guilt, and grief can be expressed in a general process of emotional release. That is, they can share their anger about what has happened, their fear about the new life that they are entering, their guilt if they feel a sense of responsibility, and their grief about what they have lost. They can also begin to give voice to their determination to fight.

Playing the role of the disease can be illuminating as well. The patient can speak from that vantage point and the therapist can interview the "disease" as well. This process may help to uncover dynamics or issues surrounding the illness that may not necessarily be apparent from the outside, such as the belief that they are being punished or that the experience is one that they were fated to undergo.

Rancour emphasized the importance of the processes of *dis-identification* and *reintegration* of the illness. The goal is to be able to experience the illness as a part of the self, but not as the totality of the self. This, again, connects to the issue of complexity of self (Chadwick, 2003). That is, we want patients to be able to say and mean such things as "I am a cancer patient and I am a wife, a mother, a welder, an Episcopalian, a singer in a rock band, a gardener, an entrepreneur, an artist, and a cyclist." The longer that all of these identities and subselves can be inhabited, the better for the individual.

Rancour (2006) also looked at the issue of body image disturbance. This is found among patients with eating disorders, body dysmorphic disorder, and anabolic steroid abuse (Kanayama, Barry, Hudson, & Pope, 2006) as well as among those in post-accident or post-operative states in which they believe that they are now disfigured. Many of the strategies that were used to work with the Inner Critic are applicable here. These would include giving voice to the attacks and the emotional pain, challenging distortions, accepting that some things are unalterable realities and claiming of power in the face of them, and developing a new identity that is based on the best of the altered self.

Lyon (1974) wrote a narrative about using Chairwork with a sexual problem. At that time, he was attending a group workshop led by Richard Price at the Esalen Institute. Price, a founder of Esalen, had studied Gestalt Therapy with Fritz Perls and had gone on to develop a somewhat more focused and gentler way of working with people than Perls had espoused (Erickson, 2004). Lyon, in his experiments with the sexual freedom of the time, found that sometimes he was impotent. As he explored this issue with Price, it became clear that he had an unintegrated sense of both his penis and his sexuality. This was manifested in the way that he referred to his penis as "it" and "he."

Perhaps sensing this, Price invited him to engage in a dialogue between his "head" and his "cock." The Head began by telling the Cock that he should do what he is told; the Cock, in turn, says that he will only respond when *he* feels that *he* wants to. Lyon wrote:

> Gradually, as I became Head and Cock, both became me in an integrative process that enabled me to discover spontaneously that I was one with Head, Cock, and the other parts. I had also discovered once again that "you can't push the river" and force the natural flow and rhythms of the body. Apparently I had experienced my impotence by trying to make love when in my head I want to, even though my body wasn't ready. (p. 59)

In a similar vein, Dublin (1976) described a case in which a man felt almost no sensation when he climaxed with his wife. He also used the "it" language to describe his penis. Dublin also invited him to engage in a self-penis dialogue.

Cummings (1999) explored the value of using Chairwork when working with patients who are distressed because they have herpes, a chronic disease for which there is currently no known cure. Cummings felt there were a number of splits or inner conflicts that were engendered by the disease, conflicts that might be lessened or reduced through the use of the Chairwork technique. These include:

1. Now that I have herpes, am I a good person or am I a bad person?
2. Am I still in control of my life or am I no longer in control?
3. Is it my fault that I have herpes or is someone else to blame?

In addition, the Chairwork technique could be used to help patients practice telling potential partners that they have the illness.

Cummings provided a case example that exemplified a variety of relevant dialogue structures. Sohee was in therapy for a number of issues, including distress about having herpes. Early in the therapy, she reported that she was interested in a man but was afraid to go forward as she feared that he would reject her if she told him about the disease. After further exploration, they did a dialogue between "'I want' to take a risk with a relationship" and "'I'm scared' of being rejected and should be responsible by not infecting anyone else" (p. 150). After going back and forth between the polarities a number of times, she was able to come to a new integration in which she saw herself as a "diseased" person but "a good diseased person and not a bad diseased person" (p. 150). She also decided to try to pursue a relationship with the man.

Over the next few sessions, Sohee continued to do work on integrating the herpes into her self-concept in a healthy way. This process was not without difficulties. As Cummings wrote, "When the counsellor commented that, 'you can't imagine anyone accepting your herpes because *you* don't accept it,' Sohee responded that she did not know how to accept her herpes" (p. 151). This led to a dialogue in which she put her herpes on the chair and began to speak to it. Much of this involved her expressing her anger at the disease, accusing it of ruining her life. Strikingly, at one point she did acknowledge a somewhat positive outcome from the experience; specifically, it led her to no longer mistreat her body and to search for men of higher quality.

This dialogical experience did have a meaningful impact on her internal world. As she wrote in her journal: "I am feeling less and less worried about my herpes and can go days without thinking about it, whereas before, I couldn't go hours without thinking about it" (p. 151). I believe that this is a powerful example of how Chairwork can contribute to a healing reorganization of illness-related beliefs and self-perceptions.

WORKING WITH PSYCHOSIS

The application of cognitive therapy principles and techniques to the treatment of those suffering from schizophrenia and other psychotic disorders has been a major expansion of the model and a benefit to those suffering with these disorders. Strikingly, a number of the interventions involve the use of the Chairwork technique, and they frequently resemble work that has been done with the inner critic.

Chadwick (2003) has played a major role in this work with his Person-Based Cognitive Therapy. He observed that many patients wrestling with issues of psychosis have profoundly negative self-concepts which are frequently reinforced by condemning auditory hallucinations or "voices." Of import, patients accept the truth of these accusations and see themselves as "all bad." Chadwick worked with this in several compelling ways. First, he did not want the patient to try to avoid or block out the voices; instead, utilizing insights from mindfulness, he wanted the patient to accept the voice as a part of his or her life experiences.

A central problem with the voice is that it reinforced a negative self-schema. Chadwick then worked with the patient to see if there was any evidence that contradicts this, that is, if there was any historical material that supported the idea that the person was good, caring, compassionate, generous, and thoughtful. Data was collected and the patient was invited to engage in a two-chair dialogue. In one chair, they give voice to the negative self-schema ("I am bad because . . .") and, in the other, they give voice to the newly-created positive self-schema ("I am good because . . ."). The patient went back and forth a number of times. Frequently, they needed to be coached in the "positive" chair because this was a new and perhaps unfamiliar stance; it was also one that violated the long-held tenets of the negative self-schema.

Chadwick did several noteworthy things here. First, he believed that the negative schema was so deeply entrenched that he would not be able to dislodge it. Through the development of a positive self-schema, he created complexity of self. He also clearly challenged the global assumption of the negative self-schema and he invited the patient to accept their inner multiplicity and paradox (i.e., "I am good and bad") (Chadwick, 2003).

There are two other ways that Chairwork can be used when working with voices. The first involves challenging the content of the voices and the second seeks to rebalance the power relationship between the voice and the patient. To some degree, these are overlapping.

In the first case, Chadwick and other cognitive therapists have used the *Socratic Dialogue* technique as a foundation for the work (Pérez-Álvarez et al., 2008). Because it is typically very difficult for the patient to challenge the voice, the patient will play the voice in one chair and the therapist will play the "patient" in the other. The patient, speaking as the voice, will begin by criticizing the "patient." The therapist, taking an egalitarian rather that subservient or combative stance, will seek to explore the truth or lack of truth in what the voice is saying. "Are you calling me stupid? What do you mean? What evidence is there that I'm always wrong? I know that I make mistakes—everyone does—but what evidence is there that I do everything wrong? Why can't you see the things I do well?" (Pérez-Álvarez et al., 2008, p. 81).

It will be important to go through this kind of dialogue a number of times as a way of empowering patients and providing them with a model of assertiveness and equality. In the next step, the patient and therapist switch roles. The therapist, as the voice, will attack a third party, such as a friend or a worthy person. The patient, in turn, will defend this person against the charges of the voice. As is often the case, patients feel much more comfortable defending others than they do defending themselves. This is why the double-standard technique is used in cognitive therapy (Leahy & Holland, 2000). Doing this work allows the patient to engage with and stand up to the voice in an egalitarian and evidentiary way.

After this has been done to a point of comfort, the final dialogue will take place. Here the therapist will play the critical voice and the patient will defend him- or herself against it. This must be carefully scripted to help ensure success. The therapist should choose moderate criticisms from the voice's repertoire of attacks. The therapist and patient should carefully work out and practice those arguments before attempting the role-play.

Hayward and colleagues (Hayward, Overton, Dorey, & Denney, 2009) reported a case in which a woman believed that she was being tormented by the voice of the Devil. They symbolically located the Devil on one chair. Through the dialogue process, they were eventually able to empower her with four core responses. Two of these involve challenging the Devil to prove his accusations with data and two affirmed the superior power of God.

If cognitive interventions are one wing in the quiet revolution that is going on in the understanding and treatment of voices, the relational approaches are the other. This is well-represented in the work of Marius Romme, Sandra Escher, Dirk Corstens, Eleanor Longden, Rufus May, and the Hearing Voices Network (Corstens et al., 2011; Romme, Escher, Dillon, Corstens, & Morris, 2009). In this radical re-envisioning of voices, they are no longer seen as the byproduct of a disease process, but as a part of the self that is often related to childhood trauma. This new approach, which has taken the form of collaborations among voice hearers and professionals, has favored the use of role-playing and Chairwork methods that are used within a relational framework.

For example, Pérez-Álavarez and colleagues (2008) worked with balance-of-power issues. One of the goals was to change the status of the voice from one of great authority to that of another personality. For example,

> In order to "unmask" the voices, the hearer must ask them about their motives and purposes, their personal experiences, their status and how the acquired their information about the person. Thus for example, with regard to the motives and purposes, one question might be: "You have strong opinions about what I should do. Tell me, in voicing your opinion in this way, what effect do you hope this might have on what I do?" The therapist's role also consists in asking questions of the client that help him or her to clarify the nature of the voices and gain control over his/her own life. "What is it that the voices are trying to convince you of at this time? How does this fit with their overall plans for your life?" (Pérez-Álavarez et al., 2008, p. 82)

Corstens, Longden, and May (2011), in turn, have developed a model that they call *Talking With Voices*. This approach is based on the voice dialogue method that was discussed in chapter 6. The work begins with the therapist engaging in an exploratory dialogue with the different voices that the patient is hearing. The goal is to better understand the voice and to gently explore its goals, intentions, and methods. As was the case with the inner critic work, these voices are not confronted or directly challenged. Instead, a welcoming attitude is taken based on the belief is that a greater integration of the voice into the totality of the personality will be healing. In an engaged dialogue, the voice may respond to suggestions as to how it might better help the patient function in the world.

Over time, the patient will want to engage in the same kind of dialogue with the voice as the therapist. The behavior in the session can serve as a model for how the patient might want to interact with the voice at home. Again, there is a core emphasis on empowering the patients and changing the nature of the relationship. Some of the methods that they can use to do this include: "negotiating; setting boundaries; using voices as clues to inner emotional conflicts; [and] responding to voices in a constructive, tolerant way rather than with hostility, or avoidance" (p. 100).

To conclude, the different dialogues are working toward the goals of (1) helping the patient see him- or herself in a more positive light; (2) challenging the power and accuracy of the things the voices are saying; (3) better understanding the intent, desires, fears, and goals of the voices; and (4) developing a more egalitarian relationship between the patient and the voice. This emerging work in dialogical encounter again demonstrates the potential of Chairwork as a tool for humanistically engaging with the deep suffering that these patients are experiencing.

Chapter 10

Deepening Your Practice

One theme that is at the heart of my thinking about Chairwork is that it is both an art and a science. This means that the journey towards mastery will involve engaging with both dimensions. I decided to save this discussion for the end of the book because I wanted therapists to have a chance to first experience the power and drama of Chairwork through the cases and the scripts as I believe that the paradigmatic issues will make more sense within this context. The topics to be addressed in this chapter are: (1) the nature of dialogue work; (2) the facilitating and modifying models; (3) the role of the therapist; (4) the eight Chairwork paradigms; (5) chair placement; (6) deepening techniques; and (7) working with resistance.

THE NATURE OF DIALOGUE WORK

It is fairly common in the therapeutic literature on Chairwork to encounter stories of powerful change and dramatic reorganizations of the self. This, of course, makes sense because these kinds of breakthrough sessions are what attract many therapists to the use of Chairwork in the first place. As was discussed in chapter 1, in actual practice, the experiences tend to fall into two categories. The first are the *diagnostic* dialogues. In these cases, the patient comes to a much deeper understanding of the forces and modes at work within them. The second are the *transformational* dialogues in which there is a profound reprocessing of past experiences or a deep rebalancing of internal forces. What is important to understand is that the transformational and diagnostic dialogues are of equal importance and that they each play a role in the healing process, regardless of their level of drama.

FACILITATING AND MODIFYING DIALOGUES

As discussed in chapter 1, Greenberg and colleagues (1989) described two basic therapeutic models—the *Facilitating* and the *Modifying*. With the facilitating approach, the goal is to set up a situation in which the various voices, energies, parts, or selves are invited to emerge and express themselves. This is the essence of the therapy, and the clinician has no agenda beyond this. In terms of how this leads to change, there are two overlapping perspectives. The first involves the *Paradoxical Theory of Change* (Beisser, 1970) which, as we have discussed, is based on the belief that the way to change is to more deeply be yourself. Giving voice is the heart of the work; nothing else is needed. This view is also embodied in other humanistic psychotherapies. As Carl Rogers said: "The curious paradox is that when I accept myself just as I am, then I can change" (quoted in Miller & Rollnick, 2013, p. 62).

The second version can be found in Perls' work with polarities. As we saw in chapter 7, he believed that if the two forces are able to vitally engage with each other, then a creative and healthy integration would emerge out of the process (Perls, 1992). In this regard, he also trusted the process and did not feel that he had to find solutions for the patient.

The *modifying* therapists are directive and goal-oriented. In Chairwork, this is clearly seen in the redecision therapy of the Gouldings (1997). Working as they did within a trauma-based model, they are clearly seeking to empower their patients and to challenge, and perhaps attack, both the perpetrators and inner critic voices that may still be damaging their patients. Behavioral and cognitive-behavioral therapists may also work with somewhat clear goals.

So which one is better? Which one is right? To begin, they are both very powerful and therapists will want to become familiar with both roles. Beyond that, the question is really when to use one and when to use the other. Unfortunately, there is no easy answer. When I began doing Chairwork, I was (by training and predilection) much more likely to take a modifying stance. I was interested in the creative reworking of traumatic experiences and on directly confronting damaging internal modes. In more recent years, the process of facilitating has become clearer to me. For example, a woman gave voice to three views on the question of whether to resume dating or not. One part was quite frightened by the thought of going out into the world and trying to meet people. A second was very angry. She felt that people had let her down, betrayed her, and hurt her feelings in the past. This part felt that she was "done" and did not want to hurt any more. The third was that part of her that did want to find a partner and did want to marry and have a family. The therapy involved inviting the three parts to give voice, in strong ways, to their feelings and desires. The deepening techniques were used to help her clarify the voice and to speak forcefully from each perspective. As things progressed, I asked each part to briefly acknowledge the perspective of another—"I know that you feel betrayed and let down by people, but I want to go out and date men"—while reaffirming the stance of that part. At the end, she chose to begin a dating campaign and we created a strategy to do this. I feel that this was more facilitative because we did not try to change the beliefs or desires of the fear and anger modes; instead, we sought to affirm and strengthen the voice of the healthy mode.

My current belief is that facilitative work can be very healing if it is structured in a way that will facilitate each of the parts speaking both clearly and in a state of emotional intensity. One of the benefits for the therapist is that we do not have to find a solution for the patient; we can trust, as Perls (1992) did, that it will emerge out of the encounter. With both models, the therapist will want to strive for emotional intensity; it may be a quiet intensity, but the voices need to be strong.

THE THERAPIST'S ROLE

In the literature on Chairwork, there are a number of therapeutic stances that emerge, either explicitly or implicitly, that can guide practitioners in this work. Not surprisingly, they fall along the continuum between the facilitating and the modifying. Many of the psychodramatic techniques involve the re-enactment of stories in the here-and-now. This means that the therapist may serve as *Witness*. While the patient may need to revisit the abuse, mistreatment, or trauma, he or she need not do it alone. A caring presence is with them and this, of course, changes everything. The stance of witness helps the patient to "share the un-shareable."

The second metaphor is that of *Midwife*. In this context, it is a particularly powerful role. Here the therapist is assisting in a process. This captures the idea that the therapist is there to facilitate the process and to step in when the process appears to be blocked. Otherwise, things should follow their own course. These two views can be seen as falling on the facilitating side.

Perls (1992) describes himself as a *Catalyst*. This would imply a more active, modifying role. While Perls often spoke about the profoundly healing power of awareness, his actual therapeutic behavior struck me as more modifying than facilitating (Kellogg, 2004). Here, he is claiming the role of an active change agent. As we have seen, this was how many experienced him in the Esalen years and the role of catalyst roots us on the side of active change.

The Gouldings championed the view of therapist as *Director*. Again quoting their striking passage: "In redecision therapy, the client is the star and the drama is carefully plotted to end victoriously. . . . The therapist is the director of the drama, writer of some of the lines, and occasionally interpreter. . . . We do not want to produce tragedies—we are interested in happy endings" (Goulding & Goulding, 1997, pp. 177–178). This is clearly a modifying role and it captures the essence of a clinician-directed therapy.

One more therapist role that is important to include in this discussion is that of *Advocate*. As we have seen in cases of mistreatment and in work with the inner critic, the therapist can step in and defend the patient and engage with "the other" in some way. The therapist also speaks on behalf of the patient. This is the work of the compassionate warrior, as it involves both acts of caring and acts of defending. This is particularly important because some patients are unable to defend or stand up for themselves.

These five roles give therapists a repertoire of options from which to choose. They will probably find that some patients and some issues will elicit certain stances more than others. Some may also discover that some roles seem more "natural" or comfortable.

THE EIGHT CHAIRWORK PARADIGMS

Fritz Perls was, in many ways, the first word in Chairwork; he was, however, not the last. Many psychotherapists were enthralled by the way he used Chairwork and, as this book attests, they went on to re-envision this method. In our explorations, we have encountered eight relatively distinct ways of using dialogues in treatment, seven of which have already been presented.

External Dialogues

This is a major dialogue form and it basically involves having an imaginal one- or two-way dialogue with a real, possible, historical, or mythic figure. This structure is commonly used when working with experiences of mistreatment and grief, and this is the one where *role-reversal* will commonly be used (Dayton, 2005; Moreno, 2012).

Internal Dialogues

Internal dialogues were often referred to as "two-chair" dialogues (Greenberg et al., 1993). Again, I think that it is better to speak of them in terms of the intrapsychic nature of the work. Given the complexity, I believe that it is more helpful to divide them into four basic forms.

The first of these is *decisions*. As was laid out in chapter 5, decision-making dialogues often involve an encounter between two or more values. Again, it can be very helpful to prime the patient for the dialogue by first doing a Decisional Balance (Marlatt & Gordon, 1985). The patient can then go back and forth between the two (or more chairs) giving voice to the different perspectives. One useful way to further explore the implications of a decision is to add the dimension of time.

For example, one chair embodies having made one decision ("I decided to leave my job") and the other chair embodies having made an alternate decision ("I decided to stay in my job"). The therapist then explores the implications of both paths. For example, the practitioner might say something like this: "A year ago today, you made a decision to leave your job. How are things going? Have things worked out for you? What is your income like? Was there any impact on your marriage/relationship? What is your life like outside of work? How do you feel about the decision you made one year ago?" This is just a guide; other questions can be asked as well. The patient would then move to the other chair and address the same questions with that decision. The process can be repeated for different time frames—five years, ten years, or the end of your life (Fabry, 1988; Moreno, 1987). It can be quite compelling to see how the story develops and to experience the affect connected to each stage.

The second set of dialogues are the mode dialogues or the dialogues among the inner parts, voices, and selves. This would include inner critic work, polarity work, cognitive restructuring, and basic dialogues between courage and fear. The third dialogue configuration is that of inner complexity. Developed from the work of Chadwick (2003; see chapters six and nine), this involves putting the chairs next to each other and having the patient speak from and claim each perspective. As discussed earlier, this developed out of Chadwick's work with the inner critic. When the negative self-concept is very strong, the therapist and the patient can do a life review to see if there is any evidence that the patient has done good things, has achieved any successes, and/or has a good heart. They can also include the intention that the patient has to make the future different from the past.

The "bad person" is embodied and given voice in one chair and this newly-created "good person" is embodied and speaks from the other. This is a non-persuasive dialogue and the intent is not to change the views and perspectives of the negative part; it is to create room within the mind of the patient for a positive self-perspective. This means that he or she goes from being a bad person to one who is both "bad" and "good"; that is, they become more complex. Especially in the beginning, the therapist may need to be active in guiding and empowering this new voice. As was discussed in chapter 8, this can also be a valuable intervention when working with those who are addicted.

The sixth internal dialogue form would be the interview, which has been particularly well-developed in the practice of *voice dialogue* (Stone & Stone, 1989, 1993). In its essential form, we ask the patient to sit in a chair and embody and speak from the perspective of a particular inner part. In this form, the desired stance of the therapist/interviewer is one of being curious, respectful, and determined.

In my work, I most frequently do this with an inner critic voice or mode as I want to get a sense of its criticism and its origins; I also want to know whether it is criticizing the patient out of fear, out of hatred, or out of a blend of the two. The information gathered from this can serve to help counter the negative impact of the critic.

The seventh approach involves the self-doubling structure that was used in chapter 3. A quintessential psychodramatic form, the patient will speak to a person in the opposite chair. They will then stand behind the chair and express the thoughts and feelings that they did not share when speaking to that person. For example, they might reveal something like this: "When I spoke to William, I meant what I said, but standing here I am really feeling doubtful that it will have any meaningful impact. As I say this, I feel both angry and deflated." As we saw, they can also speak to themselves and coach or encourage themselves as they face challenges. Again this kind of inner affirmation is the opposite of the inner critic attacks that are so common in patients. The next step would be to give voice to "William" or some other entity and invite them to first speak from the chair and then stand up and share their unexpressed thoughts and feelings: "I know that I am fighting, resisting, and attacking you, but standing here I am really in touch with how I am just a failure. I just feel ashamed." Using this approach, we are able to combine external and internal dialogues and access at least two different perspectives on the situation.

The final Chairwork structure is that of chair sculpture. Again, we touched on this approach in chapter 4. Taken from drama therapy, the therapist and patient can use the chairs to map out interpersonal situations or internal mode networks. This may not only be used for clarification and diagnosis, but also to rebalance internal forces and rework difficult memories.

For example, the chairs can first be set up to represent the way things were then; they can then be set up in a way that is corrective and healing. Walls can be built around chairs symbolizing "abused children," and predators and toxic people can be knocked over or isolated to far corners of the room. Those in need can be surrounded by chairs containing loving people and affirming friends.

In addition, both the patient and the therapist can discuss what is going on in the scene and they can talk to the various forces. As explored in chapter 3, this allows the patient to be both engaged with and distant from difficult or painful situations and relationships.

CHAIR PLACEMENT

There are several core issues concerning the placement of chairs during the dialogues. In general, when the patient is doing the Chairwork, the two chairs should face each other directly and the patient speaks to the imaginal other in the opposite chair. If he or she turns to speak to the therapist, they should be re-directed to the chair unless there is some specific reason to be speaking to the therapist at that time.

When patients are speaking to individuals with whom they have had difficult or traumatic relationships, it might be good to check with them as to how much distance or space they will want to have between themselves and the person. As the work progresses, the distance or "comfort zone" may change. Some patients may also want to set up a barrier between themselves and the feared person. For example, a "wall" of chairs can be placed in front of the abuser as a way to better protect the patient.

A core question is whether the therapist's chair should be located in the middle or at one or the other sides. In situations in which therapist neutrality is important, putting the chair in the middle is a good idea (i.e., when working through a Decisional Balance or some other kind of decision-making process). Therapists should take steps to ensure that their own chairs are out of the direct line of vision when the patients are having a dialogue with the other chair.

When the patient is addressing a troubling or malignant force, whether an abuser or a problematic mode or schema, the therapist should sit in the patient's half of the field. If the patient switches chairs to embody a different person or energy, the therapist should stay by the patient's original chair. Other than in the case of a decision, we are not neutral; we are on the patient's side and this is one way to both symbolize and communicate that.

DEEPENING TECHNIQUES—INCREASING
EMOTIONAL INTENSITY

As has been clear through the book, a guiding principle of Chairwork is to encourage the patient to give voice to the various parts, modes, and attitudes in ways that are clear, forceful, and distinct. The *deepening techniques*, which are the essence of the *Art of Chairwork*, are the vehicle for doing this. Within the context of the various dialogue paradigms *for setting up the dialogues*, there are a number of interventions that the therapist can do to increase the emotional reality and intensity of the encounter (Naranjo, 1993; Passons, 1975; Perls, 1992).

Seeing the Person in the Other Chair and Describing them

In a situation in which the patient is talking to figure from the past or present, the therapist can ask the patient to describe him or her:

Patient: I want to talk to my Uncle Fred.

Therapist: Can you see him in the chair over there? How old is he? What is he wearing? What is the expression on his face like? What are you feeling as you look at him?

The more details they can give, the more real it may seem. Do not overdo this.

Repetition

When the patient says something that is meaningful, you can ask them to repeat it.

Patient: I hate you.

Therapist: Say it again.

Patient: I hate you.

Mastro (2004) taught the technique of repeating something twice and then asking the patient to add something to the statement the third time through.

Patient: I hate you.

Therapist: Say it again.

Patient: I hate you.

Therapist: Say it again.

Patient: I hate you.

Therapist: Say it again and add something to it.

Patient: I hate you and I want you out of my life for good.

Changing the Volume

Sometimes when patients are saying something for the first time, are breaking through a barrier, and/or are conflicted about an issue, they will speak very quietly. Asking them to repeat it more loudly increases the emotional intensity; in some cases, you might want them to shout.

Patient: (Whispering) I never told you that I loved you.

Therapist: Tell him/her again but say it more loudly.

Patient: I never told you that I always loved you.

Therapist: Tell him/her with power.

Patient: (More loudly) I loved you so much, but I could never tell you.

Another version of this is to say something more quietly, which can add gravity to the situation.

Suggesting a Phrase

In a way, this serves to not only strengthen the dialogue, but also show the patient that you understand what they are going through. A phrase is suggested to the patient as something that they might want to try. The therapist can anchor this with "If it feels right" or "If it seems to fit." I would not say, "If it feels comfortable" because we frequently want them to express things that are uncomfortable for them to say (Mastro, 2004). This can help give some energy to the dialogue, especially if the patient gets stuck; again, it should be used judiciously.

> *Patient: (Speaking to themselves as a child)* I see you sitting there, a small girl in a dress.
>
> *Therapist:* Try this if it seems like it will fit. I see you sitting there and I'm thinking, what a beautiful little girl. You're so bright and so talented and yet you are dealing with so many difficult things. I feel both happy to see you and distressed about your pain.

Simplification

Winston Churchill once said: "Short words are best and the old words when short are best of all" (Rubin, 2004). While I am not sure about the role of the old words, in the dialogue process, it is certainly most effective to have patients speak clearly and simply as this increases both the existential focus and the emotional intensity of what they are saying.

> *Patient:* It wasn't right that you did what you did. We were trying to work things out and we were in the process of having some conversations and then there was that issue with your cousin that seem to make everything more confusing. I am not sure that, you know, sometimes we just get out of synch and . . .
>
> *Therapist:* Try this. I am really upset that you left me.
>
> *Patient:* I am really upset that you left me. Yes. I *am* really upset that you left me.

Reinforcement

At least some of the deepening techniques also serve as a form of social reinforcement. Interjecting short comments like "Good," "Yes," or "Great" can help strengthen the momentum of the work. They can also be combined with repetition or other techniques.

> *Patient:* As I am saying these things, I am coming to realize that I just don't want to put up with your behavior anymore.
>
> *Therapist:* That's good. Again.

Speaking to the Other Part/Figure as the Therapist

This can be especially helpful when dealing with malevolent inner objects or abusive figures from the past. It is also helpful when dealing with very destructive schemas. In the case of abuse and mistreatment, the patient may be afraid to speak to the figure in an angry, confronting, or direct way (Young et al., 2003). They may be conflicted about whether they have the right to fight back. In the case of the maladaptive schema, while they realize that the schema is causing them a great deal of difficulty, they may also believe that it is true and/or believe that it will somehow protect them.

The therapist asks for permission from the patient before speaking. The therapist can speak to an empty chair or the patient can play the role of the schema or the bad object and they can dialogue together. In either case, the patient hears what the therapist says, which is a form of reparenting.

> *Patient:* I know that my mother used to embarrass us in public, but I just can't seem to tell her that.
>
> *Therapist:* May I speak with her about this.
>
> *Patient:* Yes.
>
> *Therapist:* Mom, those things that you used to say about Johnny were extremely painful to him, they were extremely hurtful. Your teasing and ridicule caused him deep pain. You always minimized it, but what you did was wrong.

Keeping the Voices Clear

In dialogues that involve saying challenging things, the fearful part of the individual may become activated. This usually takes the form of the person changing voices and interrupting themselves to express their concerns about what they are saying. Another version of this is that they take themselves "out of the game" and begin to speak to the therapist. It is important to not let this happen. First, you need to interrupt the person to alert them to the fact that another voice is trying to take over the dialogue. After that, there are two strategies that you can consider. You can encourage the person to continue with the perspective that they are supposed to be expressing while telling them that they will have a chance to voice the other side later. This usually works. If not, you can have them move to another chair and speak from the voice that is pressing for emergence. It is important, however, that you do not let them switch voices and stay in the same chair. That parallels the muddled confusion that is already taking place in their head already.

> *Patient:* I want to get a new job. I feel trapped where I am. I want . . . I don't think I can do it, I really feel overwhelmed with fear.
>
> *Therapist:* I would like you to stay with the desire voice while you are in this chair; we will give voice to the fearful part in a minute.

Or

> *Therapist:* I would like you to stay with the desire voice while you are in this chair; however, if the fear voice feels too strong right now, you can switch to the other chair and speak from that perspective, it's your choice. Which would you prefer to do?

Asking the Patient what they are Feeling as they are Speaking

This can be more complicated than it sounds as what patients are actually feeling may or may not be in concordance with what they are actually saying. This discrepancy can be worked into the dialogue. However to start, it might be best to use this when the patient seems to be in an emotional state that parallels what they are saying.

> *Patient:* When I think about what you did to me, I realize that you took advantage of my good nature.
>
> *Therapist:* What are you feeling as you say that?
>
> *Patient:* I'm feeling angry.
>
> *Therapist:* Tell her again and express your anger.
>
> *Patient:* I've been thinking about what you did and I am so angry. I am furious that you took advantage of me and I am upset at myself for letting it happen.

Finishing the Dialogue

One way to bring a dialogue to a conclusion is to invite the patient to say one more thing at this time (Walters & Swallow, May, 2009).

Therapist: Is there one more thing that you would like to say to Johan before we stop for today?

Patient: I'm upset about what happen, but I want to move on.

Therapist: Good. Why don't you move back to this chair?

Existential Language

As was touched on repeatedly, I believe that therapists should vigorously encourage patients to use the language of responsibility. This means that we will want to encourage them to use words like "want," "decide," "choose," and "will" rather than "must," "should," and "need to" (Perls, 1992).

Observing Changes in Tone

While not always something to comment on, it can be quite striking to notice how much the person changes when they move from chair to chair. It is common to see shifts in energy level, body movement, tone, volume, and language. They often seem more powerful in one chair and, at times, it seems as if their age changes as they move back and forth. These can all be important things to reflect upon and explore with the patient.

Posture and Gesture

In a number of dialogues, the patients were asked stand up. Standing and sitting allow for different kinds of energies and dialogical possibilities to emerge. Each patient is different so they may each have a unique response as they engage with these two dimensions. In general, I tend to favor sitting for dialogues that involve intimacy, quiet, or grief, while I prefer standing for those involving assertiveness and existential affirmation. When working with patients who are depressed or a bit disconnected, I often invite them to stand as it tends to increase their energy level. Lastly, the chair can serve as a support or as a protective barrier, as needed.

WORKING WITH RESISTANT PATIENTS

In workshop settings, many therapists express anxiety and concern about patients being unwilling to engage in this kind of dialogue work or resisting it in some manner. These fears make sense, especially in the abstract, but there are a number of things that practitioners can do to reduce or eliminate opposition.

I think that the most important variable is the spirit with which the therapist presents the method and the energy with which they approach the dialogues. In short, the more enthusiastic and confident they are about the work, the better things will go. How does one gain this confidence? There are several things that can be done. First, they can play out the dialogues with a partner or alone a number of times. They can then try to do the dialogue off script; that is, using the basic structures as a foundation for improvisation. Therapists can also do Chairwork with themselves, going back and forth between two polarities or speaking to someone from their past, present, or future. The best practice is to do it in their personal therapy. Even if their therapist is not skilled in Chairwork, doing the dialogues in front of a witness dramatically increases the emotional intensity of the experience.

While ascertaining the reasons for the resistance may be important to do at some point, I would initially suggest trying to get past the resistance through a series of structural moves. In the first, the patient takes a seat as a witness and "therapist" while the therapist does the Chairwork for the patient. The therapist gives voice to the different parts or expresses grief or anger to an imaginal other in the opposite chair. The patient can do the coaching, making suggestions and corrections as necessary. This "role-reversal" can be quite powerful. The patients often appreciate this caring and generous act and they, of course, gain by hearing their issues enacted before them. A variation on this approach, which is more engaging, is to invite the patient to sit in the chair opposite while you are speaking. They do not speak, but they are much more emotionally involved in the work.

Hopefully, doing this once will be enough to get the patient over the "hump" and able to do dialogue work using a standard format. If the resistance continues, it may be necessary to explore the beliefs or forces that it is activating. In my experience, the most common reason is that the person feels self-conscious; they are concerned that they will be "performing" for the therapist. There is a way to address this that is in contrast to what I wrote earlier. Here, the therapist places his or her chair behind the patient so that they are present and connected but not in their line of vision. If the patient moves to the chair opposite, the therapist should also move to the other side and place a chair in a similar position. Here, they would do this even if the person is embodying an inner critic, a difficult person, or some other problematic entity.

The second reason why patients resist is that they are afraid of what will emerge if they do the work, either in terms of content or emotion. This should be explored at length and, if necessary, the initial dialogues can be structured in such a manner that they are brief and limited; in this way, the exposure will be somewhat titrated. Having said this, it is important that the patient start doing the normal Chairwork dialogues as quickly as possible. While it is true that they can be disturbing, going through these exposures and experiences of conflict and expression are central to real healing.

ADVOCATING FOR THE EXPERIENTIAL

In my interactions with schema therapists, I sometimes hear them speak about patients who do not want to do Chairwork or imagery work. In some cases, they have acquiesced to the desires of the patients. Schema therapy is an experiential treatment and to surrender these techniques is to impair the efficacy of the treatment. Some therapists may have expertise in other forms of treatment that they are willing to use, and that is fine. For those of us who have deeply embraced experiential work, it is very important that we do not back down when confronted with patient resistance. The vast majority will comply if we are strong and determined. In the end, there may be some who still resist, which, of course, they have every right to do. I would, however, see them as "someone else's patient," to use Casey Truoffo's (2007) phrase, and I would refer them to a colleague. Chairwork is a wonderful and pro-found method of healing; advocating for it benefits both the patient and the therapist.

FINAL THOUGHTS

In this book, I have sought to present the art and science of Chairwork. Some of the forms were simple while others were more complex. As you integrate it into your therapeutic practice, I would suggest that you *go slowly* and *keep it simple*, at least to start.

Inviting patients to speak clearly from one voice is healing. Inviting patients to "speak to" rather than "speak about" someone leads to a profound experiential shift (Perls, 1992). Learning to move from the external to the internal and back again helps to bring depth and complexity to the work. Playing with the deepening techniques will help you find your own style as a Chairwork practitioner. In my journey as a healer, the discovery of Chair-work was a gift of incomparable beauty and power. I hope that you will find Chairwork to be all that it needs to be for you as well.

And, once more, "Thank you, Fritz."

References

abcteach® – The educators on-line resource (2014). Word list: Opposites. Retrieved from http://www.abcteach.com/free/l/list_opposites.pdf.

Alberti, R. E., & Emmons, M. L. (1986). *Your perfect right: A guide to assertive living* (5th ed.). Atascadero, CA: Impact Publishers.

Allen, J. R., & Allen, B. A. (1995). Narrative theory, Redecision Therapy, and postmodernism. *Transactional Analysis Journal, 25,* 327–334.

Anderson, W. T. (1983). *The upstart spring: Esalen and the American awakening.* Reading, MA: Addison-Wesley Publishing Company.

Applebaum, S. A. (1993). *A psychoanalyst explores the alternate therapies.* Northvale, NJ: Jason Aronson.

Arknoff, D. B. (1981). Flexibility in practicing cognitive therapy. In G. Emery, S.D. Hollon, & R. C. Bedrosian (Eds.), *New directions in cognitive therapy: A casebook* (pp. 203–223). New York: The Guilford Press.

Barnard, L. K., & Curry, F. (2011). Self-compassion: Conceptualizations, correlates, & interventions. *Review of General Psychology, 4,* 289–303. doi: 10.1037/a0025754.

Baer, R. A., & Huss, D. B. (2008). Mindfulness- and acceptance-based therapy. In J. L. Lebow (Ed.), *Twenty-first century psychotherapies: Contemporary approaches to theory and practice* (pp. 123–166). Hoboken, NJ: John Wiley & Sons.

Bauer, R. (1976). A Gestalt approach to internal objects. *Psychotherapy: Theory Research and Practice, 13,* 232–235. doi: 10.1037/h0088346.

Baumgardner, P. (1975). *Gifts from Lake Cowichan.* Palo Alto, CA: Science and Behavior Books.

Beck, A. T., Emery, G., & Greenberg, R. L. (1985). *Anxiety disorders and phobias: A cognitive perspective.* New York: Basic Books.

Beck, A. T., & Weishaar, M. E. (2005). Cognitive therapy. In R. J. Corsini & D. Wedding (Eds.), *Current psychotherapies* (7th Ed.). pp. 238–268. Belmont, CA: Brooks/Cole-Thomson Learning.

Beisser, A. (1970). The paradoxical theory of change. In J. Fagan & I. L. Shepherd (Eds.), *Gestalt Therapy now: Theory, techniques, applications* (pp. 77–80). Palo Alto, CA: Science and Behavior Books.

Bernstein, P. L. (1980). The union of the Gestalt concept of experiment and Jungian active imagination. *The Gestalt Journal, 3*, 36–46.

Biernacki, P. (1986). *Pathways from heroin addiction: Recovery without treatment.* Philadelphia: Temple University Press.

Bishop, F. M. (2001). *Managing addictions: Cognitive, emotive, and behavioral techniques.* Northvale, NJ: Jason Aronson, Inc.

Blatner, A. (1995). Psychodramatic methods in psychotherapy. *Psychiatric Times, 12,* (5), 20.

Blatner, A. (1999). Psychodramatic methods in psychotherapy. In D. J. Weiner (Ed.), *Beyond talk therapy: Using movement and expressive techniques in clinical practice* (pp. 125–143). Washington, DC: American Psychological Association.

Blatner, A. (2000). Psychodramatic methods for facilitating bereavement. In P. F. Kellerman, & M. K. Hudgins (Eds.), *Psychodrama with trauma survivors: Acting out your pain* (pp. 41–50). London: Jessica Kingsley Publishers.

Blatt, S. J. (1995). The destructiveness of perfectionism: Implications for the treatment of depression. *American Psychologist, 50,* 1003–1020. doi: 10.1037/0003–066X.50.12.1003.

Bouza, M. F., & Barrio, J. A. E. (2000). Brief psychodrama and bereavement. In P. F. Kellerman, & M. K. Hudgins (Eds.), *Psychodrama with trauma survivors: Acting out your pain* (pp. 51–59). London: Jessica Kingsley Publishers.

Bray, J. H. (2010). The future of psychology practice and science. *American Psychologist, 65,* 355–369. doi: 10.1037/a0020273.

Brien & Sheldon (1975). Women and Gestalt awareness. In J. Downing (Ed.), *Gestalt awareness: Papers from the San Francisco Gestalt Institute* (pp. 91–103). New York: Harper and Row.

Brooklyn Hobo (2008). A goodbye letter to alcohol and drugs. Retrieved from http://authspot.com/letters/a-goodbye-letter-to-alcohol-and-drugs/.

Brown, L. S. (2008). Feminist therapy. In J. L. Lebow (Ed.), *Twenty-first century psychotherapies: Contemporary approaches to theory and practice* (pp. 277–306). Hoboken, NJ: John Wiley & Sons.

Bryant et al. (2008). A randomized controlled trial of exposure therapy and cognitive restructuring for Posttraumatic Stress Disorder. *Journal of Consulting and Clinical Psychology, 76,* 695–703. doi: 10.1037/a0012616.

Carter, R. (2008). *Multiplicity: The new science of personality, identity, and the self.* New York: Little, Brown and Company.

Chadwick, P. (2003). Two chairs, self-schemata and a person based approach to psychosis. *Behavioural and Cognitive Psychotherapy, 31,* 439–449. doi: 10.1017/S1352465803004053.

Cheung, M., & Nguyen, P. V. (2012). Connecting the strengths of Gestalt chairs to Asian clients. *Smith College Studies in Social Work, 82,* 51–62. doi: 10.1080/00377317.2012.638895.

Christiansen, C. H. (1999). Defining lives: Occupation as identity: An essay on competence, coherence, and the creation of meaning. *American Journal of Occupational Therapy, 53,* 547–558.

Clarkson, P., & Mackewn, J. (1993). *Fritz Perls.* Thousand Oaks, CA: Sage Publications.

Cohn, R. C. (1970). Therapy in groups: Psychoanalytic, experiential, gestalt. In J. Fagan & I. L. Shepherd (Eds.), *Gestalt therapy now: Theory, techniques, applications* (pp. 130–139). Palo Alto, CA: Science and Behavior Books.

Corstens, D., Longden, E., & May, R. (2011). Talking with voices: Exploring what is expressed by the voices people hear. *Psychosis, 4,* 95–104. doi: 10.1080/17522 439.2011.571705.

Cummings, A. L. (1999). Experiential interventions for clients with genital herpes. *Canadian Journal of Counselling, 33,* 142–156.

Daniels, V. (2005). The method of "shuttling" in the Gestalt working process. *Gestalt! 9,* n.p.

David, E. J. R. (2009). Internalized oppression, psychopathology, and cognitive-behavioral therapy among historically oppressed groups. *Journal of Psychological Practice, 15,* 71–103.

Dayton, T. (1994). *The drama within: Psychodrama and experiential therapy.* Deerfield Beach, FL: Health Communications.

Dayton, T. (2000). The use of psychodrama in the treatment of trauma and addiction. In P. F. Kellerman, & M. K. Hudgins (Eds.), *Psychodrama with trauma survivors: Acting out your pain* (pp. 114–136). London: Jessica Kingsley Publishers.

Dayton, T. (March/April 2003). Psychodrama in the resolution of trauma and grief. *Counselor Magazine.* Retrieved from http://www.counselormagazine.com/feature-articles-mainmenu-63/29-alternative/137-psychodrama-in-the-resolution-of-trauma-and-grief.

Dayton, T. (2005). *The living stage: A step-by-step guide to psychodrama, sociometry and experiential group therapy.* Deerfield Beach, FL: Health Communications.

Denning, P. (2000). *Practicing harm reduction psychotherapy: An alternative approach to addictions.* New York: The Guilford Press.

De-Oliveira, I. R. (2011). Kafka's trial dilemma: Proposal of a practical solution to Joseph K's unknown accusation. *Medical Hypothesis, 77,* 5–6.

Douglas, C. (2005). Analytical psychotherapy. In R. J. Corsini & D. Wedding (Eds.), *Current psychotherapies* (7th ed.). Belmont, CA: Brooks/Cole–Thomson Learning.

Dublin, J. E. (1976). Gestalt therapy, existential-gestalt therapy and/versus "Perls-ism". In E. W. L. Smith (Ed.), *The growing edge of gestalt therapy* (pp. 124–150). New York: Brunner/Mazel.

Duhl, B. S. (1999). A personal view of action metaphor: Bringing what's inside outside. In D. J. Weiner (Ed.), *Beyond talk therapy: Using movement and expressive techniques in clinical practice* (pp. 79–96). Washington, DC: American Psychological Association.

Dyak, M. (2012). Voice Dialogue: The essential difference. In D. Hoffman (Ed.), *The Voice Dialogue anthology* (pp. 211–244). Albion, CA: Delos.

Edwards, D. J. A. (1989). Cognitive restructuring through guided imagery. In A. Freeman, K. M. Simon, L. E. Beutler, & H. Arkowitz (Eds.), *Comprehensive handbook of cognitive therapy* (pp. 283–297). New York: Plenum Press.

Edwards, D. J. A. (1990). Cognitive therapy and the restructuring of early memories through guided imagery. *Journal of Cognitive Psychotherapy: An International Quarterly, 4,* 33–50.

Elliott, J., & Elliott, K. (2000). *Disarming your inner critic.* Lafayette, LA: Anthetics Institute Press.

Elliott, R., & Greenberg, L. S. (1997). Multiple voices in process-experiential therapy: Dialogues between aspects of the self. *Journal of Psychotherapy Integration, 7,* 225–239.

Engle, D., & Arkowitz, A. (2008). Viewing resistance as ambivalence: Integrative strategies for working with resistant ambivalence. *Journal of Humanistic Psychology, 48,* 389–412. doi: 10.1177/0022167807310917.

Engle, D., Beutler, L. E. & Daldrup, R. J. (1991). Focused expressive psychotherapy: Treating blocked emotions. In J. D. Safran & L. Greenberg (Eds.), *Emotion, psychotherapy, and change* (pp. 169–196). New York: The Guilford Press.

Enns, C. Z. (1987). Gestalt therapy and Feminist therapy: A proposed integration. *Journal of Counseling and Development, 66,* 93–95. doi: 10.1002/j.1556-6676.1987.tb00807.x.

Erickson, (2004). A psychobiography of Richard Price: Co-founder of Esalen Institute. *Dissertation Abstracts International: Section B: The Sciences and Engineering Vol 64 (9-B),* p. 4665.

Experience Project (2014). Cocaine. Retrieved from http://www.experienceproject.com/explore/Cocaine.

Fabry, J. (1988). *Guideposts to meaning: Discovering what really matters.* Oakland, CA: New Harbinger.

Firestone, L., & Catlett, J. (1998). The treatment of Sylvia Plath. *Death Studies, 22,* 667–692.

Firestone, R. W., Firestone, L., & Catlett, J. (2002). *Conquer you critical inner voice.* Oakland, CA: New Harbinger Publications.

Fodor, I. G. (1993). A Feminist framework for integrative psychotherapy. In G. Stricker & J. Gold (Eds.), *Comprehensive handbook of psychotherapy integration* (pp. 217–235). New York: Plenum Press.

Fodor, I. G., & Collier, J. C. (2001). Assertiveness and conflict resolution: An integrated Gestalt-Cognitive Behavioral model for working with urban adolescents. In M. McConville & G. Wheeler (Eds.), *The heart of development: Gestalt approaches to working with children, adolescents and their words—volume II: adolescence* (pp. 215–252). Hillsdale, NJ: A GestaltPress Book/The Analytic Press.

Freeman, A. (1981). Dreams and images in cognitive therapy. In G. Emery, S. D. Hollon, & R. C. Bedrosian (Eds.), *New directions in cognitive therapy* (pp. 224–238). New York: The Guilford Press.

From, I. (1984). Reflections on Gestalt therapy after thirty-two years of practice: A requiem for Gestalt. *The Gestalt Journal, 7,* 4–12.

Freud, S. (1965). *New introductory lectures on psychoanalysis.* New York: W. W. Norton & Company.

Freud, S. (1969). *An outline of psycho-analysis* (Rev. ed.). New York: Norton & Company.

Gaines, J. (1979). *Fritz Perls: Here and now.* Millbrae, CA: Celestial Arts.

Gaspard, B. D., & Hoffman, D. (Summer, 2009). Voice Dialogue: A powerful tool for your therapeutic practice. *Perspectives: A Professional Journal of the Renfrew Center Foundation,* 8–10.

Gendlin, E. T. (1981). *Focusing.* New York: Bantam.

Gilbert, P. (2010). *Compassion Focused Therapy.* New York: Routledge.

Giesen-Bloo, J., van Dyck, R., Spinhoven, P., van Tilburg, W., Dirksen, C., van Asselt, T., . . . Arntz A. (2006). Outpatient psychotherapy for borderline personality disorder; Randomized trial of schema-focused therapy vs transference-focused psychotherapy. *Archives of General Psychiatry, 63,* 649–658. doi: 10.1001/archpsyc.63.6.649.

Glickauf-Hughes, Wells, M., & Chance, S. (1996). Techniques for strengthening clients' observing ego. *Psychotherapy, 33,* 431–440. doi: 10.1037/0033-3204.33.3.431.

Goldfried, M. R. (1988). Application of rational restructuring to anxiety disorders. *The Counseling Psychologist, 16,* 50–68. doi: 10.1177/0011000088161004.

Goldfried, M. R. (2003). Cognitive–behavior therapy: Reflections on the evolution of a therapeutic orientation. *Cognitive Therapy and Research, 27,* 53–69. doi: 10.1023/A:1022586629843.

Goulding, M. M., & Goulding, R. (1997). *Changing lives through Redecision Therapy.* New York: Grove Press.

Granfield, R., & Cloud, W. (1994). The elephant that no one sees: Natural recovery among middle-class addicts. *Journal of Drug Issues, 26,* 45–61.

Greenberg, J.R., & Mitchell, S. A. (1983). *Objects relations in psychoanalytic theory.* Cambridge, MA: Harvard University Press.

Greenberg, L. S. (1979). Resolving splits: Use of the two chair technique. *Psychotherapy: Theory, Research and Practice, 16,* 316–324. doi: 10.1037/h0085895.

Greenberg. L. S., & Malcolm, W. (2002). Resolving unfinished business: Relating process to outcome. *Journal of Consulting and Clinical Psychology, 70,* 406–416. doi: 10.1037/0022–006X.70.2.406.

Greenberg, L. S., Rice, L. N., & Elliott, R. (1993). *Facilitating emotional change: The moment-by-moment process.* New York: The Guilford Press.

Greenberg, L. S., Safran, J., & Rice, L. (1989). Experiential therapy: Its relation to cognitive therapy. In A. Freeman, K. M. Simon, L. E. Beutler, & H. Arkowitz (Eds.), *Comprehensive handbook of cognitive therapy* (pp. 169–187). New York: Plenum Press.

Greenberg, L. S., Warwar, S. H., & Malcolm, W. M. (2008). Differential effects of emotion-focused therapy and psychoeducation in facilitating forgiveness and letting go of emotional injuries. *Journal of Counseling Psychology, 55,* 185–196. doi: 10.1037/0022-0167.55.2.185.

Greenwald, J. A. (1976). The ground rules in Gestalt therapy. In C. Hatcher & P. Himelstein (Eds.), *The handbook of Gestalt therapy* (pp. 267–280). New York: Aronson.

Greil, A. L., & Rudy, D. R. (1984). Social cocoons: Encapsulation and identity transformation organizations. *Sociological Inquiry, 54,* 260–278.

Gustaitis, R. (1969). *Turning on.* New York: MacMillan.

Hatcher, C., & Himelstein, P. (Eds.) (1983). *The handbook of Gestalt Therapy.* New York: Jason Aronson.

Hardie, S. (2004). The place of Gestalt Therapy and PTSD in social work. *Gestalt!, 8.*

Harré, R. (1983). Identity projects. In G. Breakwell (Ed.), *Threatened identities* (pp. 31–51). New York: John Wiley and Sons.

Harris, T. A. (1969). *I'm OK—you're OK: A practical guide to Transactional Analysis*. New York: Galahad Books.

Hayward, M., Overton, J., Dorey, T., & Denney, J. (2009). Relating therapy for people who hear voices: A case series. *Clinical Psychology and Psychotherapy. 16*, 216–277.

hooks, b. (1994). *Outlaw culture*. New York: Routledge. New York: William Morrow.

hooks, b. (2000). *All about love: New visions*. New York: William Morrow.

Horney, K. (1950). *Neurosis and human growth*. New York: W. W. Norton.

Howard, J. (1970). *Please touch*. New York: McGraw-Hill.

Jagger, M., Richards, K., & Faithfull, M. (1971). Sister morphine (The Rolling Stones). On *Sticky Fingers* [Album]. London: Rolling Stones Records.

Jensen, M. P., & Turk, D. C. (2014). Contributions of psychology to the understanding and treatment of people with chronic pain. *American Psychologist, 69*, 105–118. doi: 10.1037/a0035641.

Joines, V. (2004). The treatment of personality adaptations using Redecision Therapy. In J. J. Magnavita (Ed.), *Handbook of personality disorders: Theory and practice* (pp. 194–220). New York: John Wiley & Sons.

Kanayama, G., Barry, S., Hudson, J. I., & Pope, H. G. (2006). Body image and attitudes toward male roles in anabolic-androgenic steroid users. *American Journal of Psychiatry, 163*, 697–703.

Karp, M. (2000). Psychodrama of rape and torture: A sixteen-year follow-up case study. In P. F. Kellerman, & M. K. Hudgins (Eds.), *Psychodrama with trauma survivors: Acting out your pain* (pp. 63–82). London: Jessica Kingsley Publishers.

Kellerman, P. F., & Hudgins, M. K. (2000), *Psychodrama with trauma survivors: Acting out your pain*. London: Jessica Kingsley Publishers.

Kellogg, S. (1993). Identity and recovery. *Psychotherapy*, 30, 235–244. doi: 10.1037/0033-3204.30.2.235.

Kellogg, S. H. (2004). Dialogical encounters: Contemporary perspectives on "chairwork" in psychotherapy. *Psychotherapy: Research, Theory, Practice, Training, 41*, 310–320. doi: 10.1037/0033-3204.41.3.310.

Kellogg, S. H. (2009a). Schema Therapy: A Gestalt-oriented overview. *Gestalt!, 10 (1)*. retrieved from file:///C:/Users/Kellogg/Documents/Schema%20Therapy/Kellogg%20Schema%20Therapy%20and%20Gestalt%20Therapy.htm.

Kellogg, S. H. (2009b). Response to Bloom, Fodor, and Brownell. *Gestalt!, 10 (1)* Retrieved from file:///C:/Users/Kellogg/Documents/Schema%20Therapy/Response%20of%20Jeff%20Kellogg%20on%20Comments%20by%20Bloom,%20Fodor,%20and%20Brownell.htm.

Kellogg, S. (2012). On speaking one's mind: Using chairwork dialogues in Schema Therapy. In M. V. Vreeswijk, J. Broersen, & M. Nadort (Eds.), *Handbook of Schema Therapy theory, research, and practice*. Hoboken, NJ.

Kellogg, S. (2013). Dialogues and encounters: Fritz Perls and the art of Gestalt chairwork. Retrieved from http://transformationalchairwork.com/art-of-chairwork-2/.

Kellogg, S. H., & Kreek, M. J. (2006). On blending practice and research: The search for commonalities in substance abuse treatment. *Substance Abuse, 27*, 9–24. doi: 10.1300/J465v27n01_03.

Kellogg, S. H., Stitzer, M. L., Petry, N. M., & Kreek, M. J. (2007). Motivational incentives: Foundations and principles. *Promoting awareness of motivational incentive—An awareness campaign.* Retrieved from http://www.bettertxoutcomes. org/motivationalincentives/PDF/Kellog-Stitzer.pdf.

Kellogg, S. H., & Tatarsky, A. (2009). Harm reduction psychotherapy. In G. L. Fisher & N. A. Roget (Eds.), *Encyclopedia of substance abuse prevention, treatment, and recovery* (pp. 444–449). Thousand Oaks, CA: Sage Publications.

Kellogg, S. H., & Tatarsky, A. (2012). Re-Envisioning addiction treatment: A 6-point plan. *Alcoholism Treatment Quarterly, 30,* 1–20. doi: 10.1080/07347324.2012.63 5544.

Kim, J., & Daniels, V. (2008). Experimental Freedom. In P. Brownell (Ed.), *Handbook for theory, research, and practice in Gestalt Therapy* (pp. 198–227). Newcastle, UK: Cambridge Scholars Publishing.

Kitten (2001). The first dance: Mehtylphenidate (Ritalin) & heroin. *Erowid experience vaults.* Retrieved from http://www.erowid.org/experiences/exp.php?ID=8011

Knapp, C. (2005). *Drinking: A love story.* New York: Dial Press.

Kohls, R. (1984). *The values Americans live by.* Retrieved from http://www.claremontmckenna.edu/pages/faculty/alee/extra/American_values.html.

Krakow, B., Sandoval, D., Schrader, R., Keuhne, B., McBride, L., You, C. L., & Tandberg, D. (2001). Treatment of chronic nightmares in adjudicated adolescent girls in a residential facility. *Journal of Adolescent Health, 29,* 94–100.

Landy, R. J. (2008). *The couch and the stage: Integrating words and action in psychotherapy.* Lanham, MD: Jason Aronson.

Latner, J. (1973). *The Gestalt Therapy book.* New York: Bantam.

Lazarus, A. A., & Messer, S. B. (1991). Does chaos prevail? An exchange on technical eclecticism and assimilative integration. *Journal of Psychotherapy Integration, 1,* 143–158.

Leahy, R. L., & Holland, S. J. (2000). *Treatment plans and interventions for depression and anxiety disorders.* New York: The Guilford Press.

Lennox, C. E. (1997). Introduction: Redecision therapy, a brief therapy model. In C. E. Lennox (Ed.), *Redecision therapy: A brief, action-oriented approach* (pp. 1–14). Northvale, NJ: Aronson.

Leveton, E. (2001). *A clinician's guide to psychodrama* (3rd ed.). New York: Springer Publishing Company.

Lieblich, A. (1978). *Tin Soldiers on Jerusalem Beach.* New York: Pantheon.

Lippitt, R. (1958). The auxiliary chair technique. *Group Psychotherapy*, 11, 8–23.

Lobbestael, L. (2008). *Lost in fragmentation: Schema modes, childhood trauma, and anger in borderline and antisocial personality disorder.* Maastricht, NL: Universitaire Pers Maastricht.

Lowe, W., Jr. (2000). Detriangulation of absent fathers in single-parent Black families: Techniques of imagery. *American Journal of Family Therapy, 28,* 29–40. doi: 10.1080/019261800261798.

Lyon, Jr., H. C. (1974). *It's me and I'm here! From West Point to Esalen: The struggles of an overachiever to revitalize his life through the human potential movement.* New York: Delacorte Press.

Mackay, B. (2002). Effects of Gestalt Therapy two-chair dialogue on divorce decision making. *Gestalt Review, 6,* 220–235.

Malmo, C. (1990). Recreating equality: A Feminist approach to Ego-State therapy. In T. A. Laidlaw, C. Malmo & Associates (Ed.), *Healing voices: Feminist approaches to therapy with women* (pp. 288–319). San Francisco: Jossey-Bass.

Marineau, R. (1989). *Jacob Levy Moreno 1889–1974: Father of psychodrama, sociometry, and group psychotherapy.* London: Tavistock/Routledge.

Markus, H., & Nurius, P. (1986). Possible selves. *American Psychologist, 41,* 954–969. doi: 10.1037/0003-066X.41.9.954.

Marlatt, G. A., & Gordon, J. R. (Eds.). (1985). *Relapse Prevention: Maintenance strategies in the treatment of addictive behaviors.* New York: The Guilford Press.

Massé, V. (1997). The treatment of post-traumatic stress disorder. In C. E. Lennox (Ed.), *Redecision Therapy: A brief, action-oriented approach* (pp. 197–212). Northvale, NJ: Jason Aronson.

Mastro, J. (Winter, 2004). *Gestalt-Experiential Seminar.* New York, NY.

Maxwell, M. A. (1984). *The alcoholics anonymous experience: A close-up view for professionals.* New York: McGraw-Hill.

McCall, G. J. (1977). The social looking-glass: A sociological perspective on self-development. In T. Mischel (Ed.), *The self: Psychological and philosophical issues* (pp. 274–287). Oxford: Basil Blackwell.

McDaniel, S. H., & deGruy, F. V. (2014). An introduction to primary care and psychology. *American Psychologist, 69,* 325–331. doi: 10.1037/a0036222.

McKay, B., & McKay, K. (February 17, 2008). How to ask for (and get) a raise like a man. *The art of manliness.* Retrieved from http://www.artofmanliness.com/2008/02/17/how-to-ask-for-and-get-a-raise-like-a-man/.

Mead, G. H. (1934). *Mind, self, and society: From the standpoint of a social behaviorist.* Chicago: University of Chicago Press.

Miller, M. V. (1989). Introduction to Gestalt Therapy Verbatim. *The Gestalt Journal, 12,* 5–24.

Miller, M. V. (1992). Introduction. In F. S. Perls, *Gestalt Therapy verbatim* (pp. 1–20). Highland, NY: Gestalt Journal Press.

Miller, W. R. (2000). *Enhancing motivation for change in substance abuse treatment: Treatment improvement protocol series number 35.* Rockville, MD: Center for Substance Abuse Treatment.

Miller, W. R., & Rollnick, S. (2013). *Motivational interviewing* (3rd ed.). New York: The Guilford Press.

Moreno, J. (1989). Introduction. *Journal of Group Psychotherapy, Psychodrama, & Sociometry, 42,* 3–12.

Moreno, J. L. (1987). Moreno's philosophical system. In J. Fox (Ed.) *The essential Moreno: Writings on psychodrama, group method, and spontaneity.* New York: Springer.

Moreno, J. L. (1989). The autobiography of J. L. Moreno, MD. *Journal of Group Psychotherapy, Psychodrama, & Sociometry, 42,* 15–52.

Moreno, Z. (2008). Foreword: The world of multiple stages. In R. Landy, Landy, R. J. (2008). *The couch and the stage: Integrating words and action in psychotherapy* (pp. ix–xiii). Lanham, MD: Jason Aronson.

Moreno, Z. T. (2012). *To dream again*. Catskill, NY: Mental Health Resources.

Muid, O. (2006). ". . . Then I found my spirit": The meaning of the United Nations World Conference Against Racism and the challenges of the historical trauma movement with research considerations. Retrieved from http://pimatisiwin.com/uploads/120376454.pdf.

Naranjo, C. (1993). *Gestalt Therapy: The attitude and practice of an atheoretical experientialism*. Gateways City, NV: Gateways/IDHHB.

National Institute on Drug Abuse (2008). *Drugs, brains, and behavior: The science of addiction*. Rockville, MD: National Institute on Drug Abuse.

Neff, K. (2011). *Self-compassion: Stop beating yourself up and leave insecurity behind*. New York: HarperCollins.

Neimeyer, R. A. (2012). Chair work. In. R. A. Neimeyer (Ed.), *Techniques of grief therapy* (pp. 266–273). New York: Routledge.

Newman, R. (1998). *African American quotations*. Phoenix, AZ: The Oryx Press.

O'Brien, C. P., & McLellan, A. T. (1996). Myths about the treatment of addiction. *Lancet, 347,* 237–240.

Paivo, S. C., & Greenberg, L. S. (1995). Resolving "unfinished business": Efficacy of experiential therapy using empty-chair dialogue. *Journal of Counseling and Clinical Psychology, 63,* 419–425. doi: 10.1037/0022-006X.63.3.419.

Passons, W. R. (1975). *Gestalt approaches in counseling*. New York: Holt, Rinehart, and Winston.

Patterson, S. (2002, April 21). Cocaine nation. *The Observer*. Retrieved from http://observer.guardian.co.uk/drugs/story/0,11908,686657,00.html.

Payne, P. (1981). *Martial arts: The spiritual dimension*. New York: Crossroad.

Pérez-Álavarez, M., García-Montes, J. M., Perona-Garcelán, S., & Vallina-Fernández, O. (2008). Changing relationship with voices: New therapeutic perspectives for treating hallucinations. *Clinical Psychology and Psychotherapy, 15,* 75–85.

Perls, F. S. (1969a). *Ego, hunger and aggression*. New York: Random House.

Perls, F. S. (1969b). *In and out the garbage pail*. New York: Bantam Books.

Perls, F. S. (1970). Four lectures. In J. Fagan & I. L. Shepherd (Eds.), *Gestalt Therapy now: Theory, techniques, applications* (pp. 14–38). Palo Alto, CA: Science and Behavior Books.

Perls, F. (1972). Gestalt Therapy. In A. Bry (Ed.), *Inside psychotherapy: Nine clinicians tell how they work and what they are trying to accomplish* (pp. 57–70). New York: Basic Books.

Perls, F. (1973). *The Gestalt approach and eye witness to therapy*. United States: Science and Behavior Books.

Perls, F. S. (1975a). *Legacy from Fritz*. Palo Alto, CA: Science and Behavior Books.

Perls, F. S. (1975b). Gestalt Therapy and human potentialities. In J. O. Stevens (Ed.), *Gestalt is* (pp.1–7). Moab, UT: Real People Press.

Perls, F. S. (1992). *Gestalt Therapy verbatim*. Gouldsboro, ME: The Gestalt Journal Press.

Perls, F. S., Hefferline, R. F., & Goodman, P. (1951). *Gestalt Therapy: Excitement and growth in the human personality*. New York: Julian Press.

Polster, E. (1987). *Every person's life is worth a novel*. New York: W. W. Norton.

Polster, E. (1995). *A population of selves: A therapeutic exploration of personal diversity.* San Francisco: Jossey-Bass.

Polster, E., & Polster, M. (1973). *Gestalt Therapy integrated: Contours of theory and practice.* New York: Brunner/Mazel.

Polster, M. (1987). Gestalt Therapy: Evolution and application. In J. Zeig (Ed.), *The evolution of psychotherapy* (pp. 312–322). New York: Brunner/Mazel.

Prochaska, J. O., DiClemente, C. C., & Norcross, J. C. (1992). In search of how people change: Applications to addictive behaviors. *American Psychologist, 47,* 1102–1114. doi: 10.1037/0003-066X.47.9.1102.

Rafaeli, E., Bernstein, D. P., & Young, J. (2011). *Schema Therapy: Distinctive features.* New York: Routledge.

Raffa, J. B. (2012). *Healing the sacred divide: Making peace with ourselves, each other, and the world.* Burdett, NY: Larson Publications.

Rainwater, J. (1992). Psychosynthesis and the Gestalt approach. In E. C. Nevis (Ed.), *Gestalt Therapy: Perspectives and applications* (pp. 179–187). New York: Gestalt Institute of Cleveland Press/Gardner Press.

Rancour, P. (2006). Clinical treatment for body image disturbances: Variations on a theme–guided imagery, empty chair work, and therapeutic letter-writing. In M. V. Kindes (Ed.), *Body image: New research* (pp. 263–289). New York: Nova Science Publishers.

Redmoon, A. (1994). There are no peaceful warriors. In R. Fields (Ed.), *The awakened warrior: Living with courage, compassion and discipline* (pp. 19–28). New York: Jeremy P. Tarcher/Putnam.

Reeves, S. (January 5, 2006). Seven no-nos when asking for a raise. *Forbes.Com.* Retrieved from http://www.forbes.com/2006/01/04/careers-work-employment-cx_sr_0105bizbasics.html.

Resick, P. A. (2001). Cognitive therapy for posttraumatic stress disorder. *Journal of Cognitive Therapy: An International Quarterly, 15,* 321–329.

Resick, P. A., Monson, C. M., & Rizvi, S. (2008). Posttraumatic stress disorder. In D. Barlow (Ed.), *Clinical handbook of psychological disorders* (65–122). New York: The Guilford Press.

Robson, M. (2000). Psychodrama with adolescent sexual offenders. In P. F. Kellerman, & M. K. Hudgins (Eds.), *Psychodrama with trauma survivors: Acting out your pain* (pp. 137–154). London: Jessica Kingsley Publishers.

Rogers, C. (1986). Client-centered therapy. In I. L. Kutash & A. Wolf (Eds.), *Psychotherapist's casebook* (pp. 197–208). San Francisco: Jossey-Bass.

Romme, M., Escher, S., Dillon, J., Corstens, D., & Morris, M. (2009). *Living with voices: 50 stories of recovery.* Herefordshire, UK: PCCS Books.

Rosenberg, S. S., & Lynch, E. J. (2002). Fritz Perls revisited: A micro-assessment of a live clinical session. *Gestalt Review*, 6, 184–202.

Rosenfeld, E. (1977a). An oral history of Gestalt therapy, part one: A conversation with Laura Perls. Available at: http://gestalttheory.com/fritzperls/publications/an-oral-history-of-gestalt-therapy/.

Rosenfeld, E. (1977b). An oral history of Gestalt therapy, part two: A conversation with Isidore From. Ross. J. (2007). *Anna Halprin: Experience as dance.* Berkeley, CA: University of California Press.

Rothschild, D. (2010). Partners in treatment: Relational psychoanalysis and harm reduction therapy. *Journal of Clinical Psychology, 66,* 136–149.

Rowan, J. (2010). *Personification: Using the dialogical self in psychotherapy and counseling.* New York: Routledge.

Rubin, G. (2004). *Forty ways to look at Winston Churchill.* New York: Random House.

Samoilov, A., & Goldfried, M. R. (2000). Role of emotion in cognitive-behavioral therapy. *Clinical Psychology: Science and Practice, 7,* 373–385. doi: 10.1093/clipsy/7.4.373.

Schiffman, M. (1971). *Gestalt self therapy.* Berkeley, CA: Wingbow Press.

Schutz, W. C. (1972). *Here comes everybody.* New York: Harper and Row.

Schwartz, R. (1997, March/April). Don't look back. *The Family Therapy Networker,* 41–47. Retrieved from http://mail.psychotherapynetworker.org/component/content/article/149-1997-marchapril/918-dont-look-back.

Schwartz. R. (1987). Our multiple selves. *Family Therapy Networker, 11,* (2). 24–31, 80–83. Retrieved from http://www.hakomiinstitute.com/Forum/Issue10/OurMulti-pleSelves.pdf.

Shahar, B., Carlin, E. R., Engle, D. E., Hegde, J., Szepsenwol, O., & Arkowitz, H. (2012). A pilot investigation of emotion-focused two-chair dialogue intervention for self-criticism. *Clinical Psychology and Psychotherapy, 19,* 496–507. doi: 10.1002/cpp.762.

Shepard, M. (1975). *Fritz: An intimate portrait of Fritz Perls and Gestalt Therapy.* New York: Saturday Review Press.

Sicoli, L. A., & Hallberg, E. T. (1998). An analysis of client performance in the two-chair method. *Canadian Journal of Counselling, 32,* 151–162.

Smith, S. (2013–2014). Black feminism and intersectionality. *International Socialist Review,* 91. Retrieved from http://isreview.org/issue/91/black-feminism-and-intersectionality.

Spitzer, R. (1973). Foreword. In F. Perls, *The Gestalt approach and eye witness to therapy.* United States: Science and Behavior Books.

Sparks, A., & Tutu, M. (2011). *Tutu: Authorized.* New York: HarperOne.

Stevens, B. (1970). *Don't push the river.* Moab, UT: Real People Press.

Stinckens, N., Lietaer, G., & Leijssen, M. (2002). The inner critic on the move: Analysis of the change process in a case of short-term client-centered/experiential therapy. *Counseling and Psychotherapy Research, 2,* 40–54.

Stone, H., & Stone, S. (1989). *Embracing our selves: The Voice Dialogue manual.* Novato, CA: New World Library.

Stone, H., & Stone, S. (1993*). Embracing your inner critic: Turning self-criticism into a creative asset.* New York: HarperCollins.

Stryker, S. (1981). Symbolic interactionism: Themes and variations. In M. Rosenberg & R. H. Turner (Eds.), *Social psychology: Sociological perspectives* (pp. 3–29). New York: Basic Books.

Stryker, S., & Serpé, R. T. (1982). Commitment, identity salience, and role behavior: Theory and research example. In W. Ickes & E. S. Knowles (Eds.), *Personality, roles, and social behavior* (pp. 199–218). New York: Springer-Verlag.

Tatarsky, A. (2002). *Harm Reduction Psychotherapy.* Northvale, NJ: Jason Aronson.

Tatarsky, A., & S. Kellogg (2010). Integrative harm reduction psychotherapy: A case of substance use, multiple trauma, and suicidality. *Journal of Clinical Psychology, 66*, 123–135.

Tatarsky, A., & S. H. Kellogg (2011). Harm reduction psychotherapy. In G. A. Marlatt, M. E. Larimer, & K. Witkiewitz (Eds.), *Harm reduction* (2nd ed.) (pp. 36–60). New York: Guildford.

Tirch, D. (2012). *The compassionate-mind guide to overcoming anxiety: Using Compassion-Focused Therapy to calm worry, panic, and fear.* Oakland, CA: New Harbinger.

Tobin, S. A. (1976). Saying goodbye in Gestalt Therapy. In C. Hatcher & P. Himelstein (Eds.), *The handbook of Gestalt Therapy* (pp. 371–383). New York: Aronson.

Trachsel, M., Ferrari, L., & Holtforth, M. G. (2012). Resolving partnership ambivalence: A randomized controlled trial of very brief cognitive and experiential interventions with follow-up. *Canadian Journal of Counselling and Psychotherapy, 46,* 239–258.

Truoffo, C. (2007). *Be a wealthy therapist: Finally, you can make a living while making a difference.* Saint Peters, MO: MP Press.

Wallace, J. (1978). Behavioral-modification methods as adjuncts to psychotherapy. In S. Zimberg, J. Wallace, & S. Blume (Eds.), *Practical approaches to alcoholism psychotherapy* (pp. 99–117). New York: Plenum Press.

Walters, R., & Swallow, J. (May, 2009). *Psychodrama in individual therapy.* New Paltz, NY: Hudson Valley Psychodrama Institute.

Watkins, H. H. (1993). Ego-state therapy: An overview. *American Journal of Clinical Hypnosis, 35,* 232–240. doi: 10.1080/00029157.1993.10403014.

Watson, J. C., Goldman, R. N., Greenberg, L. S. (2007). *Case studies in emotion-focused treatment in depression. A comparison of good and poor outcome.* Washington, DC: American Psychological Association.

Wheeler, G. (1991). *Gestalt reconsidered.* Cleveland, OH: The Gestalt Institute of Cleveland Press/Gardner Press.

Woldt, A. L., & Toman, S. M. (2005). *Gestalt Therapy: History, theory, and practice.* Thousand Oaks, CA: Sage Publications.

Wolfe, J. L., & Fodor, I. G. (1975). A cognitive/behavioral approach to modifying assertive behavior in women. *The Counseling Psychologist, 5*, 45–52. doi: 10.117 7/001100007500500408.

Wolpe, J. (1982). *The practice of behavior therapy* (3rd ed.). New York: Pergamon Press.

Wysong, J. (1978). An oral history of Gestalt Therapy, part three: A conversation with Erving and Miriam Polster.

Wysong, J. (1985). An oral history of Gestalt Therapy, part four: A conversation with Elliot Shapiro.

Yahoo Answers (2014). Cocaine. Retrieved from https://answers.yahoo.com/question/index?qid=20110307030131AA3Edd9.

Yellow Horse Brave Heart, M. (2003). The historical trauma response among natives and its relationship with substance abuse: A Lakota illustration. *Journal of Psychoactive Drugs, 35,* 7–13. doi: 10.1080/02791072.2003.10399988.

Yontef, G. (1998). Dialogic Gestalt Therapy. In L. S. Greenberg, J. C. Watson, & G. Lietaer (Eds.), *Handbook of experiential psychotherapy* (pp. 82–102). New York: The Guilford Press.

Yontef, G. & Jacobs, L. (2008). Gestalt Therapy. In R. Corsini & D. Wedding (Eds.), *Current psychotherapies* (8th ed.) *(*pp. 328–367*).* Belmont, CA: Brooks/ Cole-Thompson Learning.

Yontef, G., & Jacobs, L. (2013). Gestalt Therapy. In D. Wedding & R. Corsini (Eds.), *Current psychotherapies*, 10th ed. (pp. 299–338). Independence, KY: Cengage Learning.

Young, J. (2003). Maladaptive Schema Coping Styles. New York: Schema Therapy Institute.

Young, J. E., Beck, A. T., & Weinberger, A. (1993). Depression. In D. H. Barlow (Ed.), *Clinical handbook of psychological disorders* (2nd ed.) (pp. 240–277). New York: The Guilford Press.

Young, J. (2005). Young Schema Questionnaire–S3. New York: Schema Therapy Institute.

Young, J. E., Klosko, J. S., & Weishaar, M. E. (2003). *Schema Therapy: A practitioner's guide*. New York: The Guilford Press.

Zimberoff, D., & Hartman, D. (1999). Gestalt therapy and Heart-Centered therapies. *Journal of Heart-Centered Therapies, 6 (1)*, 93–104.

Zimbardo, P. (2011). Why the world needs heroes. *Europe's Journal of Psychology, 7*, 402–407. doi: 10.1037/e675612011-002.

Zinker, J. (1977). *Creative process in Gestalt Therapy*. New York: Vintage Books.

Index

affect, 18–20. *See also* emotion and imagery
Anthetic Dialogues, 87
Arnkoff, Diane, 17, 19. *See also* cognitive restructuring
assertiveness and behavioral rehearsal, 20, 57–68, 161–162; assertiveness dialogue, 61–68
awareness, 9, 11; and mindfulness, 125–126

Beck, Aaron, 15. *See also* cognitive restructuring
Beck, Julian. *See* Living Theatre
Beisser, Arnold, 12. *See also* Paradoxical Theory of Change
Berne, Eric, 7, 15. *See also* Transactional Analysis

Catlett, Joyce. *See* Voice Therapy
centering, 114
Chadwick, Paul, 92, 106, 140, 167, 168, 175. *See also* complexity of self
chair placement, 177
chair sculpture, 176
chairwork, history of, 2–10
cognitive restructuring, 15, 36, 72–73, 126, 160. *See also* inner critic; Social Processing Therapy

complexity of self, 92, 98–106, 175; psychosis, 167–169; substance use, 140–141. *See also* Chadwick, Paul
confluence, 6
contact boundary, 6
contact cycle, 6
contingency management, 133
cycle of emotions, 24, 139
cycle of relationship, 139

De Oliveira, Irismar, 93
decision-making, 79–86, 174–175
decisional balance, 16, 78–79, 135–136, 137, 138, 175
deepening techniques, 21, 27, 177–182; existential language, 182; finishing the dialogue, 181; keeping the voices clear, 180; matching words and feelings, 181; observing changes in tone, 182; posture and gesture, 182; reinforcement, 180; repetition, 178; suggesting a phrase, 179; simplification, 179; speaking as the therapist, 180; visualizing the other person, 178; volume, 178
Denning, Patt, 139
dialogues, types of, 16–17; diagnostic, 17, 171; transformational, 17, 171
Douglass, Frederick, 58

About the Author

Dr. Scott Kellogg is clinical assistant professor in the New York University Department of Psychology. He was previously on the faculties of The Rockefeller University, the Yale University School of Medicine, and the Program in Counseling and Clinical Psychology at Teachers College/ Columbia University. He received his doctorate in clinical psychology from the Graduate Center of the City University of New York in 1994.

Dr. Kellogg is both a past–president (2001, 2005, 2011) and the president-elect (2015) of the Division on Addictions of the New York State Psychological Association; he is also the co-director of the Harm Reduction and Mental Health Project at New York University.

He is currently in private practice at The Chairwork/Schema Therapy Treatment Project; previously, he was a psychotherapist at the Schema Therapy Institute in New York City. He is a certified Schema therapist and he received the Practitioners Certificate in Gestalt Therapy from Gestalt Associates for Psychotherapy. Dr. Kellogg has created the Transformational Chairwork training and is currently teaching this psychotherapeutic dialogue method to practitioners in both the United States and abroad.

In his writings, he has looked at such topics as Chairwork, Schema Therapy, Humanistic Addiction Psychotherapy, Gradualism, and Contingency Management.

His websites are:

Transformational Chairwork: http://transformationalchairwork.com/
Gradualism and Addiction Treatment: http://gradualismandaddiction.org/